Cuarteto Music and Dancing from Argentina

Florida A&M University, Tallahassee
Florida Atlantic University, Boca Raton
Florida Gulf Coast University, Ft. Myers
Florida International University, Miami
Florida State University, Tallahassee
University of Central Florida, Orlando
University of Florida, Gainesville
University of North Florida, Jacksonville
University of South Florida, Tampa
University of West Florida, Pensacola

Cuarteto Music and Dancing from Argentina

In Search of the *Tunga-Tunga* in Córdoba

Jane L. Florine

University Press of Florida

Gainesville · Tallahassee · Tampa · Boca Raton
Pensacola · Orlando · Miami · Jacksonville · Ft. Myers

Copyright 2001 by Jane L. Florine
Printed in the United States of America on acid-free paper
All rights reserved

06 05 04 03 02 01 6 5 4 3 2 1

Library of Congress Cataloging-in-Publication Data
Florine, Jane L.
Cuarteto music and dancing from Argentina: in search of the tunga-tunga in
Córdoba / Jane L. Florine.
p. cm.
Includes bibliographical references (p.), discography (p.), videography (p.),
and index.
ISBN 0-8130-2087-5 (alk. paper)
1. Cuarteto (Music)—Argentina—Córdoba—History and criticism. 2. Dance
music—Argentina—History and criticism. I. Title.
ML3417 .F66 2001
781.64—dc21   2001027592

The University Press of Florida is the scholarly publishing agency for the State
University System of Florida, comprising Florida A&M University, Florida Atlantic
University, Florida Gulf Coast University, Florida International University, Florida
State University, University of Central Florida, University of Florida, University of
North Florida, University of South Florida, and University of West Florida.

University Press of Florida
15 Northwest 15th Street
Gainesville, FL 32611–2079
http://www.upf.com

To *cuarteto* lovers everywhere

Nuestro Estilo Cordobés

Yo sé que hay gente
que rechaza la verdad,
y se avergüenza de esta pura realidad.
Al ritmo nuestro no lo van a sepultar,
porque es muy puro,
tiene estilo natural.
Y defendemos con orgullo
y mucho amor,
aquella herencia que mi Córdoba
    me dio.
Y desde entonces late
    en mi corazón,
y lo percibe una nueva generación.

Buenos Aires tiene el tango,
y La Rioja con la chaya,
los salteños con la zamba,
en Corrientes el chamamé;
en Santiago del Estero, gozan de la chacarera
Nosotros, los cordobeses,
cuarteteamos hasta morir.
Al tunga, tunga, tunga no lo van a sepultar
el ritmo del cuarteto, nunca, nunca morirá.

No, no, no, nunca morirá,
no, no, no, será siempre inmortal.
Sí, sí, sí, siempre vivirá.
Sí, sí, sí, te lo puedo asegurar.
San Luis, San Juan y Mendoza
con sus cuecas y sus tonadas.
Jujuy, su carnavalito.
La Patagonia, ritmo surero.
Santa Fe, Entre Ríos, Misiones,
guarañas y chamarritas.
Nosotros, los cordobeses,
cuarteteamos hasta morir.

(JIMÉNEZ—VERÓN—DELSERI)
(Mero 1988:189)

Our [Musical] Style, from Córdoba

I know there are people
who reject the truth
and are ashamed of this pure fact.
They are never going to bury our rhythm,
Because it is very pure,
[And] has a natural style.
And we defend with pride
and lots of love,
That inheritance which my Córdoba
Gave me.
And [which] from that time on beats/has beaten
in my heart
and a new generation feels/has felt.

Buenos Aires has the tango
and La Rioja the *chaya*
Those from Salta the *zamba,*
in Corrientes the *chamamé,*
in Santiago del Estero, they enjoy the *chacarera.*
We, the people of Córdoba,
will dance *cuarteto* to death (until we die).
They are never going to bury the *tunga, tunga, tunga,*
the *cuarteto* rhythm will never, never, die.

No, no, no, it will never die,
no, no, no, it will always be immortal.
Yes, yes, yes, it will always live.
Yes, yes, yes, I can assure you of that.
San Luis, San Juan, and Mendoza
with their *cuecas* and *tonadas.*
Jujuy, its *carnavalito.*
Patagonia, [its] southern rhythm.
Santa Fe, Entre Ríos, Misiones,
guarañas and *chamarritas.*
We, the people of Córdoba,
will dance *cuarteto* to death (until we die).

CONTENTS

FIGURES

PREFACE

This book could not have been written without the help and support of an incredible number of people; my *cuarteto* research has been a group effort from the start. Due to the warmth of my new friends in Córdoba, Argentina, especially those from the *cuarteto* world, the ten months I spent doing fieldwork in Argentina and my follow-up trips were some of the happiest and most rewarding times of my life. Unfortunately, since hundreds of people have assisted me in my work, I cannot thank them all individually here. This does not mean, however, that I have forgotten about their contributions.

I must begin by thanking the Fulbright Commission for having funded the major part of my research, from September 1994 through May 1995. Although I was not in Buenos Aires very much, I came to appreciate all that the Fulbright staff members there did for me. Gabriela Cosentino, my educational advisor, and María Cristina Muntaabski deserve special thanks. Osvaldo Hepp, of Córdoba, helped me with the paperwork necessary to win the grant and gave me initial guidance with my project.

In August 1995, I made a month-long return trip to Argentina in order to read a paper on my research at the X Jornadas Argentinas de Musicología; this trip was partially funded by the Florida State University Musical Associates and the Florida State University Congress of Graduate Students. I gratefully acknowledge this financial assistance as I was able to do follow-up research in both Córdoba and Buenos Aires during my stay. Funding for the writing of my dissertation, on which this book is based, was provided by a Florida State University Dissertation Fellowship. The members of my committee (Dale A. Olsen, Michael B. Bakan, J. Anthony Paredes, and Robert Smith), as well as others at Florida State (Douglass Seaton, Patty Herrington, the late Ashenafi Kebede, and David Darst), were instrumental in my obtaining financial support and completing the manuscript.

In June and July of 1998 I made another trip to Argentina, this time to both Buenos Aires and Córdoba, to obtain the copyright clearances and releases necessary to publish this book; this trip was partially funded by Chicago State University, from which I have received reassigned time to complete the manuscript as well. Miguel A. Delmontes and Lito Bosio, both of the Sociedad Argentina de Autores y Compositores (SADAIC), helped me with the copyright process in Argentina, and a Grant-in-Aid from Mu Phi Epsilon was later used to cover part of the publication costs.

Others to be thanked are my parents, Dorothy O. Florine and the late Dr. M. Clifford Florine; Marcia Eggers; Jean Johnson and family; Suzanne Flandreau; Nancy de Cordero and family; Sergio and Viviana Blatto and family; Osvaldo and Chola Ferri and family; María Aldecoa and family; Susana Espeche; Adriana Alba and family; Elizabeth and Héctor Zardini; Miriam Nachtigall; Alberto Paulín; Liliana Sábato; and Marga Gual.

Special help was given to me by members of the Argentine musicological community, including Héctor Rubio, Leonardo Waisman, Gonzalo Biffarella, Irma Ruiz, Alejandra Cragnolini, Ricardo Salton, Pablo Kohan, and Bernardo Illari. Silvia Barei, José Aldo Guzmán, and Mario Bomheker, all of the Universidad Nacional de Córdoba, must also be thanked for their support.

Meredith Morris-Babb of the University Press of Florida, my editor, has made a great effort to bring this book to its final stages of publication. From the time she first saw the manuscript in its dissertation form, her input and suggestions have been invaluable.

Last but not least, I must acknowledge all those members of the *cuarteto* community who gave up hours of their time to help me. In particular, I owe special thanks to the members of the six groups who allowed me to share in their work: Carlos Jiménez and his entourage, Rubén and Carlos Bottalló and the crew of Santamarina, Edgar and Karina Fuentes (Gary), Chébere (Eduardo "Pato" Lugones in particular), Manolo Cánovas and Tru-la-lá (and the four founders of La Barra who were formerly with Tru-la-lá), and the members of La Banda del "Negro" Videla (Ángel Videla). In all these cases, I extend my gratitude to the owners, arrangers, singers, instrumentalists, and other personnel who came to know me well. Special friends I made in the groups were Osvaldo Morales, Augusto Bruchmann, Sergio Yanotti, and Abraham Vásquez-Martínez.

Others who must be thanked for their help are Emeterio Farías and his staff at Mejor Propaganda. It was with the assistance of Farías and his employees that many necessary doors were opened for me in the *cuarteto* world. I also spent countless Sunday afternoons at the FM radio station

La Ranchada with Antonio Díaz and his colleagues, such as Marcelo Danieli and Ricardo Valdano. Without their initial guidance with recordings and general information, I could not have done my later research. I must also mention the special assistance of Pablo León and his staff at the Estadio del Centro.

I would like to thank all of the following people and agencies, who are listed in alphabetical order, as well: Gabriel Ábalos and *A diario,* Luis Acevedo, José Adamo, Alción Editora, La Barra, Karl Barton, Juan Belfonte (BMG), Paul Berliner, Biblioteca Córdoba, Efraín Bischoff, Alfredo Blatto, Philip Bohlman, Rubén Omar Bravi, La Canción, Reyna Carranza, La Casa del Fotógrafo, Víctor Yunes Castillo, Luis Cima and Radio Suquía, Martha Ellen Davis, Susana Degoy, Juana Delseri, Marcela Depiante and family, John de Vries, Ethnoise! (University of Chicago Ethnomusicology Workshop), Juan Farías and La Banda 10, Fernando, Blanca Fior and CISPREN, Héctor Frías, Juan Pablo González, Carlos Giraudo, Héctor Grande and LV2, Luis Gregoratti, Sergio Guerrero, Donald Hill, María B. Huerta, Instituto de Musicología Nacional Carlos Vega, Elizabeth Jelín, Aldo Kustin, Laura Lara, Bernardo, Analía, and Cristián La Montagna, Adolfo C. Linardi, Eduardo "Pato" López, Santiago Loza, Miguel Machuca, Juan Carlos Maldonado, Laura Mancilla, Marito, Miguel Martí and Blanco y Negro, Claudia Maté, MJ Musical, Vicente Moncho, Dante Moyano and Orly, Gogo Muñoz, La Nueva Banda del Guapachoso, Elena Padin Olinik, PAMSCO (María Mercedes Sorroza), Oscar "Pato" Pedano, Pelusa, Piquí, Ariel Ramírez, Carlos and César Rolán and their groups, SADAIC, Daniel Salzano, Sandra, Víctor Scavuzzo, SCD (Santiago, Chile), Sebastián and Patricia, Tomacó, Cristina Vallari de Spada, Jorge Villarreal, Warner Chappell, and Mónica Zuvela and family.

I must also mention that parts of this book have appeared elsewhere: portions of chapters 1, 2, and 7 were published in "Carlos Jiménez: Reflecting the Power of the People in Argentine *Cuarteto* Music," in *Popular Music and Society* 22, no. 3 (fall 1998):61–114. Published articles I have written which are related to material contained in this book are as follows: "El cuarteto cordobés: análisis de un fenómeno social, masivo, y bailable," *Actas del II Congreso Latinoamericano IASPM International Association for the Study of Popular Music,* Santiago, Chile (March 1999), 177–90; "*Cuarteto:* Pop Music of Argentina," *Garland Encyclopedia of World Music,* vol. 2: *South America, Mexico, Central America, and the Caribbean* (October 1998), 706–20; and "*Cuarteto:* Dance-Hall Entertainment or People's Music?" *Latin American Music Review* 19, no. 1 (spring/summer 1998):31–46.

Map of Argentina and Córdoba. Artwork by John de Vries, 2000.

Introduction

Córdoba, Argentina, the capital of a centrally located province of the same name, is the home of a regional type of dance music called *cuarteto* (see frontispiece).[1] According to *cuarteto* followers, the genre dates to 1943, when Leonor Marzano, the pianist of the Cuarteto Leo, the first *cuarteto* group, invented the underlying *tunga-tunga* pattern, *cuarteto* music's identifying feature (Hepp 1988:60, 67).

Considered to be "low-class" music by many Argentines, *cuarteto* is a mass social phenomenon associated with the area; almost 20,000 people dance to it every weekend in Córdoba alone, and from 1,500 to 2,000 fans are often present at each dance (Hepp 1988:97; Gregoratti 11 March 1995:2C). One feature of the special dance style associated with this music is that both couples and small circles of people revolve counterclockwise, out on the dance floor, like a big wheel. Dances, which last four hours, normally run from about 12:30 A.M. to approximately 4:30 A.M. The genre, sometimes called the "folk music" of Córdoba—although middle- and upper-class people from Córdoba for the most part dissociate themselves from it owing to its lower-class connotations—is also heard on occasions as varied as patron saint festivals, weddings, Gypsy parties (the Gypsies in the area have given up their own traditional music in favor of *cuarteto*), and political campaigns. The object of dancing to *cuarteto* music, for all those concerned, is to forget one's worries by having fun in a ritualized setting which allows dancers to feel a sense of belonging.

Except for those who frequent the *cuarteto* environment, Argentines have little concrete information about the workings of the *cuarteto* world. Although many hesitatingly admit that they would like to know more about this music, they are often afraid to go to dances. Rumors abound, for example, regarding the unsavory environment found in dance halls, and taxi drivers will often refuse to pick up *cuarteto* fans after dances are over.

Cuarteto groups were originally made up of a piano, a string bass, an accordion, a violin, and a singer who played for Spanish and Italian immigrant communities in the countryside (Hepp 1988:59–60, 65–69). The name *cuarteto*, which means "quartet," referred to the four instrumentalists; the singer was never counted. Since those early days, *cuarteto* groups have evolved in size and instrumentation—they now often have a dozen or so members—thus they could more appropriately be called "bands" or "orchestras" rather than "quartets." With urbanization and industrialization, the groups eventually penetrated the city of Córdoba, where three ensembles (Chébere, Tru-la-lá, and Carlos Jiménez) reigned supreme in 1994 (Ortiz, Gregoratti, and Arrascaeta 11 March 1995:1C). Although contemporary groups prefer to play in Córdoba, smaller ones tour the country from dance to dance in their well-worn buses.

Members of *cuarteto* groups who own their bands must spend extra hours in their offices handling such matters as publicity, promotion, and administration. In fact, *cuarteto* groups are incorporated companies. Band personnel are often labeled as follows, according to their "importance": owners (this category includes solo singers, who own their own groups), arrangers, singers, instrumentalists, and announcers. Since groups routinely release two compact discs per year and play from three to six dances per week, *cuarteto* has become big business in Córdoba.

Instruments currently used to perform this music include a combination of electric and electronic keyboards, electric guitar, bass guitar, Latin percussion, drum set, brass, and accordion. Groups often have approximately ten instrumentalists and two singers. In bands that have two singers, one performs upbeat Caribbean-influenced selections ("*tropical*" ones) and the other sings slower songs based on rock tunes or ballads ("*moderno*" ones). Bands that have only one singer often stick to a style called *cuarteto-cuarteto*, which is more closely linked to the original *cuarteto* style than are *tropical* and *moderno.* Although the *tunga-tunga* accompaniment pattern is normally found in all *cuarteto* music—whether it be original material or covers of songs originally written in non-*cuarteto* styles to which the *tunga-tunga* has been added—there has been a definite evolution in *cuarteto* style, even in the most tradition-minded groups, since 1943; each band has its own musical style and group of followers.

Setting the Scene

Categorizing *Cuarteto*

Cuarteto has always had a different function and social milieu than more well-known genres of music from the Southern Cone, such as Chilean *nueva canción* and Argentine *rock nacional.* The *nueva canción* movement, for example, began by bringing Chilean folk songs to the national consciousness and showing the value of peasant and working-class culture; it eventually helped its middle-class followers to create a political identity associated with sociopolitical protest, labor movements, and reform. An anti-imperialist genre as well, it opposed domination by foreign powers and joined hands with other people who had a similar outlook (Moreno 1986:108). It came to have variations in almost every Latin American country and came to symbolize the 1960s pan–Latin American search for identity and the plight of the Latin American (Tumas-Serna 1992:139, 146). Regarding Argentine *rock nacional,* this genre became a phenomenon which from 1976 to 1983 helped Argentine young people who opposed the military dictatorship in power to create and inhabit a space of their own that was protected from the regime. *Rock nacional* was associated mostly with youth from Buenos Aires; it was not very popular in Córdoba or elsewhere in the interior at first and only eventually caught on nationally (Marzullo and Muñoz 1987:29). Over time, an identity was constructed within which rock singers "became leaders who, through the lyrics of their songs, gave form to an alternative, countercultural music that challenged the ideology of the dictatorship" (Vila 1992:209).

Cuarteto more correctly belongs to a group of musics to which Keil has referred as "people's musics," that is, musics such as reggae, samba, tango, polka, and *jùjú* that fit between the categories of folk (rural, illiterate) and popular (mass-mediated) music and which evolved "in the wake of massive and disruptive rural to urban migration" in the twentieth century (Pacini Hernandez 1995:231; Keil 1985:119). More specifically, *cuarteto* fits into a newer type of "people's musics," such as *bachata, brega,* and *chicha,* that developed in Latin America in the 1960s with the onset of migration, urbanization, and industrialization. These musics were considered very low class and were rejected until they exhibited some economic potential. Originally created by internal migrants living on the fringes of cities who combined rural traditions with newer urban ones, they were considered low class due both to their followers' low socioeconomic status and their hybridity. Excluded from the mainstream media at first, they flourished through informal networks of distribution until they were later reluctantly "accepted" (Pacini Hernandez 1995:232–37).

The Area of Córdoba

Córdoba, Argentina's second largest city (it numbers approximately 1,200,000), has many features besides *cuarteto* that give it a special personality (Cinti 1992:20). One of the tourist capitals of Argentina, the province receives thousands of visitors every summer who come to enjoy its rolling sierras, flat pampas, and various cultural and musical festivals; the regional economy is also based on the automotive industry, agriculture, and cattle. The lasting influence of the Jesuits and other ecclesiastical groups can be seen in the religious conservatism and the numerous churches and chapels found in the area (Ball 1990:145–50; Bischoff 1979:76). A center of learning from the beginning, the city's Universidad Nacional de Córdoba, founded by the Jesuits in 1613, was the first university established in Argentina and the second one founded in Latin America (Cinti 1992:20; Ball 1990:32). Some of the most beautiful examples of colonial architecture in Argentina, both sacred and secular, are also found in Córdoba (Ball 1990:145). The area has long had the reputation of being a center of rebellion as well: a revolt by students led to reforms at the Universidad Nacional in 1918, for example, and many protest movements have been cradled in Córdoba's labor unions (Cinti 1992:20–23).

Renowned for their special type of humor, people from Córdoba have the ability to laugh at themselves, to make others look ridiculous, and to invent short nicknames for everybody they know (Hepp 1988:227–50).

Comedians are standard fare at the National Folklore Festival held in Cosquín, Córdoba, every January because humor is considered to be a part of the province's folklore ("El humor de los cordobeses" 1995:C1). Since *cordobeses* (people from Córdoba) speak with a special accent or drawl, Argentines who are not from the area—especially those from Buenos Aires—often poke fun at or even deride how they speak. The phrase *voy a* becomes *vúa* in Córdoba, for example (Cinti 1992:22).

Because of its central location in the heartland of Argentina, Córdoba has been the crossroads of many travel and trade routes since its founding in 1573. While traffic to and from the Río de la Plata estuary was not openly permitted, for example, manufactured goods from Spain went through Córdoba on their way to the rest of Argentina from Panama, Peru, and Chile (Scobie 1971:53). The city served as a customs office and slave distribution center for a time, and early mail routes went through the region (Ball 1990:32, 38; Bischoff 1979:68–73; Scobie 1971:58, 255). Córdoba's importance began to decline after Buenos Aires became the fiscal and administrative center of the Viceroyalty of the Río de la Plata in 1776. Following a long series of events (the signing of the declaration of independence, the resolution of some civil wars, and the drawing up of a federal constitution), Buenos Aires was turned in 1880 into a federal district much like the District of Columbia, and from then on has been Argentina's major center of power (Ball 1990:32–33, 37; Romero 1968:100, 152–58).

Class and Ethnic Considerations regarding Córdoba and Argentina

When the Spaniards arrived in the River Plate region, they for the most part established their communities by basing them upon extant ones of agrarian Indian peoples. The *comechingones* of Córdoba, for example, who had a semi-agricultural economy, were easily absorbed as a labor force (Scobie 1971:48). By taking it for granted that the natives should serve them, the Spanish fulfilled their need to rule over others without having to do manual labor themselves—an aversion to which was brought over from Spain (Scobie 1971:29–30; Ratier 1971:36–38). The weakness of the Indian value system allowed them to impose Hispanic culture and Catholicism with little resistance, especially on *reducciones* (mission communities); the Indians were clearly considered as inferior beings (Romero 1968:23, 25). Non-agrarian areas without established native communities generally remained in the hands of hostile Indians who lived by hunting and could not be dominated (Andrews 1980:15; Endrek 1966:22; Mörner 1992:213; Scobie 1971:36).

The first African slaves arrived to Córdoba in 1588, and from that time on, there was much miscegenation among the three races, Spanish, Indian, and African. According to the 1779 census, for example, there were 17,340 Spaniards, 5,482 Indians, 14,892 free blacks/mulattoes, and 6,338 black slaves in Córdoba (Bischoff 1979:69–71; Endrek 1966: 12–13). Since many Indians had died massively in the early 1700s from disease brought from abroad (Arcondo 1993:71–77), most of Córdoba's early inhabitants of mixed blood were of combined European and African ancestry (Endrek 1966:22). Over time, especially in the countryside, Córdoba's population started to become "whiter." It is surmised that this decline in the black population was in part due to the practice of calling a person *"trigueño"* (wheat-colored) and counting him as white once his skin color had become light through miscegenation and he displayed no African physical features (Andrews 1980:83–85).

The general terminology that came to be used was *moreno* for blacks and *pardo* for all categories of mixed bloods, be they *mestizo, mulatto, zambo,* or other (Andrews 1980:9). At first the elite (white) Spanish ruling class accepted and recognized their *mestizo* offspring as equals (Endrek 1966:5, 21; Scobie 1971:46). However, as the group of racially mixed people, especially those of illegitimate birth and African blood, quickly became very large, this ruling class began to establish regulations to maintain its superior status (Endrek 1966:7). The Spaniards controlled government administration, access to education, and social privileges (Andrews 1980:46; Endrek 1966:54–68). Those at the bottom of the social pyramid (blacks, especially unfreed slaves) found it almost impossible to rise above the station of life into which they were born; generally speaking, the darker one's skin, the worse his economic and social position (Andrews 1980:17–18; Endrek 1966:27–29; Scobie 1971: 46–48; Szuchman 1980:48–49, 60–61).

After conversion, the Spaniards could no longer justify their domination of both the Indian and slave populations by saying they were heathens without souls. As a result, physical and personal factors came into play, which resulted in a mixture of racial and social prejudice (Endrek 1966:4, 94). The lower-class, darker-skinned population that did manual labor began to be deemed illiterate, dishonest, morally loose, vagrant, and lazy, and dark skin color and nonwhite body characteristics came to be seen more than ever as signs of inferiority (Ratier 1971:19–20). These stereotypes became so firmly embedded in the consciousness of the population that after slavery was abolished and skin color was no longer a consideration, the social structure of prejudice already put into place remained (and still remains) fixed in people's minds (Andrews 1980:39, 207; Endrek 1966:24, 96, 98; Ratier 1971:41, 44).

Skin color was not the only factor determining social class. A person with very white skin could be classified as a *mulatto* if he had ancestors who had been manual laborers, for example, and to the contrary, a dark-skinned person whose economic situation was good could be "white" (Andrews 1980:17; Endrek 1966:23–24; Ratier 1971:28, 44). Indians, who were considered as a separate racial category from the castes, "acquired a legal status midway between that of the whites and the slaves" (Andrews 1980:45).

When European immigrants began arriving in the country as a mandate of the 1853 constitution and Enlightenment ideals, most remained in the littoral regions (Andrews 1980:20–21; Ball 1990:39; Bischoff 1979:289; Szuchman 1980:3–9, 49). As a result, the population of Buenos Aires was three-quarters foreign-born by 1910 and became much "whiter" than before (Scobie 1971:33, 134). The countryside remained much more *mestizo* (i.e., darker), traditional, and conservative than the capital city, and its social elite and caste structure remained in place much longer (Andrews 1980:22; Scobie 1971:31–32, 150; Szuchman 1980:32, 49, 60). The immigrants who did make it to the interior frequently became internal migrants to urban centers because the promises of land originally made to them were often not honored (Fogal 1978:272–73; Ratier 1971:30; Szuchman 1980:36–38, 46, 78, 101). Others became tenant farmers, since most of the land was already held by large landowners (Mörner 1992:231; Ratier 1971:30; Scobie 1971:130–31; Szuchman 1980:77). As a result, these foreigners became artisans, manual laborers, and businessmen instead of the *pardos*, who had absorbed the disdain of manual labor of their masters and preferred to work as domestics (Andrews 1980:183–84; Fogal 1978:272–73; Mörner 1992:231).

Much of the original motivation for encouraging immigration to Argentina had racial and cultural overtones (Andrews 1980:103–105; Ratier 1971:21–23; Szuchman 1980:74). When Argentine intellectuals promoted immigration, it was because they felt the background and lasting accomplishments of native Argentines and Spaniards had led to inferior results when compared with those made by famous European and U.S. writers, artists, and scientists (Weinberg 1977:58–61, 66–71). The solution, as they saw it, was to import new blood of a superior, Anglo-Saxon race to show Argentines the way toward law, order, reason, progress, and a more advanced type of life (Bunkley 1948:5–7, 34–35; Fogal 1978:272; Szuchman 1980:75–77). The magic transformation of Hispanicism did not materialize, however, since no real plan to change Argentine mentality via immigration was implemented (Bunkley 1948: 38–42; Szuchman 1980:75–76, 172). Not only that, it was mostly Italians, Spaniards, and French who arrived in Argentina—not Anglo-Saxons (Bunkley 1948:25–26).

From the 1780s on, the extant gulf between Buenos Aires and the interior grew larger (Scobie 1971:26–27, 49–50, 58–63). While the capital was a white, cosmopolitan, European-oriented, bustling, and liberal city of inhabitants who rejected Church temporal powers, as well as a financial, cultural, and commercial center, the rest of the country lagged behind in its placid, conservative world of Hispanic-creole-native values and Church-dominated life (Scobie 1971:136, 209). The color division between Buenos Aires and the interior became quite evident many years later, during the Depression and the two world wars, when millions of people from the interior became internal migrants to the cities seeking work in the newly founded factories there (Falcoff and Dolkart 1975:8–9; Fogal 1978:276; Ratier 1971:13–14; Scobie 1971:234–36). This influx of workers caused some city dwellers—especially in Buenos Aires—to feel afraid, since the new arrivals were different in skin color and mannerisms from the generally white population there (Andrews 1980:209–10; Ratier 1971:44–45). Demeaning expressions showing the "inferiority" of the man from the interior thus arose, *cabecita negra* (literally, black little head) being one of the most common in the 1930s and '40s (Ratier 1971:9, 32–33). *Cabecitas* were automatically assumed to be *peronistas* (followers of Juan Domingo Perón) as well—another reason for *porteños* (inhabitants of Buenos Aires) to be afraid of and despise them (Fogal 1978: 279; Ratier 1971:14; Scobie 1971:247–49). The expression *cabecita negra* gradually faded in favor of "*hermanitos del interior*" (little brothers from the interior) or "*pobres*" (poor people), phrases used in a patronizing fashion.

Regarding the indigenous population, many Araucanians, in particular, were killed off in the Conquest of the Desert in the late 1880s, a government plan to rid Patagonia of warlike Indians to free up land for farming and grazing (Ratier 1971:9; Scobie 1971:14, 39, 85, 115). Little is published nowadays regarding the few remaining Indian groups (Andrews 1980:215). As for the black population, it also disappeared rapidly over time (Andrews 1980:4–5, 79–93, 109). Race and ethnicity continue to be major concerns in Argentina: *porteños*, in particular, proudly talk of their European ancestry, which supposedly makes them "different" from the rest of Latin Americans (Andrews 1980:109, 212–17; Ratier 1971:10, 25). Many Argentines insist there is no racial prejudice in the country (Andrews 1980:214–15).

Over time, terminology has changed in Argentina to designate extent of "blackness": the terms *pardo* and *moreno* fell by the wayside in the mid-nineteenth century in favor of the expression *gente de color*, "people of color" (Andrews 1980:199). "*Negro*" is presently the term used by whites to refer to anyone who has African features—whether this person has light or dark skin (Andrews 1980:200–204, 210). Calling a person a "*negro*" can now even be an expression of affection, especially in the interior, but there are shades of meaning in the use of the term (Ratier 1971:77–78). A new trend is to call *mestizo* inhabitants of neighboring countries such as Paraguay, Chile, and Bolivia, who have come to Argentina looking for economic opportunities and are seen as inferior, *cabecitas* (Falcoff and Dolkart 1975:8–9; Mörner 1992:243; Ratier 1971:13). This new type of prejudice, based on skin color and foreign mannerisms, is yet another manifestation of the social and racial divisions which have long existed in Argentina (Andrews 1980:215).

Social Status of *Cuarteto*

For the most part, *cuarteto* is today looked down upon by the (white) middle- and upper-class inhabitants of Córdoba; it is considered to be a type of music associated with the poorer, darker-skinned inhabitants of the city who are descendants of racially mixed unions. These same upper- and middle-class people openly voice their disgust of how elementary the genre is (some say it is not music at all), insist they would never enter a dance hall, and generally believe that *cuarteto* dances are highly dangerous orgies and/or free-for-alls. Some hypocritical elitists, however, use a *cuarteto* tune or two to enliven their own private parties, and some university students attend dances held by certain more "acceptable" groups, such as Chébere. Famous entertainers and movie stars have hired *cuarteto* groups to perform at events they have sponsored as well.

It is commonly said and/or assumed that *cuarteteros* (*cuarteto* fans) are poorly educated people who hold jobs as office workers, domestics, day laborers, factory workers, and other poorly paid, menial positions. It is also said that many of these people live in poor parts of the city, especially the slums, and that their morals are very loose. In addition, *cuarteto* musicians are supposedly *negros* ("niggers") who perform this genre of music because they could not succeed at being professional soccer players—another form of popular culture associated with the marginalized, darker-skinned, lower classes. *Cuarteto* music and those who dance and listen to it are thus considered one and the same by this more elite sector of the population, an attitude that dates back to both the racial and social prejudice that arose during colonial times and the later predominant immigrant's scorn for the native.

As has been the fate of most types of popular music in Argentina, for the most part, musicologists have not considered *cuarteto* worthy of serious study. Little has been written about *cuarteto* by journalists, either, except to criticize various "deficient" aspects of the music and the *cuarteto* phenomenon without giving concrete reasons—only emotional and ethnocentric ones—for what is being stated (Salton 1988:1–2). As Pujol has pointed out (1989:67), this fact demonstrates a general historical intolerance in Argentina of forms of mass popular culture; only the subject of the attack has changed over time. The desire to eliminate the "other," the "unknown," and the "marginal" has been attempted through the cultivation of institutionalized mass consensus and prejudice in an attempt to "assassinate" and "amputate" what is feared and misunderstood until it gains respectability.

Kinds of popular music that have gone through a process of rejection and gradual acceptance in Argentina have included tango, jazz, folk music, and *rock nacional. Cuarteto* is only the most recent object of the attack against "otherness," this time complicated by the genre's low-class associations (Salton 1988:8–9). This process of musical acceptance in Argentina has often had a political connection as well: since the country's elite has long looked to Europe for its cultural models, "expressive forms related to traditional music have been significant in the national life only when the lower social strata were important in the nation's politics" (Fogal 1978:284). *Cuarteto* is a paradox, since it has been successful during populist regimes and with the lower classes despite its European origins.

In the case of *cuarteto*, its followers do not see it as having any political or counterhegemonic connection; they do not recognize the potential that such a mass movement could have in promoting social change, nor do they see their star singers either as leaders of a movement or as symbols of any ideology. To the contrary, dancers say they go to dance events to forget about their troubles, have a good time, and be with friends. Lyrics purposely avoid anything controversial, such as religion, protest, or politics.

Cuarteto followers, in fact, do not want their music to be discussed in this light; they do not want to be analyzed as members of a lumpen-proletariat or as actors in a class struggle described in a neo-Marxist way. Thus from the start, I promised all those who helped me that I would not write about *cuarteto* from such a perspective; my study was to be a "musical" one of the genre. It is for this reason that *cuarteto* is not addressed from a "political" viewpoint or interpreted within a political or class framework in this book. My own years in Argentina have made me hesitant to address any aspect of Argentine culture in a "political" way as well; I lived in Buenos Aires from 1975 to 1987, where I was a professional flutist in the major symphony orchestras, and continue to maintain my permanent residency status there.[2]

Objective

This book, which is an ethnography and social history of the Argentine *cuarteto* world, is the result of my adventures as a researcher, dancer, and musician in Córdoba from September 1994 to June 1995, a return trip to Córdoba in September 1995, and a follow-up trip to both Buenos Aires and Córdoba made during June and July of 1998; the musical evolution of the genre is also addressed. Throughout the book, the *cuarteto* world and its music are presented and described with an emphasis placed on musical innovation and the roles and contributions of individual actors—including my own—in this ever-changing environment. As *cuarteto* has changed in its move from the countryside, where it was a kind of immigrants' music, to its present urban setting, musical innovation has played an important role. Since the major portion of my research was carried out in 1994 and '95, I have chosen to describe the *cuarteto* world as I found it during that time period and have written about it in the present tense. What I found three years later, in summer 1998, is presented in chapter 7—this time written in the past tense—in order to reinforce the aspect of constant change which is an inherent part of the *cuarteto* scene.

Goals and Theoretical Background of the Book

I chose to concentrate on the role of individual innovation in musical change in my ethnographic approach because several related aspects of *cuarteto* were intriguing to me. The *tunga-tunga*, for one, has been the identifying feature (symbol) of the genre since 1943 and is supposed to be present in every *cuarteto* tune; changing it would mean modifying the corresponding dance steps, which dancers do not want to do. (*"Tunga-tunga"* is often used to mean *"cuarteto."*) Despite this fact, some groups played the *tunga-tunga* quite prominently in 1994–95, whereas others tried to hide it. In the case of the band named Chébere, for example, the *tunga-tunga* was removed often enough to make people argue about whether or not the group really played *cuarteto* music at all. When Carlos Jiménez, the most famous singer of *cuarteto*, released a compact disc called *Raza Negra* (Black Race) in 1994, he created a true sensation: some selections fused *cuarteto* with African-influenced styles of music and others did not have the *tunga-tunga*. Even more interesting is the fact that Jiménez went back to the original *cuarteto* style with his very next recording, *El Marginal* (The Marginal Man).[3]

Second, innovation seemed to be encouraged as a means of preventing boredom, since the same people attended dances night after night and musicians played the same tunes over and over again for months on end; groups had to come up with two new compact discs per year. Third, since I noticed that some bands performed with written-out music whereas others played by ear, I wondered how this might affect musical change. Last of all, I observed that the hierarchical structures of each band were quite different. It seemed to me that these internal organizational structures could possibly have an effect on innovation, especially since each band had its own distinctive musical style.

While planning my research, I kept in mind the following passages by John Kaemmer, which show the relevance of what I hoped to do:

Individual motivations are a key element in decisions affecting the course of action, but individuals must work within the framework of the group in arriving at decisions involving public performance. Group decisions are an area where levels of interaction are important. . . . Understanding the processes of music change requires investigation of the incentives motivating people to choose new courses of action, as well as the constraints that motivate them to do things the customary way (1993:182–83).

Many forms of historical treatment still leave untouched the question as to why certain innovations are integrated into the musical life of a society and others are not, or why certain musical idioms disappear and others remain. An important question concerning music change is how individual behavior that is subject to social pressures can still lead to new socio-cultural norms. Examining these processes of change can substantially increase the range of explanations offered for present forms of music activity (1993: 170).

From the start I was well aware that most of the research already carried out regarding musical change has involved acculturation—not innovation—since studying innovation is difficult: it is hard to anticipate and/or document and normally takes more time to research than acculturation does (Nettl 1986b:360–73; Nettl 1992:381; Bascom, cited in Kubik 1986:57). Although I realized that work done in this area would be appreciated by ethnomusicologists, I also knew that I would not be able to rely on any extant methodology as an aid (Béhague 1986:18; Blacking 1986:12; Merriam 1964:313, 319; Nettl 1992:381).

Since I was considering musical innovation, it was logical to turn to the writing of H. G. Barnett, who has written the most important anthropological work on the general topic of innovation and has stressed that all cultural changes are initiated by individuals (1953:39). According to Barnett (1953:9), all innovations are recombinations of mental configurations; in other words, all that is "new" is based upon something that is "old." The mental content of new ideas is socially defined and its substance is for the most part dictated by tradition, he writes, but the manner of treating the content, the altering and reordering of it, is determined by the potentialities and liabilities of the human mind (1953:16). At times it is different types of personal motivation, in the form of self-wants, or needs (for ego gratification, prestige, creativity, avoidance of problems, and/or personal relief), that lead to innovation, he says (1953: 97–181). Innovation also depends on such things as individual differences (attitudes toward experimentation, character and personality, capacity for meaningful observation, ability to retain knowledge, and the talent to analyze everyday experiences and turn them into something new), the concepts held by a culture toward change, and "opportunity differentials," that is, differences in cultural surroundings (1953:20). Innovation occurs more often when it is expected, when people collaborate simultaneously while exploring possibilities which pool their ideas, and when people of differing thoughts or even from different places come together and interact (1953:40–43, 56–57). Competition and deprivation of essentials can also lead to innovation, adds Barnett (1953:72–80).

A person's cultural base, breadth and depth of personal knowledge, and experience are important factors in his innovative potential as well, says Barnett (1953:41–42). Without the necessary ingredients and concentration of data in his cultural inventory, some of which may come from cultural borrowing, a person cannot innovate; facility and extent of communication influence the accumulation of ideas (1953:40). There are also constraints to innovation: in his interaction with others, a person may face certain relations of power which limit his access to decision-making and creativity. The more freedom an individual has to explore on his own, says Barnett (1953:65–71), the more innovative he can be; dependence upon authority and restrictions make for a decrease in innovative potential (1953:65).

A model proposed by Ward Goodenough to explain culture change also seemed appropriate to apply in the study of musical innovation. According to Goodenough (1981:98), each individual has his own personal outlook, or propriospect, which amounts to his total knowledge of other cultures, his own culture, and what he has learned (and continues to learn) on his own. All of these various personal outlooks within a given culture form a reservoir of skills and resources, that is, a "culture pool," upon which the members of that particular culture can draw. By studying the processes governing the makeup and selective use made of knowledge from a society's culture pool, it is possible to see how cultural change and evolution occur. Decisions made regarding culture pools are influenced by personal and societal needs as well as the limitations of members' knowledge, and these decisions affect the culture pool's future content, the environment, and institutional structures (1981:119).

Goodenough uses similar concepts to explain the functioning of power relationships in cultural change. In order to see how individuals, each with different wants and needs, arrive at a "shared culture," they must be looked at from a "multicultural" standpoint, he says (1978: 82–83). Individuals belong to many different group networks of interaction (microcultures) that together make up a society's larger, ordered system or "culture" (macroculture). Since each microculture allows a certain degree of variance among its members, interaction and membership in microcultural networks overlap, and most people must interact with many different microcultures, individuals are normally "multicultural." A group's "culture pool" is therefore the total knowledge of and experience with different micro- and macrocultures its members have.

In all this interaction, variance in microcultural networks is kept within certain bounds, elements in a group's culture pool gain and lose status, and overlap and size of group networks are controlled. Says Goodenough, "all of these processes involve people pursuing their various and competing interests, a consideration that brings us back to privilege and power" (1978:84). Having access to the microcultures in which one can demonstrate personal skills and knowledge is thus critical in order to have influence in cultural change (1978:86).

The only theory specifically regarding musical innovation that seemed relevant to draw upon was that of John Blacking. In his work, Blacking (1986:10) emphasized that music-making and musical products are the results of individual decision-making about "how, when, and where to act, and what cultural knowledge to incorporate in the sequences of action." As far as he was concerned, musical and cultural changes "are the results of decisions made by individuals about music-making and music or about social and cultural practice, on the basis of their experiences of music and social life and their attitudes to them in different social contexts" (1986:3).

Several difficulties arose when trying to put some of Blacking's ideas into practice. For one, he felt that every case of musical change involves a critical moment of cognitive change, and that it is important to locate when the change has taken place (1977:13–14). This moment of conscious change, that is, "decision-making," may be preceded by a period of latency, he said, which makes analysis difficult (1977:13–14). Although he acknowledged the time problem involved in obtaining the "microscopic data" necessary for this type of study (1986:14), he made no provision for locating moments of unconscious decision-making. Yet according to Barnett (1953:16), many innovations are made unconsciously and are not even wanted; others appear upon impulse.

In addition, Blacking tried to show that musical change is not the same as other types of social and cultural change, that it is something much more radical than innovation or variation. Unfortunately, he did not explain how to determine the differences in these levels of terminology or provide a way to pinpoint just what "musical" change is. And despite his insistence on the value of intensive studies regarding individual decision-making and nonmusical factors related to musical performance (1986:15), he did not explain or identify either what these decision-making processes and nonmusical factors are or how to study them (1977:18). I eventually found my own way of applying Blacking's ideas (see below).

While preparing my study, I also used Gerhard Kubik's recommendation of following a comparative case study approach focused on the individual when studying musical change that is stimulated from within a culture (1986:58) and kept in mind his idea that changes in a musical tradition are usually brought about by a (simultaneous) combination of "externally stimulated culture change" and "internally stimulated culture change" (1986:54–55). Some sort of external influence is a necessity for change, says Kubik, so external factors should not be disregarded even when studying innovation: "Human beings are naturally inclined toward cultural and psychological inertia. No one will change his patterns of thinking or his way of life without some external force exerted on him. Such a force may become effective in his close environment, e.g., family or professional milieu, but it may also originate at a great distance" (1986:58). In his opinion (1986:54–55), some external factors which may promote musical change include availability of new materials and/or technology, changes in a tradition provoked by ideological interference (religious, political, or nationalistic movements), and changes in a tradition provoked by commercial interference (the record industry, for example).

My Guidelines

After considering all of these scholars' theories, I came up with a way in which I planned to study innovation in the *cuarteto* world. I began by identifying areas in which "decision-making" and/or possibilities for innovation could be found in musical groups: musical composition, selection of repertoire and musical personnel, arranging, rehearsals, performance, and recording. I then spoke with each of the individual musicians (owners, arrangers, singers, instrumentalists, and announcers) in the six bands with which I eventually worked regarding their personal backgrounds, musical contributions, and innovations in the above-mentioned categories. Each man tailored his comments according to the degree of innovation and/or participation permitted in the band of which he was presently a member.

The six groups with which I worked were selected for specific reasons. I wanted to work with Chébere, Tru-la-lá, and Carlos Jiménez, the three most important groups in the city. I also needed to work with bands that had been in existence a fair number of years in order to be able to discuss issues of innovation with the musicians. I chose Gary (his band also goes by this name), since he works in the *bailantas* (dance halls of Buenos Aires); Santamarina, as an example of a longstanding group that has been successful in the interior; and La Banda del "Negro" Videla, since Videla is an important figure in *cuarteto* history who has only partially succeeded as a group owner and who is partner with Emeterio Farías, a key *cuarteto* promoter. The greater part of my experience in Córdoba involved the band of Carlos Jiménez. I chose to concentrate on his group and place it into perspective with the other five for three reasons: Jiménez is the city's most important singer by far, a special case of innovation occurred in his group during my stay, and I recorded with his band. Due to the circumstances, I spent much more time with this ensemble than with the others.

I eventually became a permanent fixture at dances, rehearsals, band offices, cafes where musicians congregate, radio stations, record stores, and all other locations where *cuarteto* was present. Although the men did not understand what I was doing at first and thought I was a journalist, they soon came to call me *la yanqui* (the Yankee) or *la americana* (the American woman). They were happy to have me with them and helped me in every way they could. Although many people outside the *cuarteto* world questioned what I was doing and insulted me regarding my work because of *cuarteto*'s controversial nature, I found almost everyone within my chosen dance community to be quite helpful. I came to live and breathe *cuarteto*.

Content and Organization of the Book

Regarding the content and organization of this work, time constraints obliged me to rely on the existing literature for historical information. Since I was not able to check the accuracy of these materials, there may be some errors in the historical portion of this book. It has not been possible to include page numbers or the names of some sources, either, because I obtained so much material in the form of unidentified photocopies.

Much of what is found here has been taken and/or translated from interview transcripts; all translations are my own. For reasons of space, no original transcripts in Spanish have been included. Owing to the great number of informants involved in the study and the desire of most of them to keep their comments confidential, only in isolated instances have informants been identified by name; this convention has been followed mainly in chapters 5, 6, and 7, where named individuals are interviewed at length (and listed in the bibliography), in order to show clearly that this information has not come from a published source. When published sources have been cited, interview data and my own knowledge gained while doing participant and nonparticipant observation have often been added to what is being documented. For the sake of clarity, names of recordings are italicized, whereas song titles are enclosed within quotation marks. Translations of song titles are given in parentheses, followed by names of songwriters written in upper-case letters. In the case of "El Paraguas," for example, the translation of the song title and names of the songwriters would appear as follows: ("The Umbrella"; J. MEDAGLIA—T. VALDÉZ—P. CERINI). The photographs in the book are only a small sampling of those I took in 1994–95 and 1998. All musical transcriptions are also my own.

After the initial introductory chapter, the next two chapters are devoted to a history and ethnography of *cuarteto* music and its style. Chapter 2 gives the social and musical history and evolution of *cuarteto*, fitting in ethnic, racial, and political elements which have influenced its development. Emphasis is placed on "musical" changes—not song lyrics—since *cuarteto* lyrics have never been considered an important feature of the genre. I also attempt to show why the band of Carlos Jiménez, which is to be singled out later on, is different in regard to musical style; part of this process involves a discussion of musical features of his compact disc *Raza Negra* that made it an anomaly. Although I did extensive legwork and talked with executives from the major labels in Argentina which record *cuarteto*, it was not possible to include a compact disc of musical examples with this book due to problems with copyright. For this reason, transcriptions of several *cuarteto* songs have been provided to illustrate the musical evolution of the genre, and information on where to buy *cuarteto* recordings is given in Appendices A and B. In chapter 3, I give a detailed ethnographic account of the *cuarteto* world based on my participation in it. The chapter on dancing (chapter 4) has been included because dance is such an integral part of *cuarteto* music. The dance scene of the *bailantas* in Buenos Aires is covered only enough to explain how it differs from the *cuarteto* world in Córdoba; another entire book could be written about such a huge topic.

The subsequent chapters of the book are devoted to the specifics of my individual research with band members. In chapter 5, the group dynamics and cultures of the six groups studied are described in order to put the band of Carlos Jiménez into the proper perspective. Goodenough's theories of multiculturalism and the culture pool, discussed above, are drawn upon in order to show that individual group members are subject to power relationships which affect their access to musical decision-making processes and personal contributions.

Chapter 6 is devoted to the group of Carlos Jiménez. Once again, drawing on the Goodenough culture pool concept, each individual member of the band is introduced, one at a time, in the form of a short biography complete with quotes; Carlos Jiménez is left for last. By describing each man's propriospect and opinions regarding group decision-making processes, the contents of the band's culture pool and the ways in which group members interact are documented. The influence of individual band members in the final musical product also becomes evident.

The concept of multiple voices, that of allowing each man to speak about himself and his contributions to the group, has been adopted in chapters 6 and 7 in an effort to get closer to the actors involved; it eliminates the distant and "objective" approach so often adopted by ethnographers in the past (Rosaldo 1993:15, 21). As a way of making these band members come alive, their true names are used and photographs of them are provided (except for two men from whom copyright clearances could not be obtained).

Marcus and Fischer (1986:15) have suggested that the current intellectual problem in anthropology is "to find innovative ways of describing at a microscopic level the process of change itself," not to explain change "within broad encompassing frameworks of theory"; they call for a "jewelers'-eye view of the world." And according to Merriam (1964:317), "especially important are those studies in which music change has been documented as it occurs, a relatively rare experience"; these laboratory types of situations are helpful for understanding "not only changing forms but the processes and reasons for change" (1964:318).

From 1994 through 1995, I had a chance to experience and document musical change (innovation) in process in the band of Carlos Jiménez. In September 1994, the group launched *Raza Negra,* in which *cuarteto* music was combined with African rhythms and genres. Since this type of fusion was unheard of in Córdoba, especially from a traditionalist such as Jiménez, these "changes" made to *cuarteto* music, and the risks involved, were highly publicized. In May 1995, I was fortunate enough to rehearse, perform live, and record one tune ("Penita") with this same group. In this 1995 recording, *El Marginal,* Jiménez made a conscious decision to return to the original *cuarteto* style. My participation was unique because I played piccolo, an instrument that had never before been used in *cuarteto* music.

In order to explain the stylistic changes and innovations that occurred in the band's music during my stay in Córdoba, and the decision-making processes involved, this "slice of time" is described in chapter 6 in the form of two stories preceded by a group history. The tale of how *Raza Negra* came to be recorded is told through the words of Carlos Jiménez by including long quotes taken from an interview. The story of how I performed and recorded the song "Penita" with the group is told in my own words, and my "Penita" account contains an explanation of the return to the old *cuarteto* style. I have used personal narratives not just to make chapter 6 interesting to the reader, but because they "often facilitate the analysis of social processes that have proven difficult even to perceive through distanced normalizing discourse" (Rosaldo 1993:60).

In addition, a study about any kind of change naturally implicates the notion of time. According to Paul Ricoeur, a narrative format must be adopted in processual analysis, since "time and narrative are inseparable" (Ricoeur, cited in Rosaldo 1993:135).

Jiménez is allowed to tell most of the story of *Raza Negra,* since "rather than being merely ornamental, a dab of local color, protagonists' narratives about their own conduct merit serious attention as forms of social analysis"; we also need to take "other people's narrative analyses nearly as seriously as 'we' take our own" (Rosaldo 1993:149). In my own case, an impressionistic narrative style has been adopted as the best way to convey my learning process (what I saw, heard, and felt), give a feeling of closeness, and actively involve the reader in the action (Van Maanen 1988:101–05). It has also been possible to use this type of narrative style, since the Jiménez band members have been introduced to the reader before I tell my story.

In the last chapter, I return to the scene of my research three years later and document the changes that have occurred. Once again, I follow an individualized approach in which I focus on the group of Jiménez, who in 1998 was still number one in Córdoba. I end by explaining the reasons for Jiménez's continued success and discuss the future of *cuarteto.*

The History and Musical Evolution of *Cuarteto*

The story of how *cuarteto* music was founded is common knowledge to *cuarteto* fans: it was born on June 4, 1943, when the first *cuarteto* group, the newly formed Cuarteto Característico Leo, debuted live on a late-night radio program aired on LV3, one of the two local radio stations. Due to the highly favorable response, LV3 continued to have the Cuarteto Leo play on this same program for the next two years, but at an earlier time slot. After successfully performing at a dance for a local immigrant community shortly thereafter, the group's name soon became synonymous with *cuarteto* (Hepp 1988:67–69).

The Cuarteto Leo was founded by Augusto Marzano, a railroad worker who was relocated from Santa Fe to the town of Cruz del Eje, in the province of Córdoba, for work-related reasons. Marzano, a widower, arrived in Córdoba with his daughter, Leonor (Hepp 1988:67; SADAIC 1992:9). A railroad employee by day, Marzano worked as a musician in his off hours; he played flute and piano in Los Bohemios, a twelve-person ensemble of the type that was then called an *orquesta característica,* but which also doubled as an *orquesta típica* (SADAIC 1992:9; Hepp 1988:59, 65). The distinction between *orquestas características* and *orquestas típicas* lay in the repertoire that each performed: *orquestas características* played any dance music except tangos and *milongas* (Ábalos 2 December 1994:2–3; Hepp 1988:59, 62–65). At times, such as in the case of Los Bohemios, *orquestas características* added extra musicians in order to double as *orquestas típicas,* the standard type of ensemble that played tangos and *milongas; orquestas típicas* were more common than *características* (Hepp 1988:59, 65, 201–203). The instrumentation of *orquestas características* was not fixed, but they often used accordion (Ábalos 2 December 1994:2).

Both *orquestas características* and *orquestas típicas* toured Córdoba and the neighboring provinces of Buenos Aires, Santa Fe, and La Pampa playing for groups of Spanish and Italian immigrants. The groups had to travel overland in poor conditions, transport all their own instruments, including pianos, and on occasion, play in places without electricity or water (SADAIC 1992:9–11, 24–26; Hepp 1988:59–60). At first, dances were held on Saturday evenings and were family affairs; women did not go alone (Hepp 1988:65–66, 201). Dance events sometimes stretched into the wee hours of the morning, but more organized ones began at 8:00 PM and ended at 12:00 AM. Announcements were made after every four songs, and no music was put on while the musicians rested (Hepp 1988:68–69). These occasions gave immigrants a chance to rest after a hard week of work and to forget their nostalgia of home (SADAIC 1992:9; Guzmán 1993:1–3).

Although the Cuarteto Leo came out of the *orquesta característica* tradition, it had two novelties. First of all, its repertoire was performed with a newly invented accompaniment pattern, the *tunga-tunga;* this rhythmic-harmonic figure was always heard in the piano and string bass parts. Secondly, its size had been reduced to only four instrumentalists and a singer who also functioned as an announcer. This small size allowed the Cuarteto Leo to travel easily and cheaply, as opposed to what the other groups were doing at the time (Hepp 1988:59–60).

Leonor Marzano, a piano teacher, "invented" the *tunga-tunga* (Hepp 1988:60, 67; SADAIC 1992:9). When her father founded the Cuarteto Leo, which he named after her, he asked her to join; he did not like leaving her alone at night when he went off to perform (Hepp 1988:67). Leonor adopted a style of playing that one of her piano teachers, Genoveva Medina, had taught her (Mareco 6 June 1993:F1): she accented the quarter notes that she played in her left hand (these notes, which corresponded to the syllable "*tun*," were played on the first and third quarter notes of each 4/4 measure) and only lightly played the quarter-note offbeats that she performed with her right hand (these notes, which corresponded to the syllable "*ga,*" were played on the second and fourth quarter notes of each bar). The result was a mechanical, staccato style that helped people to keep the rhythm while they danced. According to observers, Leonor's fingers jumped over the keys of the piano in a spiderlike fashion when she performed ("Un sacudón" 1994:76–77).

The instrumentation of the Cuarteto Leo consisted of string bass (Augusto Marzano), piano (Leonor Marzano), accordion (Miguel Gelfo), and violin (Luis Cabero). It is said by some people, however, that *bandoneón* (an instrument related to the concertina and which is used in tango) was used for a short time in the Cuarteto Leo before the accordion was implemented (SADAIC 1992:9). Fernando Achával acted as both singer and announcer for the group, and *güiro* and tambourine were often used for percussion accompaniment (Hepp 1988:59; Mero 1988:41). Musically speaking, the other identifying stylistic feature of the group, besides the *tunga-tunga,* was the use of the accordion. At first an Italian type of accordion was used, but Gelfo later adopted a German one for its brilliance. The rest of the groups soon followed suit; in those days, a *cuarteto* ensemble needed to have an accordion player in order to get hired. Not only that, the accordion had to be a red one—like Gelfo's (Hepp 1988:62–63).

The Cuarteto Leo, with different personnel, performs in Córdoba to this day. It is now run by Eduardo Gelfo, the son of Miguel Gelfo and Leonor Marzano, who eventually married. When Augusto Marzano died in 1961, he asked his son-in-law to keep the group going (Hepp 1988: 65). Now that his parents are dead, Eduardo Gelfo is maintaining the tradition (SADAIC 1992:9; Barei 1993:84). Although the Cuarteto Leo does not currently perform much in the city of Córdoba, it is still considered to be a symbol of *cuarteto* music. In 1987 it was invited to perform at the prestigious Festival Nacional de Folklore (National Folklore Festival) in Cosquín, Córdoba, the first *cuarteto* group to be asked to do so (Hepp 1988:74–75, 77).

The creation and development of *cuarteto* described above fits within the first of six periods in the history of the genre: 1943–55, 1955–68, 1969–73, 1974–75, 1976–81, and 1982 to the present (Hepp 1988:63–64). As will be shown below, these stylistic periods have coincided with political changes which have taken place in Argentina as well as the growth of populist movements, Peronism in particular (Mero 1988:22). When possible, the development of *cuarteto* will be tied to specific events that happened in Córdoba.

In order to understand how *cuarteto* developed from a rural to an urban genre and changed stylistically in the process, it is first necessary to see how and why such a large immigrant population arrived in the area (with its music), how ethnic considerations played a role, and how the city became an important industrial center. In truth, *cuarteto* music evolved with the arrival of heavy industry in the city of Córdoba and the internal migration that came with it.

Immigration in Argentina and Córdoba

One aspect of both the mandates of the 1853 constitution and the term (1868–1874) of President Domingo Faustino Sarmiento was the arrival of European immigrants to Argentina; most were from Spain and Italy (Ball 1990:39; Szuchman 1980:3–4; Bischoff 1979:289). This move fit in with Sarmiento's desire to remove all of the "barbaric" elements that existed in the country, the gauchos and *caudillos* (strongmen based in the interior), for example, and to promote education and learning for all (Ball 1990:39); to those who believed in the values of the Enlightenment and dreamed of a great Argentina, European culture was a sign of "civilization" (Hepp 1988:53–54).

Most of the immigrants came from 1880 onward and were still arriving in the 1910s (Ball 1990:39; Bischoff 1979:332–33; Scobie 1971: 147–48). These people were needed because the use of steamships and the development of methods for chilling and freezing had made exporting meat and grains to Europe cheaper and more feasible than before; a workforce had to be found for this new processed meat and cereals industry (Scobie 1971:115–19).

The government sought ways to attract immigrants—especially from the north and west of Europe—to the interior of Argentina. The Dirección de Inmigración (Office of Immigration), which used propaganda, arranged for and subsidized the transfer of immigrants from Buenos Aires to the provinces; it was especially proud of its record in Córdoba (Szuchman 1980:3–4). Provincial officials from Córdoba tried to recruit immigrants by going to Buenos Aires and to Europe, the provincial legislature turned over large tracts of fertile land for colonization, generous tax incentives were provided to attract new commercial and industrial establishments, and special dispensations were made to immigrants' organizations to improve relations between local elites and Europeans

(Szuchman 1980:8). With the arrival of the first immigrants to Córdoba (to Colonia Caroya), in 1878, *colonias* (immigrant towns) sprang up alongside the railroads, where for the most part these people settled (Bischoff 1979:287–88, 315).

Industrialization and Internal Migration in Córdoba

In the Depression years of the 1930s and 1940s, agricultural prices in the countryside went down and unemployment increased. Rural residents thus began arriving in Córdoba to seek work in the industries that had sprung up there when European goods had not been available during World War I (Brennan 1994:ix, 3–5, 44–45). Because of its engineering expertise, Córdoba became a popular site for armaments and munitions factories in the 1930s as well as an area where mechanical industries would later be located (Brennan 1994:3, 24–25).

Other advances that were to set the stage for the city's industrial development were undertaken from 1934 to 1940 by Córdoba's Governor Amadeo Sabattini (Brennan 1994:25–26; Bischoff 1979:453–61). Comprehensive systems of road construction, hydroelectric power development, and light industrialization were carried out under his leadership, and the textile, cement, and armaments industries grew (Brennan 1994: 25). President Juan Domingo Perón and the GOU (Grupo Obra de Unificación), a secret military lodge that sympathized with fascist sentiments, also laid part of the groundwork that was to make Córdoba a major industrial center in the 1950s (Brennan 1994:3).

The Six Periods of *Cuarteto*

The "Invention" of *Cuarteto* and Its First Period (1943–1955)

Cuarteto's initial time period corresponded closely to the processes of industrialization and internal migration that occurred in the area and Perón's emergence as a powerful figure. When Perón first appeared on the scene in 1943 as secretary of the Labor and Social Welfare Ministry, he instituted labor reforms, pensions, and the national welfare system. In addition, he constructed schools, hospitals, housing developments, and roads (Ball 1990:43; De Fleur 1970:30). By building his power base from the working class, he easily won the presidential election in 1946 (Ratier 1971:32). On the other hand, his repressive tactics and total intolerance of opposition turned the country into a police state, and his economic policies and social programs were overly ambitious (Scobie 1971:223). When he was exiled in 1955, problems with droughts, a decrease in international grain prices, and the cost of maintaining his state-provided employment and welfare programs had led to a 50 percent increase in the trade deficit (Ball 1990:43, 55; Brennan 1994:6–7).

During this time period, Córdoba became the favorite site for mechanical industries and investors, since cheap electric power was available there (Brennan 1994:28–30). Government and military factories and complexes were established in the area, and Perón succeeded in getting Fiat and Kaiser-Frazier Automobile (Renault) to establish their operations in Córdoba in 1954–55 (Bischoff 1979:513; Brennan 1994: 19, 27–32). Since all of this happened near the time of Perón's exile, it was only after his departure that true growth of the mechanical industry took place and the city came to be called "the Argentine Detroit" (Brennan 1994:ix, 6, 15, 44). One of the major rural-to-urban demographic revolutions in Argentina took place in Córdoba from 1947 to 1970, the auto boom having created the greatest concentration of industrial workers outside of Buenos Aires (Brennan 1994:39, 45). The economy slowed only in the mid-1960s (Brennan 1994:39).

When *cuarteto* first appeared in Córdoba, the city was no longer a small commercial one that depended highly on agriculture for its livelihood, nor was it yet a true industrial center. With the move toward industrialization and the arrival of so many internal migrants to Córdoba, it is not surprising that the genre appeared on the fringes of the city, in working-class *barrios* (neighborhoods), toward the end of this time period; migrants brought their music with them. Although these people had become *grasa* (industrial workers), they still needed to relax on weekends and be part of a community of people like themselves; *cuarteto* served them in the city just as it had in the countryside (Hepp 1988:203–204). At first urban dances were held only on Saturdays, but were later scheduled on Sundays as well; many of the dances were held outdoors (Hepp 1988:207–208). Both *orquestas típicas* and *orquestas características* were hired to play on important occasions, especially for holidays (Hepp 1988:202–203, 209), and *barrio* residents could also listen to *cuarteto* radio broadcasts (Hepp 1988:209).

The *Cuarteto* Setting: 1955–1968

Economically speaking, the second period in the history of *cuarteto* began with the boom of internal migration and the auto industry in Córdoba and ended with the decline of industrial growth in the city. Politically speaking, this same time period corresponded to the exile of Perón through the "Cordobazo," the greatest working-class protest in postwar Latin American history, in 1969 (Brennan 1994:ix).

After Perón departed, a new Latin American positivism in which the state encouraged foreign investment in Argentina was promoted (Brennan 1994:14–17). The ensuing economic downturn that occurred caused violence and dissent (Ball 1990:46). Because of its large concentration of students (who had traditionally been against both the government and the Church), labor unions, and working-class internal migrants, Córdoba was the epicenter of anti-government activity, especially in the 1960s and early 1970s (Brennan 1994:18, 50–53).

When General Juan Carlos Onganía took over the country after a 1966 military coup, he instated a repressive regime in which political parties were banned, the Congress was dissolved, and demonstrations were outlawed. By 1969, the economy had plunged even further, foreign ownership of companies had reached 59 percent, and workers were experiencing a real loss in buying power (Ball 1990:46). The intense discontent with the situation led to the 1969 Cordobazo, which culminated in the overthrow of Onganía (Brennan 1994:ix).

From 1955 to 1968, stylistic changes were made to *cuarteto*, which reached the outskirts of Córdoba. Beginning in the 1950s, Argentines were introduced to Caribbean-influenced types of music, such as *calypso* and *bolero*, which were generically called *música tropical* (or *tropical*). The *tropical* fervor that overtook even middle-class Argentines in the mid-1960s was due mainly to the visits of groups like Los Wawancó and Los Cartageneros to the country; the *cumbia* was the most influential genre (Lewin 1994:222). It was also in the mid-1960s that foreign record companies, such as CBS and RCA, established themselves in Argentina and promoted certain types of music in conjunction with radio stations (Lewin 1994:218). As a result, *tropical* influences began to appear in *cuarteto*.

When the Cuarteto Leo played at the El Negrito dance strip in 1956, on the outskirts of the city, it initiated the suburban *cuarteto* movement. From that time on, it played in halls around the fringes of the city, many of which were open-air, dirt-floored locales, as well as in the countryside. Dances began to be held on Fridays, and the Cuarteto Leo began to perform almost every day of the week; its "golden age" lasted from 1954 to 1975 (Hepp 1988:70–73; SADAIC 1992:10).

Musically speaking, the 1960s was also the time of the Beatles, who were imitated by young Argentines who formed rock bands. During this period of time, raids were made of events in Córdoba at which popular music was performed, certain tunes were prohibited, haircuts were enforced, and some *cuarteto* dances were terminated (Mero 1988:25–26). The first discos and disc jockeys also appeared, music in English became popular, and the use of sound equipment and lowered lighting effects was implemented. Despite these developments, Córdoba's populace kept up its tradition of holding *cuarteto* dances in neighborhood social clubs; disco and rock were taken on by only the middle and upper classes. A folklore boom also occurred in Argentina in the 1960s, but this phenomenon was a lower-middle- and middle-class one as well (Hepp 1988:120; Mero 1988:120–21).

The *Cuarteto* Setting: 1969–1973

By 1973, Argentina had become one of the lesser-developed nations in the world (Ball 1990:54). Guerrilla groups had appeared with the growth of the military, and Onganía's successor had begun to use torture and murder. When the 1973 presidential elections were held, Perón, still in exile, chose Héctor Campora to run as his proxy. Perón returned to the country because of Campora's strong showing and was reelected as president himself in the next elections; Perón's wife was made vice-president (Ball 1990:47).

From the 1969 Cordobazo to the return of Perón in 1973, the third period in the history of *cuarteto,* the genre reached downtown Córdoba. This development was initiated when the Cuarteto Leo and its singer, Carlos Rolán, performed for a Carnival celebration in a sports club, called Rieles Argentinos, in 1969. From this time on, *cuarteto* groups began performing at sports clubs in the city (Hepp 1988:80). *Cuarteto* also began to be affected by types of international music, *folklore de proyección* (folk music which combines acoustic folk instruments with electric and electronic ones and modern "jazz-type" harmonies), and protest music (Barei 1993:44), which led to eventual changes in its instrumentation. For example, when Carlos Rolán left the Cuarteto Leo in 1971 to form his own *cuarteto* group, he incorporated bass guitar and electric piano (Hepp 1988:80).

The *Cuarteto* Setting: 1974–1975

The fourth historical period of *cuarteto* music began with the return of Peronism to Argentina and ended with the military coup of 1976. When

Perón died unexpectedly in 1974, his second wife, Isabel, became president, and the country plunged into a time of economic disaster, intense corruption, and repression. The military then stepped in, removed Isabel from her position in 1976, and put a military junta in place to rule the country (Ball 1990:47).

With the return of Peronism to Argentina, *cuarteto* music made great strides: it got to the general populace and neighboring provinces via a television program called *La Fiesta de los Cuartetos,* which was broadcast to six provinces; the "Cuatro Grandes," Córdoba's four most important groups, appeared on it as did newly formed bands such as Chébere. The Cuarteto Leo was still the most prominent group during this period (Hepp 1988:64, 73–74, 80–81).

Starting in the 1970s, the foreign musical influences that had arrived in Argentina during the prior decades began to be strongly felt in *cuarteto* (Hepp 1988:78). Carlos Rolán, for example, began using *tropical* rhythms in 1974 (Hepp 1988:81). By the 1970s, groups were imitating Caribbean *sonoras* (large ensembles with brass instruments) by using trumpets, trombones, and saxophones, and were taking on elements of the *moderno* (jazz and rock-influenced) style. The use of the accordion, the symbol of traditional *cuarteto* music, declined (Mero 1988:38–39, 41).

The founding of Chébere, in 1974, was to have a permanent effect on *cuarteto* music; the group became the symbol of modernity and change, and its musical style was imitated by many bands that sprang up in its wake (Hepp 1988:78, 87). Formed by several young men who had been influenced by the Beatles, these bohemians played for the love of music (Hepp 1988:88). Innovative, Chébere was the first band to perform with their pianist standing up, to sing with microphones, to incorporate new instruments and musical sounds (the group dropped the accordion and the violin and eventually added such things as a temporary group of female backup singers, synthesizer, trumpets, drum set, electric guitar, saxophones, trombones, and Latin percussion), and to use lights and a show element in their dances (Hepp 1988:87–91; "Chébere: veinte años" 1994:1–4; SADAIC 1992:32–33). In 1976, when Chébere became the rage, the repertoire of the Cuatro Grandes was dropped for a mixture of both fast and slow *moderno* and *melódico* (ballad or *bolero*-influenced) selections, a real novelty. The group later created the present custom of alternating *moderno* and *tropical* sets and began the trend of using foreign vocalists when it hired a Brazilian singer in 1991 (SADAIC 1992:33; "Chébere: veinte años" 1994:4).

The *Cuarteto* Setting: 1976–1981

The fifth period in the history of *cuarteto* largely corresponds to the time of the *Proceso*, the years of military rule in Argentina from 1976 to 1983. It was in 1983, when civilian elections were reinstated and Raúl Alfonsín became president, that democracy returned to the country. The *Proceso* was a brutal time during which guerrillas were repressed and scores of people "disappeared." Universities were closed, since the military viewed attempts of professors and students to gain power as a form of subversion. The foreign debt soared, inflation skyrocketed, and the Falklands/ Malvinas War only made the situation worse (Ball 1990:49).

The Proceso was also an anti-*cuarteto* time: *cuarteto*, protest music, and national rock music were officially banned on May 24, 1976, by the Comité Federal de Radiodifusión (Federal Commission for Radio Broadcasting); from then on, 50 percent of broadcasts were to be of traditional Argentine folkloric music and tango (Barei 1993:46). Television coverage was eliminated, and only one *cuarteto* radio program appeared. Ads were broadcast, but had to be done without the use of music, and cost twice as much as before (Hepp 1988:81–82). It is said that some bands changed their musical style in order that their music might still be performed on radio; by adding new instruments and eliminating the accordion, their music was not considered to be of the *cuarteto* type. According to Rolán, the military men hated the sound of the accordion because of what it symbolized to them; they associated *cuarteto* music with the "marginal" people who danced to it (SADAIC 1992:24; Mero 1988:54). In order for his band to get media coverage, Rolán added trumpets in 1979–80 (Hepp 1988:82); some people say that Chébere began to use a drum set, but only in its recordings, for the same reason (Hepp 1988:90; SADAIC 1992:33; "Chébere: veinte años" 1994:2–3). Bands that began to imitate Caribbean groups, play like combos, or sing romantic songs may have had the same motivation (SADAIC 1992:24).

This change in style also occurred because dance halls were routinely raided by the military during this time period (Mero 1988:54–55), officials often appearing in order to round up everyone there (women, children, older people, and families included), take them to the police station, and book them (Mero 1988:55, 61; Barei 1993:45–46; Hepp 1988: 80–81). Although *cuarteto* enthusiasts sometimes had to outsmart the military by surreptitiously publicizing their dances and holding them secretly, *cuarteto* continued strong (Mero 1988:55–56). This situation led to the establishment of a steady dance circuit in athletic clubs, improvements in these same clubs (roofs were added to many), and the appearance of official *cuarteto* impresarios (Mero 1988:123). The lack of media publicity allowed unknown groups to appear on the scene (Hepp 1988:82).

The year 1978 was one of the worst on record for *cuarteto*. In preparation for the World Cup soccer finals, which were to be held in Argentina that same year, the military decided to "clean up" Córdoba of whatever might be ugly for tourists to experience (Mero 1988:55). Since *cuarteto* was one of these "ugly" things, only military marches and foreign music—not *cuarteto*—were allowed to be broadcast on radio stations. *Cuarteto* could not be played as background music in record stores, either, and a military official was sent to Córdoba to remove all of the *cuarteto* recordings from these same shops. Many of these prohibitions continued for as long as two years after the World Cup was over (Mero 1988:56–59). When *cuarteto* returned to radio in 1982 and to television in 1984, the connections that groups had established with their former audiences had been lost (Hepp 1988:82).

The *Cuarteto* Setting: 1982 to the Present

Cuarteto's current period began with the end of the Malvinas/Falklands War and the return to democracy in 1983. With this opening up of Argentine society, *cuarteto*, which could once again be performed and promoted publicly, began to gain a larger audience and more respectability (Barei 1993:46–47).

After Raúl Alfonsín became president, he entered into negotiations with the International Monetary Fund to get Argentina out of its inflationary spiral and foreign debt crisis (Mero 1988:88). Since the austerity measures he attempted to impose did not succeed (Wynia 1992:163–189), in 1989, Carlos Menem, a Peronist, took over the leadership of the country. Many of the economic policies instituted by Menem have brought results, thus putting Argentina on the path of recovery (Wynia 1992:194–221).

Cuarteto has made many strides since 1982–83. The year 1984 saw the creation of Tru-la-lá and Carlos Jiménez (Ábalos, "Diez años de baile" 25 November 1994:2; Mero 1988:85), which, along with Chébere, were the "Tres Grandes" (three most important groups) in Córdoba in 1995 (Ortiz, Gregoratti, and Arrascaeta 11 March 1995:C1). Carlos Jiménez, the last true defender of the traditional style with accordion, has long been, and still is, *cuarteto*'s most important figure ("¿La Mona eternamente?" 24 July 1995:C1).

A key event in both Jiménez's career and *cuarteto* occurred in January 1988 in Cosquín, Córdoba, when *cuarteto* was heard for only the second time at the Festival Nacional de Folklore, which is held in this small town northwest of Córdoba every summer (Hepp 1988:23–29; Mero 1988:7). Since Jiménez's group was chosen to perform on this historic occasion, thousands of his fans made the trip to Cosquín in special chartered buses. Estimates of the number of audience members present at this Jiménez event—most of whom were Jiménez supporters—were 12,000 to 15,000 inside the outdoor theater (where purchased seating is located), and 50,000 outside it (Mero 1988:13–14; SADAIC 1992:21). What happened on the evening Jiménez performed was later described in one newspaper as the "darkest chapter" in the history of the festival (Barei 1993:47–48). Although the Cosquín outdoor theater has approximately 9,000 fixed seats (see figure 2.1), many more tickets than this had been sold; the organizers made no effort to control the crowd (Hepp 1988:27; Mero 1988:10–11). Thousands of the fans standing outside the area where the seats are located got terribly excited when Jiménez began to perform; many of them jumped over the railings into the theater area. Others tried dancing in the aisles and rushed up on stage (Mero 1988:14–15). The intense commotion and fervor of the

2.1. The auditorium in Cosquín. Photograph by Jane L. Florine, Cosquín, Argentina, 1995.

crowd (the "riot") led to police intervention and the cancellation of the performance while Jiménez was singing his third song (Mero 1988:14–15). Jiménez quieted the crowd by telling his fans they did not want to be seen as "Indians" (Mero 1988:15; SADAIC 1992:21–22).

The newspaper reports of that evening were unfavorable. Although Jiménez was defended in *Clarín* (Leuco 17 February 1988:13; Mero 1988:5), the write-up appeared in its police reports section (Mero 1988: 144). In other articles, it was mistakenly reported that some people had been wounded and others arrested (Mero 1988:96–100, 143–45; "Escándalo en la plaza" 28 January 1988:C7; SADAIC 1992:21–22; "Lamentable saldo" 29 January 1988:A1; "Una euforia demencial" 29 January 1988:C9; Leuco 17 February 1988:13). The disturbance was not caused by pre-concert drinking of the *cuarteto* crowd, either, as was reported (Martínez 1988:n.p.; Hepp 1988:23–30; Mero 1988:12). In truth, those in charge had not wanted *cuarteto* to be performed at Cosquín again; only four of Jiménez's numbers were to be broadcast as a token gesture (Mero 1988:58). It was not reported that the authorities had harassed fans who had arrived by bus, either, mistakenly assuming they would find bottles of wine and arms (Mero 1988:12).

This 1988 Cosquín appearance ushered in a new era for *cuarteto* music. In Buenos Aires, where almost no one had known about Jiménez or *cuarteto* before the Cosquín event, both he and *cuarteto* became "famous" (Barei 1993:50–51). Jiménez was soon invited to perform in Buenos Aires, other *cuarteto* groups began to be invited to play in the *bailantas* there, and *cuarteto* started to become more "acceptable" (Elbaum 1994:193; Lewin 1994:221; Ortiz 1993:24).

When cable television arrived in Argentina in the 1980s, foreign musics arrived along with it. Later, from the 1990s on, salsa could be heard on radio stations in Córdoba and began to affect *cuarteto* greatly. It was only in 1991, however, that the Dominican merengue became influential, and especially so after a 1992 performance by Juan Luis Guerra in Argentina (Gregoratti, "El merengue mueve montañas" 1 June 1992: C1). Ángel Videla, who had left Chébere in 1990, brought four Dominican musicians to Argentina to form a merengue group in 1991. Although his experiment failed, three of the Dominicans stayed in Córdoba, later adding their musical knowledge to *cuarteto* ("Juan Luis Guerra sacude" 16 August 1994:C1; "Basta de discriminación" 3 July 1995:C1).

One of these Dominican musicians joined the band of Carlos Jiménez, which by this time had also acquired a Peruvian member; a young man from Ecuador joined the Jiménez group later on. With this expertise, and his own absorption of influences from abroad, Jiménez released his experimental compact disc called *Raza Negra* (Black Race) in 1994 ("Carlitos Jiménez presenta" 18 September 1994:C4).

Since approximately 1993, most *cuarteto* bands have stopped going to Buenos Aires; they dislike the working conditions of the *bailantas*. There has been a rapid decline in the number of people who attend *cuarteto* dances, both in Córdoba and in the provinces as well (Platía 1993:38–40). Although *cuarteto* is still big business, only about forty *cuarteto* bands are still active, whereas in 1968, eighty-three were counted (SADAIC 1992:24). In the 1970s, from thirty to fifty dances went on simultaneously in neighborhood clubs on any given evening in Córdoba; in 1995 there were only three (Ábalos, "Todo el país bailó" 2 December 1994:2–3). There is hence much speculation about the future of *cuarteto* and what will happen when Carlos Jiménez, who is middle-aged, retires. Since Carlos Jiménez "is" *cuarteto,* there are many people who feel the genre might die without his presence.

Musical Style: Evolution of the *Cuarteto* Genre

As *cuarteto* moved from the countryside to the city, it went through various types of stylistic changes. Today little remains of the original style of the Cuarteto Leo except the updated *tunga-tunga* foundation over which standard textures are used to create three umbrella styles: *moderno, tropical,* and *cuarteto-cuarteto.* Although these three styles sound quite different, it is the presence of the *tunga-tunga,* which is needed by dancers, that makes them all *cuarteto.*

A summary of the musical evolution of *cuarteto* and an explanation of how the music of Carlos Jiménez fits into this schema are given below. Although Jiménez's music, which is almost the exception to the norm nowadays, is considered to be that closest to the style of early *cuarteto,* even in 1984, when he created his own band, his music was more "modern" than that of the Cuarteto Leo. By 1994 he had fused Afro-Caribbean musical ideas with *cuarteto* via *Raza Negra,* after which he returned to his former style with *El Marginal,* released in 1995. Following the discussion of the stylistic evolution of *cuarteto* below, it will be shown what made *Raza Negra* so innovative. In the musical examples here presented, only partial transcriptions of recorded examples are given; the exact parts and instrumentation could often not be identified, since synthesizers and overlapping voices had been used.

The Original *Cuarteto* Style

"El Paraguas" ("The Umbrella"; J. MEDAGLIA—T. VALDÉZ—P. CERINI), a hit song of the Cuarteto Leo, is a good example of the early *cuarteto* style (see figure 2.2). The version of the tune discussed here (*Cuarteto Leo: 20 Grandes Éxitos* [Sony 580–708]) was recorded in approximately 1971. Although éthe Cuarteto Leo cut its first recording in 1953 (Hepp 1988:69), material recorded before 1971 is not available.

Instrumentation, Form, and Texture

Cuarteto has always been a vocal genre with instrumental accompaniment: early groups consisted of a tenor-announcer who sang with musicians playing violin, accordion, piano, and string bass (Hepp 1988: 59). *Güiro* and tambourine were sometimes added later on (Mero 1988: 23). Like "El Paraguas," *cuarteto* pieces were basically songs with an introduction, one or two verses, a refrain, and instrumental interludes (Hepp 1988:60–62; Waisman 1993:2). In these tunes, the solo accordion and/or solo violin might have performed a sixteen-bar introduction, played through one verse and one refrain without the singer (in the case of "El Paraguas," the violin plays the "verse" by itself and the accordion plays the "refrain" alone), returned to the first sixteen bars, and then accompanied the singer either in unison or heterophonically as he sang his first verse and refrain. This same procedure was followed for the next "introduction" and the second verse and refrain, after which the accordion and violin played the "introduction" as an ending (Waisman 1993:2–3).

This type of sparse texture and rigid format, with little independence or interaction among the individual voices, was typical (Waisman 1993: 2–3). Countermelodies were uncommon, but instruments sometimes played short answering-type fragments between the singer's phrases and/or paused when the singer did, as in measures 15–16 and 49–50 (Waisman 1993:2–3). The end result was a structured type of music played in "chunks" that did not flow smoothly.

Melodic and Harmonic Features

Early *cuarteto* melodies, like that of "El Paraguas," were normally diatonic, conjunct, and easy to sing. More often than not, they were composed in minor keys that conveyed a happy minor aesthetic. "El Para-

El Paraguas

2.2. "El Paraguas." By permission of SADAIC, Buenos Aires.

guas" is in D minor, for example. Note values used in melodies were often all of the same length, such as the steady quarter notes found in the refrain of "El Paraguas," and syncopations between beats or across barlines were uncommon. Verses often consisted of four phrases of four measures each. The tenor, who carried the melody in a smooth, lyric

style, used a clear voice tone and a moderate amount of vibrato. Instrumental parts alternated between staccato and legato, but not within the same measure. Modulations were rare, harmonies reached a major minor seventh chord at most, and chord progressions consisted mainly of the tonic, subdominant, and dominant. No dynamics were used, but the singer's voice came out clearly over the top. It was the loud, mechanical,

and staccato *tunga-tunga* that hegemonically controlled the flow of the music (Waisman 1993:2–4).

Rhythmic Elements and the *Tunga-Tunga*

Most *cuarteto* music has always been performed in some sort of duple time (Hepp 1988:60–62). Since modern-day *cuarteto* music is notated

with an alla breve rhythmic organization, all references made to early *cuarteto* music here are made in the same fashion. When analyzing the early *tunga-tunga,* a measure will be described as having four quarter notes in it—not four beats—and the *tunga-tunga* part of "El Paraguas" will be referred to.

In the *tunga-tunga,* the string bass and the left hand of the piano played in unison on the first and the third quarter notes of each bar; as mentioned earlier, these notes corresponded to the "*tun*" syllable of *tunga-tunga,* which is an onomatopoetic term that imitates the sound of the rhythm. The first (and perhaps the third) quarter note of each measure were usually played in octaves, and just as occurs when the word *tunga-tunga* is pronounced, "*tun*" notes were (and still are) played louder than "*ga*" notes were (and still are). As also mentioned earlier, the syllable "*ga*" corresponded to the staccato, quarter-note offbeats that were lightly played in the right hand of the piano on the second and the fourth quarter notes of each measure; each "*ga*" entrance was made up of three notes of the chord that was being outlined in that same measure. The notes played in the left hand of the piano and the string bass normally alternated between the tonic and dominant notes of the chord that was being used in any given measure, the second "*tun*" note of this tonic-dominant alternation usually being played either a fourth or a fifth below the first. The chord outlined by the bass and the piano was changed harmonically, as necessary, to fit with the melody, but chord changes could be made only at the beginnings of measures. The continuously played *tunga-tunga* pattern of early *cuarteto* often stopped abruptly at the ends of the singer's phrases (see measures 15–16 and 49–50 of "El Paraguas"). Tempi were very fast, and connecting, scalar passages which facilitated the movement of the bass part of the *tunga-tunga* appeared at the ends of phrases.[1]

Rhythmic devices were much more fixed and standardized in early *cuarteto* music than were melodic ones. For example, certain types of short rhythmic cells (combinations of eighth, quarter, and dotted quarter notes) were used, and rhythmic divisions such as triplets or syncopations occurred only within beats (Waisman 1993:3, 12).[2] A short, three-note tag ending (although not present in "El Paraguas"), which could vary in rhythm, was sometimes sung to the three syllables of the phrase *bailaló* (dance [to] it) or *se acabó* (it [has] ended) (Hepp 1988:61–62).[3]

Lyrics

The lyrics of "El Paraguas" deal with love, the most common topic of all *cuarteto* songs, both past and present (Hepp 1988:128):

Verse:
Cuando salgas a la calle
con tu novia a caminar,
no te olvides del paraguas.
Te recuerdo por favor.
Tú bien sabes que en el invierno
muy invariable el tiempo está.
Cuando menos uno piensa
ya comienza a lloviznar.

Verse [translation]:
When you go out[side] to the street
to take a walk with your girlfriend,
don't forget to take your umbrella.
Please, don't forget.
You know very well that in winter
the weather is very unstable.
When you least expect it
it starts to drizzle.

Refrain:
Abre, abre, tu paraguas,
que comienza a llover.
Si se moja nuestra ropa
ella se puede encoger.

Refrain:
Open up, open up, your umbrella;
it's starting to rain.
If our clothing gets wet
it could shrink.

Verse:
El paraguas es un invento
que se debe admirar.
El paraguas es un invento
que se debe admirar.
Porque el mismo es muy útil
también para enamorar.
Porque el mismo es muy útil
también para enamorar.

Verse:
The umbrella is an invention
that should be admired.
The umbrella is an invention
that should be admired.
Because it's something very useful
also for falling in love.
Because it's something very useful
also for falling in love.

Refrain (same as above).

Refrain [same as above].

Like "El Paraguas," early *cuarteto* songs often had fairly repetitive lyrics that painted a picture rather than telling a story; they concerned objects, people, and situations one encountered in daily life, such as bus drivers, maids, girls on their fifteenth birthdays, brooms, beds, and one's clothes (Hepp 1988:124–25, 136). Some songs were macabre enough to sound like police reports (Waisman 1993:6). Early *cuarteto* lyrics, sung by and performed for working-class populations, were sometimes deliberately sung with linguistic features that, as these men and women saw it, were used only by people with a higher-class upbringing than theirs (Waisman 1993:6–7). For example, the "*tú*" form of the second-person singular—not the "*vos*" form used in Argentine Spanish—often appeared, as it does in "El Paraguas" (see verse 1, line 5). The "*ll*," "*y*," and "*rr*" sounds might be pronounced differently in songs than they were in daily life for the same reason. Singers, however, betraying their class origins, at times unconsciously lapsed into their normal ways of speaking while they were singing (Waisman 1993:6–7).

Cuarteto Music Today

Instrumentation and Orchestration

Major changes have occurred in instrumentation and orchestration since the early days of *cuarteto*. No longer limited to four set instruments, bands now use a fairly standard type of instrumentation and have approximately eight to thirteen members. Electric pianos, electronic keyboards (synthesizers), electric guitar, bass guitar, and various types of percussion instruments are found in all of the groups. The violin has become obsolete, and extant accordion parts—if present at all—are minimal. Although some bands have added trumpets, trombones, and saxophones to their rosters, other groups create the effects of these same instruments electronically. Nontraditional sounds, such as those of oboe, violoncello, flute, and panpipes, are created with sequences, perhaps producing a thick, symphonic texture. Regarding the use of percussion, a drum set and/or drum machine is commonly used, as are *güiro* and tambourine. Latin percussion, such as congas, *timbales, tambora, güira* (a serrated metal cylinder with cone-shaped ends that is scraped with a fork-like brush), and *agôgô* (double bell) can either be performed live or simulated electronically. It is now rare to see a group perform live without *timbales* and congas on stage.

Solo singers in *cuarteto* groups are still tenors, but there are often two different singers in each band (especially in groups that alternate *moderno* and *tropical* sets). Vocal parts are still basically lyric and are sung with a moderate amount of vibrato, and the quality of the voice varies in timbre with the umbrella style being sung. A new element in modern *cuarteto* music is the frequent use of male choruses, especially on refrains (using female singers is uncommon).

Form and Texture

Arrangements of *cuarteto*, which are now often done by professionals, are integrated and polished. Although songs are still usually made up of introductions, verses, refrains, and interludes, these elements are not used rigidly. A refrain may be sung several times in a row or inserted in a song where it is not expected, for example, and introductions may be slow or in a different rhythm than the rest of the song (the *tunga-tunga* might not be heard until the lyrics start). Interludes often include unrelated material, and repeated sections are varied to add interest.

The unison and heterophonic instrumental parts that frequently doubled the vocal line in early *cuarteto* are no longer found; each instrument now has its own independent part, and contrapuntal instrumental lines are used even when the vocalist is singing the melody. Instrumental "solos," no longer limited to short, answering fragments during the singer's resting points, may be virtuosic and last for several measures. These independent, overlapping voices create a thicker texture than before and allow for the music to flow along smoothly without "holes."

Melodic and Harmonic Features

Cuarteto melodies are still basically lyric, diatonic, easy to sing, and performed in minor keys. Syncopation and ties across bar lines are now common in vocal parts, however, and singers have much more freedom than before. Four-bar phrases and sixteen-measure verses are still found, but this "rule" can be broken. Harmonically, diminished and augmented chords, as well as different types of seventh, ninth, eleventh, and thirteenth chords, are purposely used. Harmonics and glissandi often appear in guitar parts, in the style of rock or heavy metal. Although tonic, dominant, and subdominant chords are still the norm, less standard chord progressions and more frequent modulations than before may also be found. Piano parts often incorporate jazz harmonies, syncopations, and ostinato patterns of salsa music and/or a big band sound. Dynamics are now used, and articulation is not as stereotyped as before (Waisman 1993:4).

Rhythmic Elements and the *Tunga-Tunga*

Rhythmically speaking, the rhythmic cells and "*bailaló*" endings of the early *cuarteto* style are now gone. The *tunga-tunga* is still normally played using the tonic and the dominant notes of the chord (and is added to all tunes), but other notes can occasionally be used. The note corresponding to the second "*tun*" syllable of each measure is still usually played a perfect fourth or perfect fifth lower than the first "*tun*" note of each bar, and chord changes are still made only at the beginnings of measures.

Since *cuarteto* music is now notated alla breve, the notes of the *tunga-tunga* pattern played in the bass guitar and the left hand of the piano are notated either as steady half notes, as they are in this book, or as quarter notes separated by quarter-note rests. The contemporary *tunga-tunga* sounds much more connected than before because it is not played in a staccato fashion and is performed continuously throughout a song—even when the singer pauses.

In figure 2.3, five hypothetical ways of playing the *tunga-tunga* are presented; each of these independent one-measure units can be repeated until it is necessary to change to another chord that better fits the melody harmonically. Figures 2.3a and 2.3b show how the *tunga-tunga* might be played in A-minor and E-minor and the most typical movement of the bass line, and figure 2.3c gives an example of the *tunga-tunga* in a major key. Figure 2.3d demonstrates that the bass line

2.3. Five of many possible ways to play the *tunga-tunga*. The right hand of the piano plays the top line (the offbeats); the left hand of the piano and the bass play the bottom line. The *tunga-tunga* is seldom written out; the chords to be played in each measure are usually indicated with chord symbols, as is shown above, instead. Hypothetical examples by Jane L. Florine, 1996.

might move upward, and figure 2.3e shows how a seventh chord might be played.

It is the pianist who decides what the voicing and fingering of the offbeat chords will be and how to play the bass line. Fingerings/spacings are chosen so as to move the fingers as little as possible (i.e., comfortably) from one measure to the next or when one-measure units are repeated. Once the pianist has determined how he will play his part, he does not change it; there is no real improvisation in *cuarteto*.

Piano and bass players do not normally have the *tunga-tunga* completely written out for them; instead, their parts often consist of chord symbols to which they add the standard *tunga-tunga* (see the chord symbols in figure 2.3). An example of an actual *tunga-tunga* bass line is given in figure 2.6; the right-hand chords in the piano line, although present on the recording they were transcribed from, have not been notated (this procedure has been followed in all of the musical transcriptions presented in this chapter).

When one listens to a *cuarteto* tune nowadays, it is often hard to hear the *tunga-tunga* being played by the electric piano because the bass guitar line overshadows it. Some pianists no longer play their left-hand notes in octaves, either, which makes their lines less audible as well (compare the bass lines of figures 2.2 and 2.6). The *tunga-tunga* bass line is occasionally altered rhythmically, sometimes for only a few measures (to draw attention to words in the lyrics, to provide contrast, to help the performer get from one chord to the next more easily, etc.), sometimes for an entire song.[4] Groups that find it confining may hide it (by playing it softly or in an "inaudible" register) or draw attention away from it (by using overlapping rhythmic layers and percussion instruments). A running, arpeggiated bass line or an anticipated bass pattern typical of salsa might be substituted for it in certain cases.

Lyrics

The immigrant population, all types of love, feminine sensuality, the seductive macho, praise for dancing, making fun of others, the city of Córdoba, and praise of one's friends have all been common themes of *cuarteto* lyrics (Hepp 1988:127, 138–53; Barei 1993:67–71). Sexual innuendo and double meanings have traditionally been characteristic in lyrics, whereas political issues and religious allusions have been avoided (Hepp 1988:136). Complex literary symbols have not been a part of the style.

From the beginning, *cuarteto* lyrics have been criticized for being poorly written and having little content (Barei 1993:71; Hepp 1988:122–23; Mero 1988:116). Although they are still not considered to be great poetry (Hepp 1988:125; Barei 1993:71–73), nowadays their rhyme schemes and vocabulary are much better thought out than before, phrases and words are not repeated over and over, and stories are sometimes told rather than scenes described (Hepp 1988:124–25). Most lyrics now deal with love, but there has been a trend to sing somewhat occasionally about contemporary social ills or situations (Hepp 1988:124–26; Barei 1993:71–73). For example, Tru-la-lá has one song that encourages dancers to say "no" to drugs, "No a la Droga" (S.M. GÓMEZ—J.A. MOYANO—C. TOLEDO; BMG 74321–21169–4), and a few Jiménez songs have addressed topics such as wife-beating, abortion, and nuclear bombing (Hepp 1988:150–54; Barei 1993:71; Mero 1988:91–92). Lyrics with double meanings are still common, but are more typical of the style of Carlos Jiménez than the styles of other groups. In fact, since lyrics used by Jiménez are directed to people of the lowest social classes in Córdoba, the types of everyday topics he sings about (prostitutes, men in jail, poverty) make his lyrics the exception to the rule (see below).

In all *cuarteto* lyrics, the idea is to find a *gancho* (hook), a catch saying or phrase that gets the attention of the listener. "Te Compro Tu Novia" ("I Will Buy Your Girlfriend from You"; RAMÓN ORLANDO) was the title of a 1994 Tru-la-lá song (BMG 74321–24649–2), for example. Everyday sayings, such as "here today, gone tomorrow," also make good *ganchos*— especially when they are coupled with a melodic or rhythmic motive.

The *Moderno* Style

Moderno is the *cuarteto* style that has been influenced heavily by rock, jazz, and international romantic (Latin) music. Fairly slow and lyric, this music is sung with a husky, sexy vocal timbre. When a *moderno* singer performs his tunes, which are often cover versions of international hits, he is normally accompanied by only some of the instruments in his band: keyboards (synthesizers and electric piano), bass guitar, brass (or sequences imitating brass instruments), electric guitar, and drum set. No Latin percussion instruments, except perhaps congas, are used. This standard instrumentation can be seen in the fragment of "Qué Será" ("What Could It Be"; GOGO MUÑOZ) by Chébere (Clave Records CD 51413) provided below (see figure 2.4).

"Qué Será"

Form and melody in *moderno* music follow the general characteristics of present-day *cuarteto* discussed above. For example, in the case of "Qué Será," the song has an introduction, a verse and refrain, an interlude, and another verse followed by a modification of the refrain. Two formal elements especially characteristic of the style also appear in "Qué Será": a slow introduction and an extended guitar solo. This song's introduction is unusual, since it begins with a fast part that features the brass (measures 1–17), slows down for the first sixteen measures of the verse (measures 18–33, when the singer enters), and then (at measure 34) speeds up to a tempo that is maintained for the rest of the song. The *tunga-tunga* is used for measures 1–17, drops out during the slow section, and reenters at measure 34. A sixteen-measure guitar solo, which occurs right after the first refrain, serves as the interlude that leads into the second verse.

The texture of "Qué Será" is much thicker and varied than that of "El Paraguas." Instead of the unison or heterophonic interaction with the singer typical of early *cuarteto*, there is a give-and-take feeling created among the performers. The influence of big band harmonies can be seen in "Qué Será" as well, in the first seventeen bars, for example. As for the *tunga-tunga*, it is played only faintly in the right hand of the piano once it begins, and its bass line gets away from the expected tonic-dominant alternation (see measures 9–17 and 46–51). The backbeats heard in the drum set (see measures 2–15), in the style of rock or jazz, are typical to the *moderno* style (Waisman 1993:8).

Since they deal with erotic love, the lyrics of "Qué Será" are an excellent example of those most commonly used in *moderno* music:

Verse:	*Verse [Translation]:*
Quisiera juntar todas	I would like to get all my
mis fuerzas	strength together
y dejar de ser tu prisionero.	and stop being your prisoner.
No quiero ser más tu	I don't want to be your faithful
fiel esclavo,	slave anymore,
un perro celoso que no duerme.	a jealous dog that cannot sleep.
Pero cuando llegas me do-	But when you arrive you domi-
minas	nate me
con sólo tocarme con tu	just by touching me with your
aliento.	breath.
Mis dedos caminan por tu cuerpo	My fingers run down your body

y soy en tu cama águila
herida.

Navegando en tu piel de seda
soy volcán de fuego, arena
caliente.
Tú me desesperas, tú me vuelves
loco.

Refrain:
¿Qué será que no puedo escapar
de ti,
que me dejas sin corazón
y perturbas mi razón?
¿Qué será ese algo que
tienes tú
que me hace temblar de amor
en mi lecho cuando no estás,
cuando te vas? ¿Porqué será?

Verse:
A veces me enredo en otros
brazos
tratando de ahogar todas mis
penas.
Pero no consigo liberarme
y te sigo amando, no puedo
dejarte.

Navegando en tu piel de seda
soy volcán de fuego, arena
caliente.
Tú me desesperas, tú me vuelves
loco.

Refrain:
¿Qué será que no puedo
escapar de ti,
que me dejas sin corazón
y perturbas a mi razón?

and in your bed I am a wounded
eagle.

Navigating your silky skin
I am a volcano of fire, hot sand.
You make me desperate, you
drive me crazy.

Refrain:
Why is it that I cannot escape
from you,
that you take my heart [away]
and disturb my ability to reason?
What could that special something be that you have
that makes me tremble with love
in my bed when you're not around,
when you leave? Why can this be?

Verse:
Sometimes I get wrapped up in
[another woman's] arms
trying to drown all my sorrows.
But I don't succeed in freeing
myself
and I keep on loving you, I
cannot leave you.

Navigating your silky skin
I am a volcano of fire, hot sand.
You make me desperate, you
drive me crazy.

Refrain:
Why is it that I cannot escape
from you,
that you take my heart [away]
and disturb my ability to reason?

¿Qué será ese algo que
    tienes tú
que me hace temblar de amor
en mi lecho cuando no estás?
¿Qué será?

What could that special something
    be that you have
that makes me tremble with love
in my bed when you're not around?
What could it be?

Qué Será

2.4. "Qué Será." By permission of Gogo Muñoz, Santiago, Chile.

Melódico

Within the *moderno* style, there is a kind of music fans call *melódico*. This term can refer to a slow song played with the *tunga-tunga*, in the form of a ballad, for example, but it generally refers to a lyric, romantic type of tune to which the *tunga-tunga* is not added. This latter type of *melódico* song might sound very much like international *boleros* with orchestral accompaniment. Often, as his last song of the evening, a *moderno* singer will do a *melódico* number (of the type without the *tunga-tunga*) that shows off his beautiful voice and vocal style; the lights are focused on him and many people stop dancing in order to listen. Normally, no more than one or two *melódico* numbers without the *tunga-tunga* will be heard per dance.

The *Tropical* Style

Tropical, the style of *cuarteto* in which Caribbean musical influences are combined with the traditional *cuarteto* style, was created by Chébere. A *tropical* singer normally alternates sets with a *moderno* singer; since his tunes are more upbeat, syncopated, and rhythmic than are *moderno* ones, he is the person who wraps up the dance. *Tropical* singers have a tendency to dance when they sing, and their voice timbre is characteristically brighter than that of *moderno* singers. Their repertoire normally includes international cover tunes of Central American and/or Caribbean groups adapted to the *tunga-tunga*. *Tropical* lyrics often concern erotic love, but sometimes make reference to dance-related themes (Waisman 1993:7).

Formwise, *tropical* follows the updated types of song form described above. Instrumentally, it has some standard features. First of all, salsa-style brass parts, whether they are played on real instruments (trumpets, trombones, and saxophones) or synthesizers, are typical of the *tropical* style. Secondly, the electric guitar and trap set of the *moderno* style are not used. Lastly, Latin percussion, almost always at least congas and *timbales*, are added during *tropical* sets. Other instruments and/or sounds used with the *tropical* repertoire, whether they are performed live or created with a drum machine, could include *tambora*, *güira*, maracas, *agôgô*, beaded rattles, and *claves*.

Fusions

Fusions of the *tropical* style of *cuarteto* with salsa and Caribbean genres are very common, especially those done with *cumbia* and merengue.

Since both *cumbia* and *cuarteto* have four quarter notes per bar, and the bass pattern in *cumbia* is related to the pattern played by the left hand of the piano and the bass guitar in *cuarteto* music (although it is made up of a half note followed by two quarter notes that outline part of the chord), they are easy to combine.[5] When fusing the two, the *cumbia* bass line would be left intact, the *güiro* rhythm of *cumbia* would be adopted, and the offbeat, right-hand piano chords of *cuarteto* music would be used. *Cuarteto* fans recognize *cumbia* as being a subdivision of the *tropical* style, since its half-note, two-quarter-note bass line cannot be danced to using *cuarteto*-style steps.

The fact that Dominican merengue is in 4/4 time and has a bass pattern just like the one played in the left hand of the piano and the bass guitar in *cuarteto* makes it easy to fuse both genres.[6] In a "*merenteto*," as *cuarteto* musicians call this type of fusion, the *güira* and *tambora* parts of merengue would be played with these instruments themselves or with drum machines, and merengue's fast eighth-note saxophone line— *jaleo*—might be performed with synthesizers or other instruments (if it is played at all). Either "Cuban-style montuno-type" piano ostinati (Manuel 1988:45) or the normal chords that correspond to the offbeat right-hand *tunga-tunga* piano part would be added as well, perhaps in alternation. Only musicians—not dancers—can distinguish merengues or *merentetos* from *cuarteto*.

"Huelga de Hambre"

The example of *tropical* music provided here (see figure 2.5), "Huelga de Hambre" ("Hunger Strike"; GOGO MUÑOZ), is taken from the compact disc *Chébere: Ace 1994* (Clave Records CD 51413). This song is unusual because it is written in a major key (E-flat major), but its instrumentation is typical of the *tropical* style. As is seen here, *tropical* melodies are often made up of short phrases with rests between them (see measures 34–37). They feel faster and more agitated than do *moderno* tunes, partially because of the syncopated rhythmic patterns, short (answering) phrases, and layers of percussion that they have. The brass line of "Huelga de Hambre," for example, consists of short, syncopated phrases that alternate between the trumpets and trombones similar to the way call-and-response patterns are heard in instrumental sections of merengue (see measures 18–31).

A merengue texture is also created, since a saxophone-type *jaleo* programmed with sequences to sound like a glockenspiel is played in the keyboards, from measures 34 to 42, along with the vocal line; the *tunga-tunga* offbeat chords normally played in the right hand of the piano enter only when this pattern begins. In the introduction and in the portions of the song in which the brass have their answering phrases (measures 1–35), the right-hand piano *tunga-tunga* notes are not played; in these same sections, the percussion parts are given more of a major role. Although the chords used throughout consist almost exclusively of alternations between I and V, which is another feature of instrumental sections in merengue music (Manuel 1988:44–45), typical merengue percussion patterns and instruments are not used.

The *tropical* repertoire in *cuarteto* music is performed in a song format with verses and refrains; the three-part structure of Cuban music (*guía, montuno,* and *mambo*) is not followed, the *clave* pattern is not used, and no one in the group improvises (Gerard and Sheller 1989:84–85, 87–114). The lyrics of "Huelga de Hambre" are also typical of the *tropical* style: they deal with erotic love and are performed in a verse and refrain format with brass interludes:

Verse:
Te envío flores, te escribo
 poemas,
te canto canciones,
y tú ni fu ni fa.
Como una reina te admiro
 cuando pasas.
Te digo cosas
 lindas
y tú ni fu ni fa.

(Brass interlude)
Cuando caminas, meneando
 tu pollera,
todos te miran. Me muero de
 celos.
Me muero de
 celos
y tú ni fu ni fa.

Verse [Translation]:
I send you flowers, I write you
 poems,
I sing you songs,
and you don't care one way or
 the other.
I look at you like a queen when
 you walk by.
I say nice things to you,
and you don't care one way or
 the other.

[Brass interlude]
When you walk, moving your
 skirt,
everybody looks at you. I die
 of jealousy.
I die of jealousy,
and you don't care one way or
 the other.

Refrain:
Voy a hacer una huelga de
  hambre
si no te puedo conquistar,
si no te puedo conquistar.
Voy a hacer una huelga de
  hambre
si no te puedo conquistar,
si no te puedo conquistar.
Y tú ni fa, y tú ni fu ni fa.
Ni siquiera una hormona
se te mueve de aquí ni allá
y tú ni fa.
Y todas mis hormonas por tí
me hacen tucutu, tucutu,
  tucutu, tucutu, tu, tu.

Verse:
Escribo tu nombre
sobre las paredes
frente a tu casa
y tú ni fu ni fa.
Como un
  romántico,
camino por la lluvia.
Me mojo todo, todo,
y tú ni fu ni fa.

(Brass interlude)
Cuando caminas, meneando
  tu pollera,
todos te miran. Me muero
  de celos.
Me muero de celos,
y tú ni fu ni fa.

Refrain as before.

Refrain:
I'm going to go on a hunger strike
if I can't conquer you [your love],
if I can't conquer you [your love].
I'm going to go on a hunger strike
if I can't conquer you [your love],
if I can't conquer you [your love].
And you don't care one way or the
  other.
Not even a hormone [of yours]
moves from here to there
and you don't care.
And all of my hormones [desire]
  for you
make me go tucutu, tucutu,
  tucutu, tucutu, tu, tu.

Verse:
I write your name
on the walls
in front of your house,
and you don't care one way or the
  other.
Like a romanticist,
I walk through the rain [for you].
I get wet all over, all over,
and you don't care one way or the
  other.

[Brass interlude]
When you walk, moving your skirt,
everybody looks at you. I die of
  jealousy.
I die of jealousy,
and you don't care one way or the
  other.

Refrain as before.

Huelga de Hambre

2.5. "Huelga de Hambre." By permission of Gogo Muñoz, Santiago, Chile.

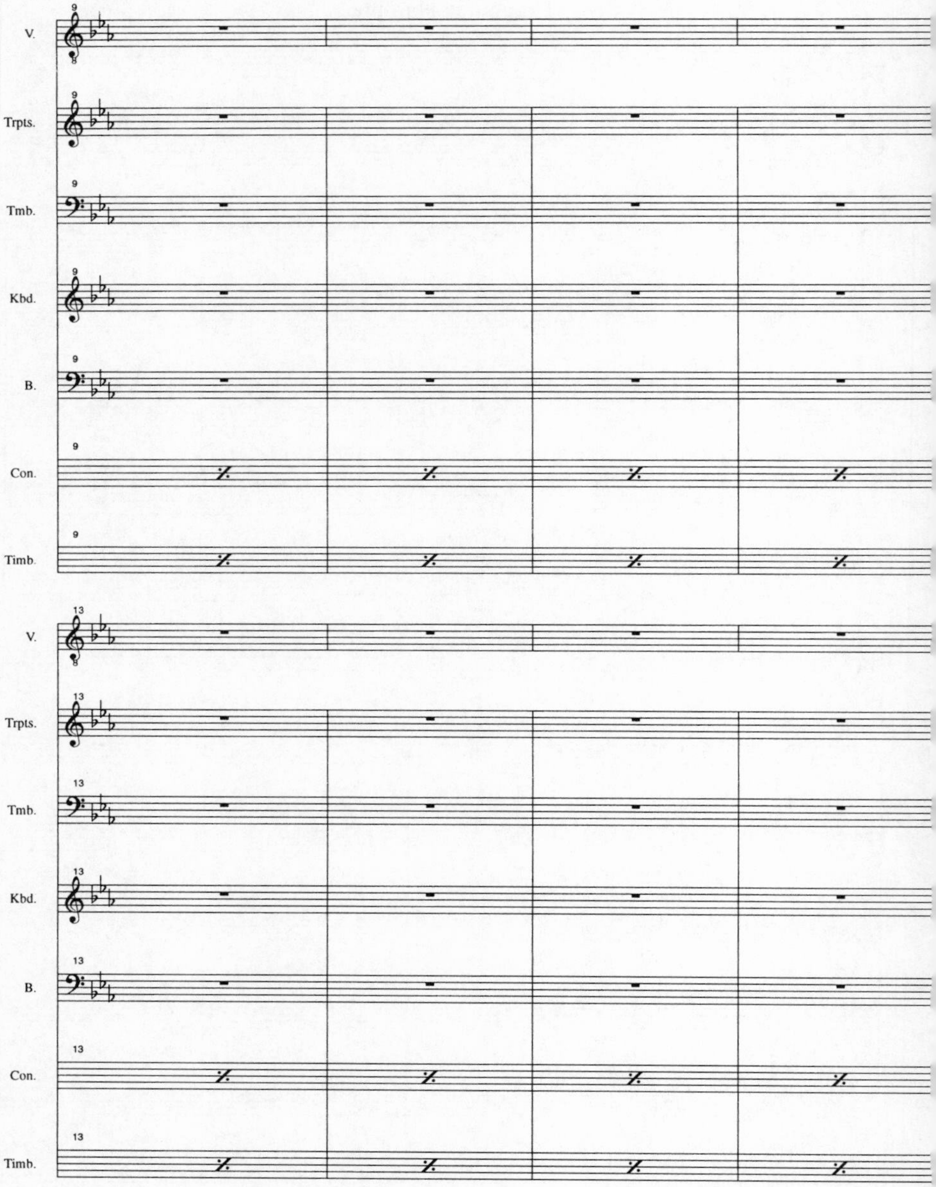
9
V.
Trpts.
Tmb.
Kbd.
B.
Con.
Timb.
13
V.
Trpts.
Tmb.
Kbd.
B.
Con.
Timb.

Carlos Jiménez and the *Cuarteto-Cuarteto* Style

The 1984 Jiménez Style

When Carlos Jiménez formed his own group in 1984, his intention was to update, yet maintain, the traditional *cuarteto* style (Mero 1988: 35–36, 45–51). This modernization of early *cuarteto* music is here called the *cuarteto-cuarteto* (i.e., "really" *cuarteto*) style. Much of this stylistic continuation is symbolic: the accordion is still used. The violin was dropped from Jiménez's group from the start and was replaced with a synthesizer (Mareco 6 September 1992:7F; Mero 1988:41, 48–51), but when the group recorded, a violinist was originally hired to play in some tunes (Hepp 1988:85–86). Jiménez changed the acoustic piano and bass for electric instruments upon founding his group as well, and conga and *timbales* were added to pseudo-Caribbean repertoire, such as *cumbias*, from the start.

"Mujer y Amante"

In Jiménez's 1984 release, *Para Todo América* (PolyGram 63263), several characteristics of contemporary *cuarteto* music were introduced; the song "Mujer y Amante" ("Wife and Lover"; JIMÉNEZ—H. AMMAN— R. VERÓN) will be used to demonstrate some of these innovations (see figure 2.6). Although the instrumentation used in "Mujer y Amante" is that of early *cuarteto* with *güiro* accompaniment, the "violin" part is produced with a synthesizer, and the piano and bass parts are played on electric instruments.

The song begins with an introduction (measures 1–38) in which the accordion has a syncopated line with some notes held over the bar lines; the violin part, instead of being in unison with it, has long, held-out chords. This independence of instrumental voices continues throughout the song, and at no time do the instrumental parts double the vocal line. At times (in the verses, from measures 41 to 55) the accordion has short answering fragments that fit into the singer's pauses, but it also plays a separate countermelody in the refrains/coda, from measures 93 to 103. The violin line consists of held-out chords in the verses (measures 57– 74) and a countermelody in the refrains/coda (measures 75–92). After the introduction, two verses are sung one after the other, and then the

Mujer y Amante

2.6. "Mujer y Amante." By permission of SADAIC, Buenos Aires.

ra - do   te   de - ja   re - gre - sar,   cuan - do   tu/e - na - mo - ra - - - do

te   de - ja   re - gre - sar.

refrain is sung twice; there are no musical interludes between any of these sections. Once the refrain has been sung these two times, the accordion introduction is used as an interlude. Next, instead of proceeding to another verse, as is expected, the refrain is again sung twice. The song ends with the accordion introduction being used as a coda.

The vocal part of this tune, which definitely comes out over the other instruments dynamically, does not consist of the steady note values heard in early *cuarteto* melodies; instead, it contains syncopated notes and others held across bar lines (see measures 39–42). The key used is a minor one (A-minor), as is to be expected, and the song does not modulate. Harmonically speaking, the chords used are still those of early *cuarteto*, but the *tunga-tunga* has now become the contemporary one described in figure 2.3 that moves along smoothly and steadily. In the recording of "Mujer y Amante," the *tunga-tunga* is prominently heard throughout the entire song; emphasizing the *tunga-tunga* line has long been a characteristic of the music of Jiménez and is a prominent aspect of the music of any group that uses the *cuarteto-cuarteto* style.

Carlos Jiménez is a tenor, but his voice quality is unlike that of *moderno* and *tropical* singers. At times he sings somewhat "out-of-tune" and almost shouts instead of singing; he also gesticulates, moves around, and dances when he sings. Since Jiménez came out of a working-class background and sings for the poorer sectors of the population, it is perhaps surprising that the tendency to make changes in the typical working-class syntax, pronunciation, and vocabulary of early *cuarteto* lyrics is still apparent in his songs (Waisman 1993:6–7). The "correct" use of the future tense is sometimes used in his lyrics instead of the more informal way of saying the same thing; for example, "I will change" (*yo cambiaré*) might be sung instead of the more familiar "I am going to change" (*yo voy a cambiar*). The "correct" form of the second-person singular, *tú*, is mixed with *vos*, the form normally used in Argentine Spanish, in his songs as well.

In "Mujer y Amante," the lyrics of which follow, some of these tendencies can be seen:

Verse:	*Verse [Translation]:*
Yo me he dado cuenta	I have found out
que intimás con	that you're being intimate with
otro	another man

fuera de nosotros,
fuera de tu hogar.
Aún nadie
   comenta,
tal cual lo presiento.
Pero es un tormento
tener que aguantar.

Verse:
Los niños desean
salir con mamita,
pero tú prefieres
a ese señor.
Es sólo un amante
que quiere tu cuerpo.
Como un pasatiempo,
te usa y se va.

Refrain:
Esposa y madre pero hoy
   mujer, mujer y amante.
Termina cuanto antes
tu relación con él.
Veo tus labios
siempre que están recién
   pintados
cuando tu enamorado
te deja regresar,
cuando tu enamorado
te deja regresar.

Refrain: repeat as before; after
   interlude, sing refrain twice more.

besides us,
outside your home.
Although nobody has said
   anything about it yet,
I can feel it.
But it is pure torture
to have to put up with it.

Verse:
The children want
to go out with their mommy
but you prefer
[to be with] that man.
He's only a lover
who wants your body.
Like a pastime,
he uses you and then moves on.

Refrain:
Wife and mother but today
   wife, wife and lover.
Break off as soon as possible
your relationship with him.
I see that your lips
have always been freshly applied
   with lipstick
when your sweetheart (lover)
lets you come home,
when your sweetheart (lover)
lets you come home.

Refrain: repeat as before; after
   interlude, sing refrain twice more.

Although the "refined" *tú* form is used (see verse 2, line 3), the word "*intimás*" (verse 1, line 2) is pronounced as it normally is in Argentina, not "*intimas*," as it should be when using the *tú* form. Other verbs in the song, such as "*prefieres*" (verse 2, line 3) and "*termina*" (refrain, line 2) are correctly used in the *tú* form though (in Argentine Spanish they would normally be "*preferís*" and "*terminá*").

Cuarteto-Cuarteto Song Lyrics

Often geared to the daily life of the working-class, lower-income population of Córdoba, the lyrics of Jiménez's songs contain themes not addressed by other *cuarteto* groups. Instead of singing purely love songs, Jiménez might sing of social relationships that involve family members (a wife, girlfriend, parents) or friends. When he sings about other individuals (a drunk, a womanizer, etc.) typical to the world of his fans, it is often in a funny way. Songs in which social commentary is made are dramatic (Barei 1993:67).

The use of humor in Jiménez's songs reflects how people in Córdoba make life pass by more easily (Hepp 1988:122–23, 133–34). For example, in "Cortáte el Pelo Cabezón" ("Cut Your Hair, You with the Big Head"; A. KUSTIN—C. RAMALÓ—TITO VALDÉZ) the singer tells someone with a "big head" to go out and get his hair cut so that he will be able to hear and so that the barber will remember what his face looks like (Hepp 1988:134). An example of social drama or commentary occurs in "Señor Juez, Un Minuto por Favor" ("Mr. Judge, Just a Minute Please"; JIMÉNEZ), in which Jiménez personifies a man about to be sentenced; speaking directly to the judge, he says he has brought his daughter along and doesn't care if he stole something, no matter what the judge decides to do (Boria 1993:154).

Jiménez song lyrics concerning love can be divided into those that deal with romantic love, those that deal with grotesque love, and those that purposefully treat love in a humorous way with double meanings (Boria 1993:162–71). Songs included in the "romantic" category involve the image of a woman in a domestic setting (Boria 1993:162), for example, those of "Mujer y Amante," which tell of an adulterous relationship.

The song "La 0 Kilómetro" ("The New Car"; JIMÉNEZ—VERÓN—VILLARREAL) is an example of grotesque love, that is, love in which physical elements of the body are treated degradingly and erotic elements appear (Boria 1993:165–66). Here (Boria 1993:166) the singer compares a woman's body to a new car: "yo quiero una 0,0 kilómetro / que sea último modelo / con flor de maquinón / que tenga las gomas nuevas / y buena suspensión / y que su carrocería / sea de lo mejor" ("I want a brand new car / it should be the latest model / with a really super engine / new tires / and a great suspension system / and its body / should be the best there is").

Lyrics with humor and double meanings are found in "Entra Durito y Sale Blandito" ("It Goes in Pretty Hard and Comes Out Pretty Soft"; ALTAMIRANO—BRITOS—RIVAROLA): "Negrita linda esta noche / te voy a invitar a cenar / para que veas como te quiero / por ti voy a cocinar / . . . Entra durito y sale blandito / adivina que es / el fideito / el fideito" ("My pretty little woman / tonight I am going to invite you over for dinner / so that you can see how much I love you / I am going to cook for you / . . . It goes in pretty hard and comes out pretty soft / guess what it is / the [my] little noodle / the [my] little noodle") (Boria 1993: 167–68).

El Marginal: The Updated Cuarteto-Cuarteto Style

El Marginal (BMG 74321-30538-2), released in mid-1995, offers an excellent example of Jiménez's updated *cuarteto-cuarteto* style. When *El Marginal* was recorded, the group consisted of Jiménez, two keyboard/ synthesizer players (one of them also operated the drum machine and the other doubled on electric piano), bass guitar, electric guitar/*güiro*, *timbales*/percussion, African dancer/percussion, congas, *tambora/güira*, accordion, and two announcers.

Although the tunes on *El Marginal* are written in song form, they are creatively put together with such features as short, slow introductions, varied repetitions, and interludes containing new material. Instrumental lines are still independent, and synthesizers are used to create sounds of instruments not traditionally associated with *cuarteto* (brass, saxophones, violoncello, etc.). The tradition of using minor keys and a "singable" vocal line with syncopated and tied notes is continued, but more modulations now occur than before and men's choruses are the norm. More sophisticated harmonies and chord progressions are used than before, the isolated use of ostinato passages from Cuban music is evident, and the modern *tunga-tunga* as shown in figure 2.3 is prominent.

"Penita"

Many of these updated stylistic elements are seen in the song "Penita" (C. JIMÉNEZ—A. VÁSQUEZ-MARTÍNEZ—R. VERÓN), found on

El Marginal.[7] The synthesizer is used to produce the sounds of trumpets and trombones, and a glockenspiel effect is created in the introduction. The accordion, although present, plays a small role, the simulated violin part consists of long held-out chords, and the use of the piccolo is a novel addition. The instruments act independently. As occurs in the introduction, the accordion and piccolo occasionally answer each other with short phrases; the accordion also performs small interjections between the singer's entrances, and the piccolo's running passages, which return throughout, add spice. In the refrain, the brass line is given a countermelody; the piccolo plays a countermelody with triplets that go between the beats when the refrain is repeated, an unusual occurrence in *cuarteto*. *Güiro* and tambourine, associated with early *cuarteto*, are the only percussion instruments used.

The verse and refrain format of "Penita" is varied with the repetitions to make it more interesting. After the initial introduction and two performances of the verse and refrain, the listener gets a surprise: the following interlude consists of only part of the introduction, and the ending of the piccolo line is changed. Unexpectedly, the refrain is next sung—not the verse—and a return is made to the introduction as if it were a coda. This last time through the introduction, the piccolo part is played up an octave to end the piece with a brilliant finish.

The contemporary *tunga-tunga* pattern described in figure 2.3 is used throughout with only one exception: a rhythmic change is made in the bass line at the beginning of the second part of each verse, on the word *"mírame"* ("look at me"), almost as a way of getting one's attention (just as the singer is trying to get the woman in the song to do to him). The men's chorus enters each time *"mírame"* is sung and sings all the lines of the refrains except for the phrase *"en mi corazón"* ("in my heart"), which is sung by Jiménez alone.

The lyrics of "Penita" deal with romantic love. The second time the verse is sung, its last line is changed in order to finish telling the story, following the current trend in *cuarteto* of doing more than just "describing":

Verse:	*Verse [Translation]:*
Pena, dejaste sólo en mi alma	You left only pain in my soul
desde el día que te fuiste,	starting the day that you left,
mujer.	woman.

Me quedé dudando triste y
   vacío.
Tú eras mi único
   abrigo.
No te engañes.
Siempre fui fiel compañero
en nuestra relación.
Mírame,
dijiste que tú me amabas,
   mi amor.
Mírame,
dijiste que tú me amabas,
   mi amor.
Y ahora,
yo no sé en qué creer,
   mi amor.

Refrain:
Pena, yo tengo mucha pena,
pena, penita, pena, dentro
   del corazón.
Pena, yo tengo mucha pena,
pena, penita, pena, dentro
   del corazón.

Verse:
Pasa el tiempo
y yo te sigo queriendo
a pesar de tu ausencia.
Yo seguiré
esperando que tú vuelvas
a este lecho de amor.
Dímelo, ¿qué haremos todos
   nuestros hijos
que fueron frutos de amor?

Mírame,
dijiste que tú me amabas,

I kept wondering sadly and
   emptily.
You were my only source of
   shelter/warmth.
Don't fool yourself.
I was always a faithful companion
in our relationship.
Look at me,
you told me that you loved me,
   my dear.
Look at me,
you told me that you loved me,
   my dear.
And now
I don't know what to believe in,
   my dear.

Refrain:
Pain, I have a lot of pain,
pain, a little pain, pain, in
   my heart.
Pain, I have a lot of pain,
pain, a little pain, pain in my
   heart.

Verse:
Time goes by
and I go on loving you
despite your absence.
I will keep on
hoping that you will return
to this bed of love.
Tell me, what will all our
   children do,
who were created out of love?

Look at me,
you told me that you loved me,

mi amor.	my dear.
Mírame,	Look at me,
dijiste que tú me amabas,	you told me that you loved me,
mi amor.	my dear.
Y me dices que no vas a volver,	And [now] you say that you're not coming back,
mi amor.	my dear.

Refrain as before, then interlude.   *Refrain as before, then interlude.*
Refrain as before.   *Refrain as before.*

Raza Negra

In September 1994, just ten months before he released *El Marginal,* Carlos Jiménez launched *Raza Negra* (BMG 74321–23116–2); according to a spoken introduction, this disc was a tribute to the "black race" and its music. When *Raza Negra* was launched, journalists deemed it one of the biggest risks ever taken to introduce innovation in *cuarteto* and said that Jiménez had consciously combined the *cuarteto* style with Afro-Caribbean rhythms and genres on it ("Siempre hay lugar" 9 January 1995:2C; Gregoratti 11 March 1995:3C). In the songs that appeared on *Raza Negra,* the normal verse-refrain format and style of *cuarteto* music were not always followed, and lyrics were not always related to "typical" *cuarteto* topics. At times the *tunga-tunga* was absent and/or fused with Afro-Caribbean-based genres. African musical elements such as African percussion instruments, layered rhythmic patterns, ostinati, syncopation, polyrhythms, call-and-response singing, and repetitive, rhythmic melodies based upon only a few notes were sometimes incorporated.

This fusion of Africanisms with *cuarteto* can be seen in the following tunes from *Raza Negra:* "Cuarte-Conga," the title of which alludes to the fusion of *cuarteto* and *conga* found in the song (DELSERI—MIRANDA —MACHUCA); "Esta Noche, Me Voy de Caravana" ("Tonight I'm Going Out from Place to Place"; JIMÉNEZ—TAPIA—VILLARREAL); "Raza Negra" ("Black Race"; JIMÉNEZ—TAPIA—VILLARREAL); and "No Soy Dios Para Perdonar" ("I'm Not God So I Can't Forgive You"; JIMÉNEZ—ROJO—A. VÁSQUEZ-MARTÍNEZ).[8]

"Cuarte Conga"

This unusual *cuarteto* tune begins with an introduction for solo conga which changes meter several times (4/4 to 5/4 to 3/4, etc.) and contains syncopations and triplets. A rhythmic piano ostinato made up of short melodic fragments then enters, followed by a men's chorus singing a chantlike, repetitive, and syncopated melody with reiterated notes and an ostinato figure; the piano ostinato is later joined in octaves by simulated saxophone and brass parts. When the solo voice part enters, the *tunga-tunga* enters with it, signaling the beginning of the song proper, and layers of percussion instruments associated with Afro-Caribbean music are introduced (*tambora, timbales,* and conga). The vocal melody is sung on a single note and, throughout the whole piece, alternates with an eight-bar male chorus that repeats the chantlike ostinato melody it sang in the introduction in a pseudo call-and-response texture. This men's chorus part, which corresponds to the conga rhythm, is fused with the *tunga-tunga* pattern throughout the entire song. The lyrics tell listeners that the conga, which was brought to Córdoba by a foreigner, can be combined with *cuarteto.*

"Esta Noche, Me Voy de Caravana"

This particular song is a *cuarteto* version of rap music in which the singer says he is going to go out from place to place that night to have a good time. After an introduction in which Afro-Caribbean layers of percussion ostinati interact with an ostinato trumpet pattern created with synthesizers, the piece truly begins; at this point, the bass enters with an ostinato, arpeggiated, running quarter-note pattern, the only figuration it plays during the entire piece (the *tunga-tunga* is not used at all). Layered ostinato percussion patterns are performed throughout, and accented notes contribute to the syncopations felt in the piece. When the men's chorus enters, its repetitive melody goes back and forth between only two pitches. Half-spoken, half-sung areas are then performed by the solo singer in an imitation of the rap style. Only short interjections are played in the accordion part.

"Raza Negra"

The title song of *Raza Negra* is a tribute to the black race and the black soil from which it sprang. In parts of the song, a typical Caribbean-influenced piano ostinato pattern can be found, as can a tied bass pattern reminiscent of salsa music. This bass pattern—not the *tunga-tunga*— is heard throughout the entire song. The accordion, which carries the melody in the introduction, has an independent line that is syncopated and tied across bar lines.

"No Soy Dios Para Perdonar"

This tune, one of the *merentetos* recorded on *Raza Negra,* begins with a salsa-style ostinato piano part over a *clave* accompaniment. The *clave* pattern performed is the *rumba clave,* which is a variation of the 3–2 *son clave* (Gerard and Sheller 1989:15; Mauleón 1993:52). Most of the instrumental parts, as well as the vocal parts, are ostinato-like, highly repetitive, and syncopated. At measure 4, the voice part, which is made up of short fragments, joins in. Shortly thereafter, a male chorus begins to answer the singer; this call-and-response texture occurs throughout.

A second section of the introduction begins at measure 21, where a trumpet-call sound is introduced with the synthesizer. At measure 27, where the "verse" part of the song begins, the standard *tunga-tunga* pattern is introduced in the piano and bass. Both the *tambora* and *güira* are used in this tune, as are *timbales,* congas, and other Latin percussion instruments. A trombone solo is later simulated very convincingly in a salsa performance style, and at one point, the right hand of the piano alternates between sections of ostinato, salsa-like patterns and offbeat *tunga-tunga* chords while the bass line does the usual *tunga-tunga* pattern. The accordion plays only a few insignificant answering fragments after the vocal part begins.

Final Comments: Stylistic Significance of *Raza Negra* and *El Marginal*

As can be seen, *Raza Negra* contains some musical selections that have strayed far from the early style of *cuarteto.* Since Jiménez is a traditionalist, it seems quite amazing that he put together such a recording at all. In fact, all of his other recordings have adhered to the *cuarteto-cuarteto* style. Still more interesting is the fact that after having completed such a massive project, he abruptly returned to an updated version of the *cuarteto-cuarteto* style in 1995 with *El Marginal.* Even considering only *El Marginal,* it is still evident that Jiménez has made great advances in instrumentation, orchestration, and use of song structure in his music as compared to the early days of the Cuarteto Leo. If Jiménez's style of *cuarteto* is the most traditional one still used today, it is logical to assume that the styles of other more "advanced" groups have undergone even more change. In any case, the style of *cuarteto* music has become much richer since the time of its creation.

3

An Ethnographic Account of
the *Cuarteto* World

Virtually everyone in Córdoba knows of *cuarteto*. Since this music is heard in locations as varied as shops downtown, apartment buildings, private parties, municipal events, and on television and radio stations, a person has no choice but to be exposed to it. On the other hand, it is a rare individual outside of *cuarteto* circles who knows more than the names of some of the most important groups and has more than a general idea of what *cuarteto* music sounds like; very few of the city's middle- or upper-class residents have ever attended a dance, for example. Despite this general lack of knowledge, rumors abound regarding the dangers of dance halls and the "low-class" people who frequent them. For the most part, those outside the *cuarteto* world are very curious about the genre; despite their fears, they would like to know more about dance halls, what Carlos Jiménez is really like, and what attracts so many people to dances.

In this chapter, an ethnographic account is provided of this unknown world by addressing group organization and administration, music-related group activities, the commercial aspect of *cuarteto* music, life in the *cuarteto* world, *cuarteto* followers, and issues that often come up regarding *cuarteto*.

Group Organization and Administration

Many types of people are involved in the functioning of a *cuarteto* group. Musically speaking, those in the *cuarteto* world label band personnel seen on stage in the following categories: owners (*dueños*), arrangers (*arregladores*), singers (*cantantes*), musicians/instrumentalists (*músicos*), and announcers (*locutores*). The level of musical influence that each type of person in a *cuarteto* group has generally falls into the order that they have just been mentioned. The category of "owners" includes *solistas*— solo singers who have formed their own bands. *Cantantes*, however, are people who sing in groups belonging to others. To members of the *cuarteto* world, singers (*cantantes*) are not "musicians," as the word *músicos* would literally be translated; *músicos* are, in fact, instrumentalists. In this book, the emic differentiation between "singers" and "musicians" will be maintained by using the word "musicians" to refer only to instrumentalists. When both types of personnel are referred to jointly, the phrase "singers and musicians" will be used. The terms "band members" and "group members" will encompass all of the categories of personnel who perform and/or travel with their respective groups, *solistas* will always be called "solo singers," and *cantantes* will be referred to as "singers."

Regarding behind-the-scenes personnel, *cuarteto* groups employ orchestra managers; administrative personnel in charge of promotion and publicity; box office personnel (*boleteros*); drivers (*choferes*); lighting personnel (*iluminadores*); sound men (*sonidistas*); and handlers (*plomos*), who carry, set up, and take down the equipment. In some cases, bands have their own lawyers, accountants, and secretaries.

Owners

Owners are extremely busy people who have a lot invested in their groups; it can cost as much as U.S.$300,000 to start a band (SADAIC 1992:34). It is true that they are quite wealthy, but owners must work seven days a week to keep their groups going. If they perform in their own bands, and compose and arrange for them as well, they have almost no free time. Since bands are incorporated companies, and each group has an office, owner(s) must often spend time there. If a band has several owners, responsibilities for musical matters, administration, public relations, and personnel may be divided up; in this case, each owner might take a turn in the office. Since so much money is involved, trusted family members (e.g., wives) might also be involved in managing a group's financial and administrative operations. Many band offices, which are normally open for only a limited period of time each day, are located downtown. Owners are often available only from Tuesday to Thursday, since their groups are traveling on weekends, but in summer, when their bands also play dances during the week, they may be available only one day per week. It is difficult for them to calculate their time or to set up appointments.

Owners deposit box office receipts, pay song royalties and taxes, arrange and pay for publicity and radio time, have video clips made, book dance engagements, and decide which areas to target. They must get photographs, posters, and other graphic material ready, prepare press releases, and buy instruments, sound and lighting equipment, and band buses. Uniforms for musicians and singers must be chosen, and T-shirts and/or sweatshirts must be purchased for handlers (see figure 3.1). Owners must also keep up-to-date on equipment and the latest developments in the field of popular music, pick repertoire, set up rehearsals, work with arrangers, think ahead to the next recording, plan for the day when their band members get older, find ways to renovate their style without alienating fans, and come up with new ideas for record distribution. Bus schedules, hotel accommodations, meals, local publicity, and dance hall setup must be arranged when traveling.

Owners manage as many as thirty-five people on their payroll. After determining the group's instrumentation, singers and musicians have to be hired; they must be *buenas personas* (good people with excellent outside recommendations) who will fit into the band's "culture"—besides being good performers. To create the group's image, they often choose men under thirty with long hair and good physiques in order to attract girls to the dances. Market fluctuation causes many changes in personnel and musical style over a short period of time, but fans expect to see the same faces on stage; constant change in a group's membership is detrimental to its future. It is the management style of owners, however, that truly sets the tone for group interaction. Some owners treat their employees like friends, create an atmosphere of democracy, and encourage band members to make musical contributions. In these groups, tunes written by group members might be recorded by the band, thus producing royalties (extra income) for these men. Owners who do everything themselves and monopolize profits from song composition often cause resentment and resignations.

Owners pay their employees much less than they keep for themselves, which is often a source of friction. Bands in Córdoba pay their musicians

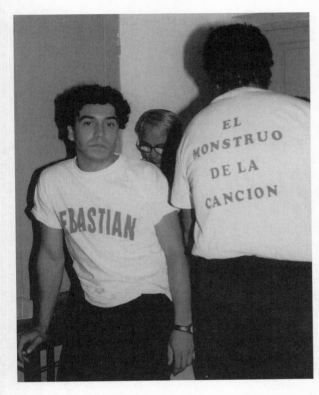

3.1. T-shirts used by *plomos* in Sebastián's group. Photograph by Jane L. Florine, Córdoba, Argentina, 1994.

approximately 80 pesos per dance, whereas those in the interior pay about 45 (at the time of writing, 1 Argentine peso is equal to 1 U.S. dollar). Since group members are paid by the dance, but only for dances that are actually performed, they are happy when their bands play extra engagements. Owners must also determine vacation times, vacation pay, and other benefits, except in the case of temporary employees or those under contract. Policies regarding smoking, behavior in hotels, how long to wait for band members at bus stops, meal allowances while traveling, drinking, whether or not to perform on holidays, conduct with the public during breaks, and grooming must be established. If band members ignore group policy, especially if they do not appear at rehearsals and/or dances and do not find a substitute, they may suffer sanctions.

Arrangers

Arrangers, who are key individuals in *cuarteto* groups, are normally told what new material to arrange. The making of arrangements might be done with a pencil and paper, by ear, or with the use of electronic equipment or keyboards and an initial sketch. Since some groups try to have weekly rehearsals, arrangers may have a set number of tunes they are assigned to prepare per week, one *moderno* and one *tropical*, for example; the arrangers normally direct these rehearsals. If an arranger is also an owner, he helps select repertoire; if he is a composer, his tunes are often recorded by the group. Once the arrangements are ready, they are copied off by hand. When singers and/or musicians play by ear, the arranger must either sing them their parts note by note in rehearsals or give them recordings or demos to listen to in order that they learn their parts.

Arrangers are sometimes actively involved in a band's recordings, perhaps preparing a diskette (in a home studio) that is taken to the recording studio, either in Buenos Aires or Córdoba; this diskette then serves as the basis of the new compact disc. In this type of recording process, only a few band members record their tracks live over the sequences that have been prepared by the arranger on the diskette. When group members' tunes are recorded, the arranger gives them a professional touch. Arrangements are chosen to fit the personal styles and ranges of the bands' singers as well. If bands do not have an official arranger, as may happen when groups play by ear, arrangements for tunes to be recorded are determined by all of the band members in an interactive process.

Arrangers play a big role in the establishment of a group's musical style, since their musical backgrounds influence orchestration. Although some arrangers have gotten professional training at conservatories or music schools, and even sometimes as far away as the United States, others are self-taught. When an arranger is not an owner, he is paid on a contract basis; in these cases, his work and style are controlled by the owner(s) for consistency. Arrangers are normally paid very well, especially if they know how to arrange for brass instruments, because good arrangers are hard to find in Córdoba.

Singers

Singers play a special role in *cuarteto* bands, since their faces are often the image of the group—especially when a singer is a solo singer. Most bands have two singers (one of whom might be a solo singer), who are both tenors: one sings *tropical* tunes and the other does *moderno* ones. It is important that these men be good-looking and have charisma. As of today, no *cuarteto* singer who is blond has ever been successful; it is thought that *cuarteto* fans, who are usually *"negros,"* can identify only with a person of their own kind. Girls often tell singers about their problems, have their pictures taken with them, and give them presents. Since it is often the (solo) singers that attract girls to dances, a group is in trouble if one of its singers leaves. Although singers earn more than musicians (they are harder to replace), they are sometimes lured away by impresarios who give them initial financial backing and convince them that they can make more money on their own.

Besides helping out by playing percussion instruments and singing choruses when they are not "performing," singers might be composers. Solo singers who do not read music usually work with the group's arranger and/or a band member who can help them; the few solo singers who do read music often arrange all of the group's material themselves. Even when singers are not *solistas,* they have influence, since they need to sing tunes that suit their voices. Solo singers have the ultimate power, however: a *solista* decides which songs he will record and may choose to put a picture of only himself on the cover of all of his compact discs, for example.

Musicians

What musicians do in *cuarteto* groups can vary greatly. Some arrange and compose songs for their bands, contribute in group compositional processes, pick the order of the tunes that are performed in the dances, and/or sing choruses besides performing on their instruments. It is common for musicians to make suggestions as to how to improve their parts and to recommend possible cover tunes. Many point out that their musical training, knowledge of performing certain musical styles, and expertise in playing their instruments (tone, technique, intonation) all contribute to make up their band's sound. Although some musicians, particularly percussionists and guitarists, have often had little formal musical training and play by ear, brass players are required to read music. Some instrumentalists' parts consist mostly of chord symbols (bass, piano, and guitar), and at times allow for a moderate amount of flexibility. In a few groups, when cover tunes are performed, all band members must play their parts by ear after having listened to a recording. In order to save in recording costs, not all musicians record with their bands; everyone plays live at dances, however.

Although some musicians have been brought up on *cuarteto* and have begun playing it professionally as youngsters (they have perhaps begun in the interior and have worked their way up to the top from smaller groups), others have attended their first dance on the occasion they have begun performing with their present bands. A few play by ear, but the majority of them have had some sort of musical training, be it from a conservatory, music school, private teacher, or youth band; it is not uncommon to find *cuarteto* musicians with official degrees in music. In fact, some band members have had to take exams to obtain a *carnet de músico*, a document that proves they know the rudiments of music, in order to get work as musicians. Generally speaking, guitarists all have rock backgrounds (some have played heavy metal) and prefer to play by ear. Drum set players are also former rock musicians. Brass players have often been trained in youth military bands and usually like jazz and salsa. The musical tastes and backgrounds of other band members are normally quite varied.

Some *cuarteto* musicians still study classical music and dream of playing in symphony orchestras, and others wish they could be rock musicians or jazz artists, but playing *cuarteto* is almost the only way to make a living with music in Córdoba. Although some of these men listen to *cuarteto* in their free time and say that it is the kind of music they prefer, the majority of the musicians listen to other genres. Educationally speaking, musicians in the *cuarteto* world range from those who have finished only grade school to those who have completed university programs. The musical taste and musical and educational backgrounds of owners, solo singers, and singers are similar to those of musicians.

Announcers

Announcers, who often have had no musical training, have usually gotten into the business because they have liked *cuarteto* and/or have worked as disc jockeys. In most groups—except if they are also owners, arrangers, and/or composers—their musical contribution amounts to playing *güiro* or tambourine, or perhaps to singing choruses; they mostly do public relations for their bands. Announcers do not normally attend rehearsals or recording sessions, but they might suggest repertoire or choose the order of songs to be performed during a dance. During dances, they are passed scraps of paper (dirty business cards, packaging from cigarettes, bottle labels, etc.) on which fans have written greetings for others who are in attendance; the announcer reads these messages out loud between songs to all those present (see figure 5.4). These messages may amount to birthday wishes, salutations to employees of a certain establishment, recognition of the people from a particular neighborhood who have come to a dance, comments about soccer teams and their supporters, and well-wishings to special guests. Performers might also send their greetings to friends. Since the announcer begins to talk right after a tune is over, there are no real pauses until a set ends. He creates a family atmosphere by greeting "regulars" and making jokes.

Other Personnel

Each group divides up its administrative work differently. Administrative assistants, who may answer the telephone and tentatively book dances, are sometimes the people who take care of all publicity and travel arrangements. Orchestra managers, bookkeepers, and box office personnel, who normally travel with their bands, have usually done related work at soccer games or in the corporate world.

Bus drivers and the men who are responsible for light, sound, and equipment handling know all the ins and outs of the business; many of them have worked with several different *cuarteto* groups and have done the same kind of work for years. At times, *plomos* have been known to have worked their way up in bands, having become musicians (usually percussionists or keyboardists who play by ear; see figure 5.6). Although *plomos* are sometimes "promoted," it is almost impossible for a musician to ever become an owner. To do so, he would have to break away from a group and form his own band. Since it is so expensive to start up a group, only in rare cases have musicians ever become owners or part-owners of their own bands.

Cuarteto Groups in Córdoba

At the present time, there are only forty or so *cuarteto* bands that still play in the Córdoba area (SADAIC 1992:24). Of these forty, three reigned supreme in Córdoba in 1994: Carlitos Jiménez ("Carlitos" is the diminutive form of "Carlos"), Tru-la-lá, and Chébere. Since a group called La Barra has been very successful (its four owners broke off from Tru-la-lá), it was speculated in 1994 that there might soon be four top bands in the city ("La Barra del desafío" 16 January 1995:1C; Ortiz,

Gregoratti, and Arrascaeta 11 March 1995:1C). These three or four groups play at the major halls in Córdoba on weekends and have a fairly steady dance circuit. Other groups, such as La Banda del "Negro"Videla and Santamarina, play almost exclusively in the interior and other nearby cities and provinces. Gary is a group that is rarely heard in Córdoba, yet is known all over the country. Other smaller groups would be Pelusa, Fernando, Orly, Alberto Tosas, Carlos and César Rolán, Heraldo Bosio, the Cuarteto Leo, Jorge Daniel, La Nueva Banda del Guapachoso, Noelia, and Adamo. The singer Sebastián used to be very popular, but was rejected by the public when he left Córdoba to perform almost exclusively in Buenos Aires.

Of the many *cuarteto* groups that have been created, many have died within a few months of their founding. For this reason, musicians are often seen one day in one band and the next day in another. When openings appear for singers or musicians, owners can either look for people who have lost their jobs and are doing temporary work, find young men playing in "amateur" *cuarteto* groups sponsored by *cuarteto* promoters, or get musicians from the interior (usually from the province of Córdoba).

Music-Related Group Activities

Members of *cuarteto* groups normally engage in similar types of musical activities: repertoire selection and composition, rehearsals, recording, and live performances.

Repertoire

Although every group performs its own specific repertoire, cover versions of current rock tunes, ballads, or Caribbean selections to which the *tunga-tunga* accompaniment pattern has been added are often played; these can be either local hits or songs recorded by international artists (Wilfredo Vargas, Juan Luis Guerra, etc.). Recently, even Afro-Caribbean genres, rap, and blues have been adapted to the *cuarteto* rhythm. Once cover tunes are chosen, they are classified as being either *moderno* or *tropical* and assigned to the appropriate singer (in the bands that use these two styles).

Songs might also be composed by band members or local composers. In order to be able to earn royalties, which is a lucrative possibility, they become members of SADAIC (Sociedad Argentina de Autores y Compositores), the national association for songwriters and composers. When group members contribute compositions, the owners generally modify them and are thus listed as coauthors (and earn royalties on them).

Since the market is competitive, owners go to great lengths to find new material. If they like the melody of a song sung in another language, for example, they might have it translated. Owners might travel abroad, order new recordings through record stores, or be in contact with someone who can send them tunes from foreign sources as well (tapes of Latin radio broadcasts from Miami, for example). Since it is unstated policy that the first group to record a tune is the only band that can record that particular song, it is important to get to new tunes before the other groups do. All bands play versions of hit songs in their dances though.

Repertoire must be renewed because the same people always come to the dances; since the same tunes are repeated over and over, both dancers and band members can quickly get tired of the same selections. Some older tunes can be played at locations in the interior, but groups that play regularly in Córdoba must release a new recording every six months. Before new songs are recorded, they are sometimes tested out at dances to get audience feedback.

Rehearsals

When *cuarteto* groups rehearse, it is to learn new tunes—not to polish what they already know. By learning a song or two every week, as some bands try to do in their fairly regular weekly rehearsals, new material will be ready by the time that a recording needs to be made, and popular cover tunes can be introduced at dances periodically. Although most bands try to rehearse once a week, this is impossible when they have a heavy performance and travel schedule. Many groups have a set time of day when they hold rehearsals, but the day of the week changes owing to their fluid commitments. Standard rehearsal spots might be in a garage next to a band's office, a vacant studio, an abandoned dance hall, the owner's house, or the arranger's home. It is also possible that a group might rehearse immediately before a dance by using the facility in which it will be performing as a rehearsal hall. Since the date, time, and place of rehearsals can change frequently, band personnel must constantly check in; rehearsals can be called almost without prior notice or canceled once equipment has already been set up at the rehearsal site.

Bands that are constantly on the road rehearse only when they are preparing tunes for their next recording. When the time comes, they shut themselves away for days, and for hours at a stretch, in order to prepare the material. Even so, it is possible that all of the new songs might not have been completely finished before the recording sessions begin. In this type of situation, parts of the arrangements are semi-improvised in the recording studio. After the compact disc has been made, the group then imitates in its dances what has been "invented" and recorded in the studio.

Although some groups rehearse and perform with music, others use written-out parts only to learn and/or memorize the tunes, and yet others may always play by ear. Written-out parts may consist of notes and/or chord symbols, depending on the instrument that one plays. Rehearsals are sometimes informal, with people walking in and out. When people take breaks, they often talk, drink beverages such as *mate* (a special kind of tea that is drunk with a straw), and eat light snacks. Meals might even be served in cases where band members work for long stretches at an owner's home.

Although some groups do not rehearse for a set period of time, and may practice all night, other bands limit the number of hours of rehearsal time. Arrangers might rehearse in an organized fashion, having some performers arrive early to go over difficult sections of the new tunes. If new group members have been taken on, the arranger might come with a list of compositions that must be gone over. Singers and *solistas,* because they normally do not read music, have learned their parts and transcribed their lyrics ahead of time by listening to the selection(s) to be rehearsed.

Although some arrangers run their rehearsals as though they were conductors of a symphony orchestra, asking for dynamic changes and other details in a directive fashion, in other bands, the members all decide among themselves what the final details, such as timbre, will be. In this latter case, it is the band members who determine which tunes will be rehearsed and when this will be done. In these more "democratic" groups, the composer of each song directs the rehearsal of his own material; the owner, if he is a solo singer, might not attend rehearsals until the band is ready for him.

Recordings

When groups release new recordings, as they must periodically, a sense of renovation is involved. It is true that bands earn most of their income from dances, but releasing compact discs provides a way for fans to learn song lyrics and for bands to make additional earnings in royalties. Although recordings are sometimes done live at dances, it is more common for them to be done at studios in Córdoba or, better yet, in Buenos Aires (one group has made a recording in Los Angeles, California). Mixing is normally done in Buenos Aires, but has also been done in the United States.

Some groups do still record live, but it has become popular to prepare most of the sound tracks (sequences) electronically, in the arranger's home. At times, bands use recording sessions as a time to invite in either special guest artists of perhaps international renown (musicians who play with Madonna and Phil Collins, for example), in order to boost their self-esteem, or studio musicians who can help them to do unique types of orchestrations. The problem of having guest artists perform unusual instruments on a band's recordings is that it might not be possible to reproduce these sounds later on, when the guest artists are no longer available. Recordings also give solo singers a chance to introduce repertoire they have always wanted to sing (non-*cuarteto* selections might perhaps be recorded).

In order to get known, it is critical for brand-new groups to sign with a major label, such as BMG, Sony, or Warner. Once a band has signed a contract, its owners can normally record whatever they want to; however, if its recordings do not sell, the group will be dropped by the record company. On the other hand, if its recordings do well, another label might come in, lure the band away, or buy out its contract. Record companies often hold special promotional parties to which owners and record-store salesmen are invited; at these events, they woo new bands and encourage salesmen to display and sell their products. *Cuarteto* groups also depend on good relationships with sales personnel, since they are given only a few free recordings.

A band's choice of record label is important because record companies are in charge of distribution (see Appendix B). If a company distributes *cuarteto* recordings only locally, in Córdoba, bands might arrive to perform in other provinces and discover that no one has heard their latest repertoire. Once a group has left a particular record company, it is common for that label to put together recordings of that band's biggest hits and/or previously unreleased material in order to make money after the fact. Most of the large *cuarteto* groups record with BMG—which makes a yearly compilation containing two selections by each band on its roster—or with Sony. In 1995, BMG also produced a special television program, with a local comedian, on which all of its *cuarteto* groups were featured ("Doña Jovita" 6 March 1995:1C). Some bands distribute internationally (to Chile, Mexico, Uruguay, and other nearby countries), but it is their dream to make it in the U.S. Latin market.

Recordings are normally released for important dates when fans must buy gifts, such as Mother's Day or Christmas, or in July and December, when workers are paid bonuses. Special launching ceremonies, at times attended by as many as ten thousand people, are heavily promoted through the media. At these events, new uniforms and special stage decorations are used. Bands try to have their recordings in the stores a few days before the launching ceremonies, if possible, in order that their fans already know the new lyrics by the time they are held. In the case of recordings released by Carlos Jiménez, fans often reserve copies in advance or begin to wait in line outside of record stores early in the morning on the day that his newest recording is to arrive; they are informed of these dates on special *cuarteto* radio programs, which also give weekly sales statistics. Quite often newly available *cuarteto* recordings achieve the status of "gold record" (*disco de oro*) or "platinum record" (*disco de platino*) before the launching ceremony is held. A special trophy is also awarded to the singer who sells the most *cuarteto* recordings.

Of every ten recordings sold in Córdoba, eight are of *cuarteto* music (Cinti 1992:22). The sale of cassettes overtakes that of compact discs by a seven to three ratio because of a big difference in price (Gregoratti 21 March 1995:1C); a cassette might cost from 8 to 10 pesos, whereas a compact disc runs from 18 to 20. Fans purchase most of these recordings at record stores on San Martín Street in Córdoba, but mostly at MJ Musical, a store that also has locales in other parts of the city (see Appendix A). Many recordings of *cuarteto* are also sold in train stations, even in Buenos Aires (the Once district). In Buenos Aires, *cuarteto* is confused with genres that are there called *tropical* and *cumbia;* as a result, *cuarteto* music is often mislabeled in Buenos Aires's record stores. Although it is usually died-in-the-wool *cuarteto* fans who purchase recordings, some hypocritical elitists purchase them telling salespeople they are buying them for their maid or hired help.

Since most new recordings are sold within a month of their release, and discs are routinely released every six months, old recordings are often on sale or can be found in remainder bins on San Martín Street; some of these stores carry outdated long plays (new recordings are no longer made in this format) for a couple of pesos. Once the entire stock of a recording is sold, it may not be possible to order a copy of it. MJ Musical has tried to remedy this situation by reediting some older releases. Since fans like to replace their older tapes with compact discs, there is also a market for reissued material (Gregoratti 21 March 1995: 1C). Copies of older recordings can sometimes be obtained from fans with large personal collections, from band owners, or from radio archives.

Sheet music of *cuarteto* tunes is not sold; instead, bands give it away as a promotional tool and in order to get smaller groups to play their repertoire (and thus generate royalties). Although some bands work with publishers, they do not see publishing their music as a profitable venture.

Live Performances

The performance schedule of *cuarteto* groups normally follows a yearly cycle. After New Year's Eve, the summer season, which is the busiest time of year for *cuarteto* groups, begins. Bands travel to all sorts of resort towns during the summer months and may perform as many as six or seven nights a week. The larger groups keep performing in Córdoba on weekends, however, to maintain their audiences. Summer is also the time of special "festivals" (the Honey Festival, the Sausage Festival, etc.) throughout the province of Córdoba, for which *cuarteto* groups perform, and when the Festival Nacional de Folklore is held in Cosquín. *Cuarteto* has not been heard at the festival proper since 1988, but it has been performed at the celebration called "Febrero en Cosquín" ("February in Cosquín"), which immediately follows the folklore festival. When the festival is going on, *cuarteto* music can be heard at small dance halls in the city and at outdoor swimming areas by the river.

After the festival season has wound down, *cuarteto* groups begin performing for the Carnival season, during which both dancers and band members sometimes dress up (see figure 3.2); some dancers come in

3.2. Eduardo "Pupi" Rojo of the Jiménez band dressed up for Carnival. Photograph by Jane L. Florine, Córdoba, Argentina, 1995.

Brazilian-style dress, complete with string bikinis and feathered headdresses. Once the Carnival season is over, *cuarteto* groups normally take a couple of weeks off, in March or April, to go on vacation. Owners may not be able to rest during their vacations, however, since they must plan for the recordings that they must get out to the public in June or July. Some band members might have to cut their vacations short in order to record.

Once the new recordings have been launched in June or July, the regular dance schedule kicks in. Many of these dances are held to celebrate patron saint festivals and birthdays (of girls who turn fifteen). In September, there are special events planned for Students' Day, which is also the first day of spring. A caravan, in which a *cuarteto* group may be included, goes through the city and ends up at Parque Sarmiento, where a huge open-air concert is held; perhaps thirty thousand people attend this event. In October, many special events that include *cuarteto* music are held for Mother's Day (see figure 4.4). These might include an open-air concert in Plaza San Martín, sponsored by a local radio station, for which chairs are set up in front of the Cabildo Building downtown. In honor of the occasion, a televised program, which includes various musical groups and fireworks, might be held at the Teatro Griego, an amphitheater in Parque Sarmiento, as well. Groups must then plan for their next recording, which will be released in a launching ceremony at the end of the year. Bigger groups rest over the end-of-the-year holidays, but smaller ones keep on playing to continue earning money.

Cuarteto music is used for all sorts of occasions, not just those mentioned in the yearly cycle. For example, Gypsies hire *cuarteto* groups to play on December 8 to honor the Virgin; they think that offering *cuarteto* music is the best possible gift that they can give to her (see figure 4.12a). School groups sometimes offer *cuarteto* nights, using recorded music, as fund-raising events. *Cuarteto* is commonly heard at wedding parties, family gatherings, birthday parties of the rich and famous, discos (one or two recorded selections might be put on per evening in order to get the dancers up), and at informal public events after the main part of the program is over. This music is also used during the upbeat portions of Pentecostal church services, especially by young people. Many associations of workers, for example, the Bakers' Society, plan a yearly, sit-down dinner for members; among the several famous ensembles and/or acts hired for the occasion are *cuarteto* groups. Although many people who attend the dinner do not know how to dance *cuarteto*-style, they dance in whatever way they can to the music.

Cuarteto music might also be heard in a concert, in conjunction with other groups (the municipal band, a tango ensemble, etc.), in outdoor summer programs planned by the municipality, or at outdoor nondance events (such as anti-drug and political rallies). Carlos Jiménez might celebrate his birthday by offering either a recital in a huge stadium or by holding a special dance in a big dance hall; for these events, a taxi or a house might be raffled off. At outdoor events, *cuarteto* fans dance to the music in the aisles or between the rows where people are seated.

Dances are held in many types of establishments, big and small, for as few as 500 people up to as many as 30,000. They are often held in huge sports clubs, small dance establishments, former movie theaters and warehouses, walled-in open-air locales with dirt floors, gymnasiums, and in *bailantas* in Buenos Aires. Dance halls in Córdoba are commonly old, hot in the summertime, and drafty in winter. Bathrooms are small and dirty, only a few tables and chairs are provided, and furnishings are

3.3. Sign outside Rincón 50, a small club where *cuarteto* is performed. Photograph by Jane L. Florine, Córdoba, Argentina, 1994.

generally dilapidated. Outside, the signs that show the names of establishments may be neon, painted, or look homemade (see figure 3.3). On Fridays, Saturdays, and the eves of holidays, dances begin at approximately 12:30 A.M. and end fairly close to 4:30 A.M. On Sundays and weeknights, they begin around 10:30 to 11:00 P.M. and end promptly at 2:00 A.M.; the 2:00 A.M. ending time is dictated by municipal regulations.

Some of the smaller dance halls are geared to the over-thirty crowd; they might have fixed house orchestras that play *cuarteto* and other types of music, or they could be halls that hire a different *cuarteto* group every week. Larger halls serve those thirty and under, the biggest population of dancers. Some of the bigger clubs are monopolized by the three or four most important bands in the city; since the men who rent these halls out know they have a sure thing with these big-name groups, they are hesitant to rent them out to smaller ones. It is mostly on weekends that the major bands perform at these clubs in Córdoba; they have to keep performing in the city so as to not lose the dancers who follow them. These large groups try to cover several areas in the city over a fifteen-day period in order to get to a larger populace. The names and locations of the halls included in the local dance circuit of downtown Córdoba are shown in figure 3.4, which is a drawing based on information that appeared in *La Voz del Interior* (Gregoratti 11 March 1995:2C). Typical attendance figures for these locales, from Thursday through Sunday, are also given in the same figure. A photograph of one of the very large dance halls, La Vieja Usina, is shown in figure 3.5.

The biggest halls are associated with specific bands. Chébere, for example, often performs in Villa Retiro and La Vieja Usina. Jiménez is in the Estadio del Centro and Sargento Cabral during one weekend and at Atenas and the Super Deportivo the next; he commonly performs at Alas Argentinas on Sundays. Tru-la-lá is at Atenas, the Super Deportivo, and the Estadio del Centro on the weekends that Jiménez is not performing at these same locations. This dance circuit does change from time to time. The largest halls are used on Saturday evenings, when the greatest number of fans go to dances. More fans usually attend Friday dances than Sunday ones, so the halls used on Fridays are a bit bigger than those used on Sundays.

Some groups cannot break into the dance hall circuit in the city. At times even important bands may not be allowed to play in certain locales because they are on bad terms with the person who rents them out or do not want to have to buy their publicity through a firm connected with a particular dance hall. In yet other cases, owners have decided not to play in certain halls because the person renting them out has demanded a larger portion of box office receipts than usual (asking for 40 percent instead of 30 percent, for example).

Groups are constantly coming up with all sorts of gimmicks in order to increase attendance at dances. Fans might be allowed to enter free if they arrive before a certain time, or free passes might be given for the following week's dance. Girls might be given special cards that always allow them to enter free; dance halls need to be full, and it is important that many young women be there. Other gimmicks include offering dancers free candy, Christmas fruitcake, cider, chocolate, beer, cake (for a singer's birthday), or parts of gold records (made of real gold). One group, when it changed its name, put up mystery signs with its new name on it all over town; only much later was everyone told what this name referred to ("Basta de discriminación" 3 July 1995:1C). On another occasion, fans were encouraged to come to a series of dances, at 9:00

Thursday	Number of Dancers
1. Gerónimo	600
Friday	
2. Estadio del Centro	2,000
3. Atenas	1,800
4. Alas Argentinas	1,800
Saturday	
5. Sargento Cabral	3,800
6. Club Huracán	2,800
7. Club Villa Retiro	5,000
8. Super Deportivo	2,500
9. La Vieja Usina	5,000
10. Comedor Universitario	3,000
Sunday	
11. Club Las Palmas	2,000
12. Sociedad Belgrano	1,500
13. Hindú Club	1,500

3.4. Names, locations, and weekly attendance figures of the main dance halls in Córdoba (Gregoratti 11 March 1995:3C). Artwork by John de Vries, 2000.

3.5. La Vieja Usina, a huge, upscale hall made out of a former warehouse. Photograph by Jane L. Florine, Córdoba, Argentina, 1994.

P.M., by getting the bands scheduled to perform later on to play one set before 12:30 A.M.

The *Bailantas*

After *cuarteto* was introduced in Buenos Aires by Carlos Jiménez in 1988, many groups began playing in the *bailantas*. Since approximately 1993, however, this practice has stopped. Owners began to feel that the effort of going to Buenos Aires was not worth it; maintenance costs were high, agents needed to be contracted in Buenos Aires, their business in Córdoba was being put at risk, and *bailanta* administrators wanted to pay them only a standard fee (not the box office receipts, or a percentage of them, as happens in Córdoba). Worse yet, at one point bands could work with only one of the two chains of *bailantas* in Buenos Aires at a time; when the owner of one chain had hired a group, the owner of the other would boycott that band.

The biggest objections of *cuarteto* groups regarded the performance conditions imposed in the *bailanta* circuit. Instead of each band playing for its own followers for an entire four hours in one hall, as happens in Córdoba, they were required to play in as many as six or seven locales per evening; performances lasted only forty-five minutes or so and were in the form of a show. Each time a band played, it was forced to set up quickly, dismantle everything as soon as possible, and rush to the next performance site. Band members did not have enough time to set up properly and felt that audience members were being cheated.

Although *cuarteto* groups enjoyed the modern facilities in the *bailantas* (they look like discos), they missed the atmosphere of Córdoba. Some of them felt so uncomfortable in Buenos Aires they did not ever stray from the block in which the hotel was located. By playing only short shows, they did not ever have a real group of steady followers or feel any connection with their audience in Buenos Aires, either. Announcers could no longer greet dancers, making the announcers' presence almost unnecessary, and band members could no longer socialize with fans in breaks. What was even stranger to *cuarteto* groups was that people who go to *bailantas* do not dance while bands perform; instead, they listen as if they were at a recital, scream when solo singers make their entrances, and throw things up on stage. It is only after a live group leaves, and recorded music is put on by a disc jockey, that they dance—but not *cuarteto*-style.

It should be mentioned that *bailantas* in Buenos Aires do not have a very good reputation, supposedly being frequented by low-income people who have migrated to Buenos Aires from the interior. Many of these locations were traditionally located next to large train stations, in places where the working-class population could access them via public transportation (Elbaum 1994:199–200, 210). Some of the biggest *bailantas* are Fantástico del Once, Metrópolis, Monumental de Merlo, and Terremoto. It is commonly said that *tropical* and *cumbia* are played in these locales, which also means *cuarteto* music in Buenos Aires. Many pseudo-*cuarteto* groups that have sprung up in Buenos Aires are only poor imitations.

The Commercial Aspect of *Cuarteto* Music

Competition and Publicity

Since *cuarteto* music is big business and involves huge sums of money (35,000 pesos—equivalent to U.S.$35,000—might be earned in a single weekend), competition is fierce (Ortiz, Gregoratti, and Arrascaeta 11 March 1995:1C). Of the three or so entrepreneurs who control the major dance hall business, Emeterio Farías is the most powerful. Farías, who rents out Atenas and the Super Deportivo, also owns a publicity agency (through which most *cuarteto* groups place their ads), a television studio (where most of the *cuarteto* television commercials are made), and a radio station (which is heavily involved with *cuarteto* programming and promotion). If it is not possible to get dance dates in the most important dance halls, such as those of Farías, bands normally have to work in the interior. At one point, however, Carlos Jiménez, who had been shut out of some of the major locales, created his own *bailanta*-style establishment in Córdoba; having La Cueva, as he called it, allowed him to avoid dealing with the major impresarios (SADAIC 1992:22).

In Córdoba, band owners normally get their money from ticket sales (minus taxes, song royalties, and a percentage of the sales that a person like Farías, who rents out a hall, might insist on keeping for himself). When they play in the interior, band owners pay much less in taxes. The owner of the dance hall (or the person who rents it out), whether it be in Córdoba or in the province, gets the money from the drinks that are sold at the bar. During better economic times, the amount of money earned from the bar was much larger than that collected in ticket sales; since drinks are expensive (a soft drink can run from 3 to 5 pesos and alcoholic beverages cost much more), consumption varies with the economy. In Córdoba, men must pay approximately 7 pesos to attend a dance; girls might pay around 2 pesos or perhaps get in free. By contrast, in the interior, everyone must pay from 10 to 12 pesos to get in. Since the economic situation in 1995 was critical, ticket prices in the interior had been lowered to approximately 5 pesos in August of that year, however. Although less money was being taken in than before, owners were still doing very well.

Because the field is so competitive, the biggest groups must spend from 4,000 to 5,000 pesos per week in advertising. If a band stops placing ads, other groups move in with more publicity than ever in order to try to pick up more business. If an important band stops playing in Córdoba on weekends, other groups try to take over its territory as well. People associated with or who work for a *cuarteto* band are not often seen at the dances of another group; it is said that spies are sent around by owners in order to see how many people appear at dances played by the competition, though. Since bands do not ordinarily plan together in order to space out the locations in which they play in the interior, dances played there often end up being performed simultaneously in places that are very near to each other. As a result, none of the groups involved draws a very big crowd. In some cases, bands plan joint dances in which each band plays two sets.

The fierce competition among groups also results in damaging rumors and accusations that are created intentionally. Many of these rumors are started in the Bon Que Bon, a bar located in the heart of the *cuarteto* district (only a few blocks away from the main *cuarteto* offices). In this bar and another, called El Padrino, performers have traditionally been able to find out about job openings. Most hiring of groups is done by impresarios in these same two locations on Tuesday afternoons, at which time the dances of the past weekend are discussed. Besides rumors, it is said that bands must worry about sabotage to their dances. One group travels with its own backup power generator in case the electricity at the dance hall it happens to be playing at "accidentally" goes out.

The Media

Radio is the type of media that most groups rely on for publicity. Some programs, such as *El Club de los Bailarines, Esperando el Baile,* and *Taxi Libre,* are broadcast on Saturdays in order to get fans up for the dances. Other daily programs, such as *Con Toda Música* on LV2 with the announcer Héctor Grande and a program on Radio Suquía hosted by Luis Cima, exist more to relay publicity about upcoming dances than anything else. On all of these broadcasts, fans participate by calling in to request and dedicate songs; at times they can win prizes. The latest gossip and "current events" important in the *cuarteto* world are also discussed. Many FM stations, such as La Ranchada, broadcast *cuarteto* music almost constantly. Others, such as Radio Nacional, never do.

The two largest radio stations in Córdoba, LV2 and LV3, have long competed in order to attract more listeners. The two stations at times sponsor events for which *cuarteto* groups are hired; they try to heavily publicize attendance figures from these performances and occasionally exaggerate them in order to come out on top. Paid *cuarteto* ads are placed on both stations, but LV3 supposedly has a more sophisticated audience than LV2 does. One morning program on LV3, run by Mario Pereyra, is used by bands as their major publicity vehicle. Others rely heavily on the program on LV2 done by Héctor Grande (and sponsored by Emeterio

Farías) or Radio Suquía (owned by Farías and devoted purely to *cuarteto*). Many *cuarteto* ads are also heard during broadcasts of soccer games. On large stations, air time must be purchased (sometimes under the table); on small FM stations, it is often free.

Newspapers rarely carry any information on *cuarteto*. Fan magazines have occasionally published dance schedules, but printed sources have never been of importance in informing fans about upcoming dances. Video clips of *cuarteto* groups on television, used in the form of commercials, are an important way to publicize dance dates and locations, though. Most of these commercials are put together at RangoTV, owned by Emeterio Farías, and are broadcast on Channel 10, which gives bands a discount. Some ads may be placed on Channel 12, although they are expensive. A television program broadcast on Saturdays, called *Ómnibus,* frequently features *cuarteto* artists, but *cuarteto* groups are not often seen on television. In the interior of the country, bands rely on posters, banners in the streets, and men who drive around in cars with loudspeaker systems on top to publicize their dances. Fans who regularly attend dances are already familiar with the standard dance hall circuits and hardly need to be informed about dance dates.

Life in the *Cuarteto* World

Personal and Daily Life

Most of the people involved with *cuarteto* music are from either the city or the province of Córdoba; only a few come from other provinces or other countries (Peru, Ecuador, Brazil, and the Dominican Republic). Upon going to a dance, one gets the impression that these men are really enjoying themselves; they laugh, tell jokes, chat with fans, and give humorous yet affectionate nicknames to each other (Grapefruit, Baby, Big Head, Rabbit, Indian, Little Bird, Pickpocket, Old Man, etc.). It is unusual to see a band member look depressed in public.

Yet underneath this façade, all those who live and work in the *cuarteto* world lead difficult, self-sacrificing lives and are often very down. They live backward from the rest of the world and do not have time for themselves. They also spend many hours on buses traveling and often do not sleep. At a moment's notice, they must be ready to drop everything and go to a last-minute rehearsal or engagement. Although many men say they are tired of living this kind of life and would like to get out of it, many of them miss the "excitement" of *cuarteto* life when they do not have it.

Those involved with *cuarteto* music often say that it is almost impossible for them to have any sort of family life, and that personal relationships get strained. Lucky men have family members who are also involved in the business; if not, it is usually only their girlfriends (whether these men are married or not) who accompany them to dances. In truth, band members' colleagues often end up being their true families.

Many band members say that they stay in the business only because of the amount of money they can make; nonmusical jobs do not pay as much. Five or six of the men in the larger groups do somehow manage to either study at the local conservatory or university or hold down second jobs, though. Since band members are often paid from dance to dance, it is common for them to live from day to day. When unpaid vacations come around, within a few days many of them call their band owners in order to get salary advances or loans. Band members often discuss their salaries and feel they are being cheated, but they rarely bring their complaints out in the open to owners; they cannot risk losing their jobs.

The Role of Women

Almost everyone in the *cuarteto* world is male; although there are some female singers and/or women singing choruses, female instrumentalists are nonexistent. There is one female soloist, Noelia, who has her own group, but she does not have a big following and does not sing in Córdoba. Female singers have occasionally been used on recordings and in bands in order to sing choruses, but only one group presently has women doing backup vocals (Gary has two women in his band; see figure 5.7). Regarding female instrumentalists, Leonor Marzano is the only one to have ever been a member of a *cuarteto* group. Until I performed live and recorded with Carlos Jiménez's group in 1995, to the best of my knowledge, no female instrumentalist had even been a guest artist with a *cuarteto* band.

This lack of female performers is made up for by the quantity of women at dances, many of whom aggressively pursue band members. These women often wait for the men during intermissions (some are allowed to go backstage) and after dances; many accompany group members to nearby hotels after the dances or have sex with them in the band bus. There are some who make it their goal to sleep with each man in the band; others might target only singers. Although there are often prostitutes at dances, most of these girls are groupies (see figures 3.6–3.7). Since so many women are constantly offering themselves to band members, it is said that few of these men are faithful to their wives. Band members brag about their conquests, point out the girls they like, and sometimes openly make fun of the young women who pursue them. Although some wives either suspect or know that their husbands are fooling around, they often say there is nothing they can do about it. What they do not like is when girls who have slept with their husbands appear on their doorsteps to tell them so. There could also be huge problems in the case of a paternity suit. Ordinarily, wives do not go to dances; when

3.6. Two "regulars" found especially at Tru-la-lá's dances. Photograph by Jane L. Florine, Córdoba, Argentina, 1994.

3.7. A young woman who frequents *cuarteto* dances of many groups. Photograph by Jane L. Florine, Córdoba, Argentina, 1994.

they do go along, groupies who like their husbands sometimes treat them badly and fabricate untrue stories in order to make them jealous.

Problems can sometimes arise among band members over women. For example, one musician was thrown out of a group because he went out with a girl who was seeing the owner. Since no man wants "his woman" to be courted or even talked to too much by another man, fights can occur when a band member thinks someone has been making advances to his girlfriend.

Traveling

Members of *cuarteto* groups spend the greater portion of their lives traveling. Their work might entail going from and returning to Córdoba each evening a dance is held. Although each one of these dances could be held in a different city, band members normally return to Córdoba immediately after each one is over (to avoid spending extra money in hotels and meals). If several dances are being performed in the same general area, bands do go to hotels; these types of trips, which generally last from two to four days, are called "tours" (*giras*). One group once went on a "tour" that lasted for a month, an unusual length of time.

Each group has a standard place in downtown Córdoba (a bar, a candy stand, a street corner, or a park) where its members congregate and wait for the band bus on days of performances. Since the pickup time often changes at the last minute, band members are informed of the pickup time for the following day at the prior evening's dance. Group members arrive a bit before the scheduled time, just in case, but pickup times of some bands are often "flexible." If a group member misses the bus, he must find a way to get to the dance. When dances are scheduled close to Córdoba, many band members prefer to drive. Some owners do occasionally fly to Buenos Aires, but most bands go there by bus, which takes approximately ten hours.

When the bus arrives at the waiting place, some band members have already boarded it; group members who live near the place where the bus is stored prefer to take it there—before it goes downtown. After the people waiting downtown are picked up, band members who happen to live on the way to the dance location might be picked up en route; girls who want to go to the dance are sometimes picked up along the way as well.

Once the group gets to the city where the dance is to be held, the band members all eat together at a restaurant; a meal has been requested for them in advance for a specific time. All of the group members usually sit around one or two long tables while they eat (see figure 3.8). If anyone wants something "extra," for example a dessert, he must pay for it out of his own pocket (some owners prefer to give band members a daily food allowance instead). After dinner, they go back to the dance hall to change into their uniforms if necessary. Some band members test out their instruments, have a drink or two (often spiked cola) to get up for the dance, and perhaps roll dice. Meanwhile, the *plomos*, the sound men, and the lighting personnel have prepared the hall.

After the dance is over, the band members change their clothes. Some of them take out pillows and blankets they have brought along so as to be able to sleep. If a group happens to have two buses, the performers' bus

3.8. Gary's entourage eating out before a performance in Buenos Aires. Photograph by Jane L. Florine, Buenos Aires, Argentina, 1994.

leaves right after the dance. If the band has only one bus, everyone must wait to leave until the equipment has been safely stored on it. After the bus arrives in Córdoba in the wee hours of the morning, the band members then find their way home. This same type of routine is followed day after day.

Drivers of band buses have often been employed by the same group for years. The buses that they drive are of the Greyhound type, not the school bus kind, and usually have the name of the band painted in large lettering on both sides. A poster of the solo singer—if the group has one—is often placed in the front window as well. These buses are not always heated and/or air conditioned, so band members dress appropriately. While the group is traveling, the driver puts on tapes of various types of music kept by his seat. Each person in the band has his own assigned seat, his home away from home. The men are seen reading, listening to music or the latest soccer games (on portable radios), drinking *mate*, and talking.

When groups go on tour, band members might entertain themselves during the day by having a barbecue or playing soccer (figure 3.9). They

3.9. The members of Santamarina and Jiménez's band take time out from playing soccer before a joint performance in San Juan, Argentina. Photograph by Jane L. Florine, San Juan, Argentina, 1994.

appear when meals are served, but otherwise are on their own. Within each band, small cliques of friends eat and room together; some owners do not fraternize with band members. Men often bring along their "girl-friends" on tours, and many prostitutes and groupies appear at hotels where bands usually stay.

Cuarteto Followers

Who Attends Dances and Why

Many people who do not attend *cuarteto* dances cannot understand why fans follow their chosen groups so faithfully; some *cuarteto* enthusiasts go to dances as many as four to five times per week and may travel to nearby cities to do so. The truth of the matter is that people who attend *cuarteto* dances regularly often do so in order to fulfill certain needs. Some of these needs are openly acknowledged by fans, whereas others are hidden and perhaps secondary to them.

Although *cuarteto* fans do not stop to think about it, dance events mirror social organization and can help to produce group solidarity and identity in urban locations. Safe in their dance halls, lower-class participants, such as *cuarteto* fans, can interact far away from city-dwellers who do not appreciate them (Hanna 1979:215). Attendees come to recognize familiar faces in a setting where they feel accepted; instead of feeling inferior, as they often do in their daily lives, they are on an equal footing with all those present.

As far as *cuarteteros* are concerned, *cuarteto* dancing is primarily done to enjoy oneself: dancers uniformly say that they go to dance events to have a good time, to experience *alegría* (happiness). Little attention is paid to dance expertise. The fact that *cuarteto* dance steps can be performed easily by almost anyone (so as to allow for maximum participation) is a typical characteristic of social dances, as are the social interaction and warm atmosphere experienced at them (Shay 1971:49, 53–54).

If too many people appear at a dance, for example, at a major record launching ceremony, and fans do not have enough space to dance, they do not have a good time; the physical action involved in dancing is a real need for them. Dancing around and around hypnotically in a counterclockwise motion, always using the same steps, helps fans to lose themselves in the music; it also enhances their feeling of participation and communion. Even when attending *cuarteto* "recitals," fans feel a need to get up and dance in the aisles or on the tops of their chairs when they hear the *tunga-tunga*.

The audience composition and number of dancers in any particular hall on a specific evening will depend on several factors. First of all, most people who attend *cuarteto* dances in the larger halls in Córdoba city are under thirty. Secondly, more dancers will be out on Saturday evenings than any other time; some fans say they prefer to go to the smaller, more intimate Sunday dances, however. Thirdly, since people from certain social classes follow specific groups with which they feel comfortable (fans normally follow one band), dance attendance at a particular hall on a specific evening depends on which band is there. Lastly, dances in the interior of Córdoba and the neighboring provinces do not attract the same kind of audience members that attend dances in the city.

Chébere, for example, is known for attracting university students who also go to discos. It is also said that Chébere dances have more of a "couples" environment than do those of other groups, so unmarried

3.10. A young singer who imitates Carlos Jiménez, both in singing style and dress. Photograph by Jane L. Florine, Córdoba, Argentina, 1994.

girls who often go to dances with groups of female friends might not care to attend them. At Carlos Jiménez's dances, it is quite evident that Jiménez's followers are not from the same social class as are Chébere fans. When Jiménez performs, he attracts people from the most economically disadvantaged sectors of the city, such as prostitutes, transvestites, and criminals. Entire families, which sometimes bring babies that fall asleep on chairs, are also in attendance at his dances. Jiménez followers, and young singers who imitate him (see figure 3.10), are often from the working class (office and factory workers, maids, manual laborers, etc.) or are unemployed. When groups—not just Jiménez's band—perform outside of Córdoba, more families attend dances than do in the city. In the interior, where dances are sporadic, it is also common for fans to follow more than one band. "Oldtimers" in the interior go to dances that are performed by *cuarteto* artists who were popular in their youth, such as Carlos Rolán, whenever they get a chance.

Cuarteto followers have often gotten hooked on *cuarteto* music starting at an early age. Some have begun going to dances because their parents, who were *cuarteto* fans or performers, used to take them along. Two young boys, for example, who are approximately four years old, get up on stage when the band Tru-la-lá performs; they "sing" into stand-up, plastic microphones as though they were singers with the group. These youngsters, whose parents hope they will become famous *cuarteto* artists someday, are dressed like the band members (their parents have special outfits made for them) and know all of the band's song lyrics; they also play tambourines. It is also common for children who have become *cuarteto* fans to do school projects on *cuarteto* if they ever get the opportunity. After girls turn fifteen, some of them begin to attend *cuarteto* dances every weekend from then on.

The Life of the *Cuartetero*

People who are avid *cuarteto* fans are commonly called *cuarteteros*. In song lyrics, it is common to describe them as being *cuarteteros de corazón* (heartfelt *cuarteto* fans). *Cuarteteros* spend most of their time thinking about, talking about, and listening to *cuarteto* music and the bands that perform it. Since they constantly listen to *cuarteto* radio programs and watch *cuarteto* commercials, they know exactly when and where all of the dances will be held from week to week—not just those of the group they prefer. Most of the time, however, they have already obtained this information on their own by going to dances, by word of mouth, and by gossiping about the *cuarteto* scene. *Cuarteteros* always know if anything about *cuarteto* has been published in *LaVoz del Interior,* the local newspaper, read whatever they can find written about it, and are up-to-date on the latest rumors. They constantly discuss which dance they next plan to attend.

Besides talking about the singers and musicians in the *cuarteto* world, *cuarteteros* constantly talk about the latest tunes that have been recorded;

they faithfully buy new recordings to add to their personal collections and learn all of the lyrics of the latest songs. They also enjoy listening to older tapes of their favorite groups and swap tapes with their friends. Many *cuarteteros* actively participate in *cuarteto* radio programs, acting as volunteer disc jockeys or calling in to request or dedicate tunes to friends and family members. Prisoners sometimes call radio stations to request songs by Carlos Jiménez.

Most *cuarteto* fans have their walls papered with posters of their favorite groups and singers; they often have and display photographs in which they have had their picture taken along with a famous person in the *cuarteto* world as well. Girls, in particular, target one band member; they might have many photographs of themselves taken alongside this person and collect posters and perhaps hundreds of photographs of him as well. Girls also keep up on the birthdays of their favorite band members and bring them birthday cakes on the appropriate days. They go to great lengths to try to obtain the phone numbers of the men they are interested in.

Very few things can keep *cuarteto* fans from going to dances. Poor weather, for example, a torrential rain storm, is about the only thing that deters them. Since the halls have no air conditioning and can get so hot that singers have actually fainted up on stage, heat waves are another possible deterrent. Unless a dance is held near the end of the month, when money is scarce (most working-class Argentines live from month to month, and from paycheck to paycheck), it is unlikely that *cuarteteros* are going to miss a dance.

Many *cuarteteros* are also avid soccer fans who frequently go to soccer matches, especially those in which their favorite team plays, besides attending dances regularly. In fact, the police officers that work at *cuarteto* dances are often the same ones that work at soccer games; they are normally assigned to games played in one particular arena and to specific dance halls. It is quite common for a particular *cuarteto* group to be associated with one soccer team, the one that the majority of its band members root for. On days that important games have been played, their outcomes are mentioned in dances either in jest or not; on these same occasions, some fans appear with hats or headbands on that are emblematic of the soccer teams that they follow (see figure 4.14). Since so many soccer fans are also *cuarteteros,* it is easy to understand why fans turn popular *cuarteto* tunes into "fight songs" by changing their lyrics.

Cuarteto fans expect bands to be sincerely committed to performing *cuarteto* music. If followers feel that a group is only out to make money (i.e., that it does not transmit anything to them or even care to do so), they stop going to that band's dances. As a result, the group soon dies out. *Cuarteto* fans also expect to be treated with respect: bands must begin to perform on time, performers must not be drunk or exhibit poor behavior, and groups must keep performing in Córdoba on weekends. Once a band has abandoned Córdoba in order to try to make it in Buenos Aires, its former followers are not very forgiving; if the band tries to return to Córdoba to perform, it will no longer be accepted. When a singer leaves an established group in order to try to make it on his own as a solo singer, something similar happens: although this singer may have been idolized prior to this time, fans normally continue to follow the established group that he has broken away from—not the new band that he has formed. In other words, elitism is rejected by *cuarteto* fans.

Issues in *Cuarteto* Music

There are certain topics of discussion which come up time after time in Córdoba when people who know little of the *cuarteto* world talk about *cuarteto* music; these are the same issues that have traditionally been addressed in the occasional newspaper articles that have been written about the genre. Times are changing, however, and people in Córdoba do seem to be modifying some of the ideas they have long had about *cuarteto*.

Cuarteto music has long been looked down on as being simple, low-class, and not worthy of much attention by musicologists and journalists. Socially speaking, however, everyone in the city has always agreed that *cuarteto* is a mass phenomenon that is very important for many people. As has also been explained, discrimination against the genre exists because upper- and middle-class people associate the music with those who listen and dance to it, a group of people they do not like; *cuarteto* is, to these better-off people, synonymous with the marginalized, dark-skinned, working-class population, slum dwellers, and the poor. *Cuarteto* goers and performers have frequently internalized this prejudice and have come to believe that they are truly inferior; they have also become suspicious of journalists and intellectuals who have tried to "study" them.

Many myths about *cuarteto* have arisen out of all of this discrimination. Besides the assumption that *cuarteto* musicians are *negros* who have not been able to make it as soccer players, it is also thought they are not really musicians at all; since *cuarteto* music is supposedly simple and musically deficient, these men must certainly be uneducated, without any musical training, and not at all professional. Very few people know or even guess that bands have professional arrangers, for example. Classical musicians express anger because *cuarteto* performers, who they assume play by ear and have almost no musical training, earn much more than they do. Many stories circulate about the knifings, killings, and orgies that occur in dance halls. It is also common to say that the dance halls are the worst possible environment in the city and that any girl who attends dances has "the brains of a mosquito."

Many of the myths about *cuarteto* also have to do with Carlos Jiménez, who is often called either "the most famous man from Córdoba" or "the most loved man in Córdoba." People constantly speak of his generosity with the poor and the fact that he gives away houses and cars at some of his dances. They also speculate about how much money he makes and talk about his "mansion" located in an exclusive part of town.

An offshoot of this discrimination against *cuarteto* is the issue of whether or not *cuarteto* is folk music; the elite does not want it to be "their" music. Since for many years no one has been able to decide what genre of music *cuarteto* is, or if it is even music at all, this is why it was not heard at the Cosquín Folk Festival, which was established in the early 1960s (Gregoratti 1 February 1995:2C; Comisión Municipal de Folklore n.d.:1), until 1987. According to Osvaldo Hepp, it was decided by some academics at a conference in Cosquín in the early 1990s that *cuarteto* is a "regional" genre of folk music. Gabriel Ábalos, a professor of folklore at the Universidad Nacional de Córdoba (UNC), is trying to have *cuarteto* music be officially included as part of the UNC's folklore program, but has so far been unsuccessful; there is still no agreement on the matter.

Another topic that frequently comes up, also in newspaper articles, is the issue of change in *cuarteto* music. It is disputed whether or not groups such as Chébere, which play with an "evolved" musical style and sometimes camouflage the *tunga-tunga,* are *cuarteto* groups or not. Some people insist that the genre, since it is no longer played with four instrumentalists, is not really *cuarteto;* instead, it is *música bailable cordobesa* (dance music from Córdoba) or *música popular cordobesa* (popular music from Córdoba). The debate continues, especially when *cuarteto* is fused with other genres. "Is this still *cuarteto* or has it changed into something else?" is a common question.

When band members talk about *cuarteto*, they have their own personal issues regarding the genre. Musicians and singers who perform in groups that play by ear think that musicians and singers in bands that perform with written-out music are not creative; a person who plays with a part does not play from the heart and cannot play with feeling, they say. In contrast, musicians and singers in groups that play with parts think that a person who performs by ear is not truly a musician or singer; it is necessary to "know" about music in order to be a true musician or singer, they insist. This intense controversy polarizes members of the *cuarteto* world.

Lastly, it must be pointed out that *cuarteto* music is an important part of Córdoba's culture—whether or not everyone in the city wants this to be the case. For one thing, all people in Córdoba, rich or poor, have something to say about it; these comments and reactions, which are

3.11. Sergio Blatto in front of a painting depicting Carlos Jiménez and what happens at a dance. Photograph by Jane L. Florine, Córdoba, Argentina, 1995.

usually strongly for or strongly against the genre, can be unsolicited and/ or extreme. For example, when the visual artist Sergio Blatto exhibited his paintings that portray scenes from *cuarteto* dances, some of his canvases were slashed with a knife (see figure 3.11). For another thing, wherever one goes in the city, he will hear *cuarteto* music being played. Since *cuarteto* is so much a part of Córdoba, when Jairo, the internationally famous singer from Córdoba, and the poet Daniel Salzano, also from Córdoba, composed a song cycle about their home town, one of the songs, "Cuarteto Corasson" (JAIRO—D. SALZANO) was done *cuarteto*-style; it was the opinion of these two men that a portrait of the city would be incomplete without the *tunga-tunga*. As Jairo and Salzano have realized, Córdoba would not be the same without *cuarteto*.

Dancing *Cuarteto*-Style

It is difficult to understand what *cuarteto* is really about without attending a dance. Since *cuarteto* is not "listening music," one should ideally learn how to dance *cuarteto*-style as well. In an attempt to assist those who cannot attend a dance in person, this chapter describes what is experienced over the course of a typical evening at a large dance hall in Córdoba, how to dance, dance etiquette, and the ritual, communal function of *cuarteto* dances. At times, comments regarding smaller dances and/or dances held in the interior (based on events observed in Villa María, Unquillo, Pilar, and San Juan) will be made. A description of what it is like to attend a performance at a *bailanta* in Buenos Aires is provided in order to give a more complete picture of the function of *cuarteto* music.

Chronology of a Dance

Before the Dance

Most *cuarteto* fans know in advance which bands will be performing in which halls; being "regulars," they have gotten this information by having attended prior dances. Posters and banners advertising dances, which are sometimes placed throughout the city, as well as ads on television, often serve only as reminders (see figure 4.1). Neither beginning and ending times of dances nor addresses of dance halls are announced publicly, but dancers know the standard times and places. Since most people, including police officers, travel to dances by bus, at approxi-

4.1. An ad for a La Barra dance to be held at the Super Deportivo. Photograph by Jane L. Florine, Córdoba, Argentina, 1994.

mately 11:30 P.M. queues of dancers can be seen forming at many bus stops.

Men generally dress informally, in jeans and a shirt, to attend dances, but girls take great care about their appearance: it is common for them to wear fashionable, tight, form-fitting clothing, extremely short skirts, and blouses or tops that are very revealing. This is not to say that they dress outrageously—it is normally only prostitutes who dress in loud, bright, outlandish clothing. Since there is seldom a place to check coats and valuables (they can sometimes be left at the box office, piled on the stage, or put on a table or chair), most dancers leave wraps at home and hide money and personal documents on their bodies.

Many *cuarteteros* follow a specific routine before going to dances. *Barras* (groups of friends) might get together to listen to special programs broadcast before dances, especially on Saturdays, and some friends drink together in order to get their spirits up before Friday dances; they continue to drink for the entire weekend—before, during, and after each dance that they attend. Some *barras* make routine arrangements regarding how they will get to dances, when and where they will meet, and who will buy the tickets ahead of time if necessary. A father might drop off a group of girls whose boyfriends are waiting for them, for example, or friends might agree to meet at a location near the dance hall and walk there together. Since many people go to dances as a way to top off an evening after having gone to a prior engagement, most people arrive at dance halls long after dances have begun.

Getting into the Dance Hall

If one gets to a dance hall early, a long line of people stretching a couple of blocks may be waiting to get in. Other people can be seen arriving on foot, getting out of taxis, and stepping off buses. A neon or painted sign with the name of the club on it might be placed above the main door of the hall. Since most dance halls are old, poorly lit, and located in modest parts of the city, the location is not normally an attractive one.

After a person pays for his ticket at the box office window—unless he gets in free, as many people do—he walks through the front door. Owners, performers, employees, and others well known at a hall often enter through a special side door or gate, however, and may spend their free time before the dance at a bar that is inaccessible to the public or in a private area backstage. In order to enter these off-limits areas, fans must have special permission. *Cuarteteros* who enter through the main door are individually searched by police officers (in Córdoba, but not in the interior); policemen search men, and policewomen search women (see figure 4.2). These officers are looking for alcohol that is being brought into the dance (no one is allowed to bring in his own beverages), not for drugs or weapons; liquor is commonly hidden in plastic bags under one's clothing. People do not normally bring food into the dances, either, despite the fact that food is only occasionally sold at them. At most, a small candy stand might be set up out in the lobby, or *choripán* (sausage sandwiches) might be sold during breaks; at dances in the interior, more types of food are sometimes sold. Birthday cakes are occasionally brought in to celebrate a *barra* or band member's birthday, however; this cake is shared inside the hall only among friends of the group at one key mo-

4.2. A policeman body-searches a young man before a dance. Photograph by Jane L. Florine, Córdoba, Argentina, 1994.

ment during the evening. Another exception to the general absence of food is that free food and/or drink (fruitcake, chocolate, cider, beer, etc.) is sometimes offered to fans as a way of increasing attendance at targeted dances.

Special permission must be obtained from both the owner of the group that is performing and the locale owner or manager in order to enter a dance hall with a camcorder, television equipment, or a sophisticated camera. A person must also have permission to videotape and to take photographs outside of a locale. If permission has not been obtained, there will be problems with the police.

After being searched in the lobby of the dance hall, one passes by a bar that is located in this same general area on the way into the dance hall itself. A sign or chalkboard on which the prices of the drinks available for purchase are listed is sometimes placed on the wall behind the counter; beer, wine, several types of hard liquor, soft drinks, and ice can usually be bought. Drinks are often poured out into paper cups or plastic bottles, but those who buy an entire bottle of hard liquor are given its original container. Wandering vendors with baskets or waiters might sometimes sell drinks inside the hall.

Inside the Main Dance Hall

Dance halls are normally rectangular in shape, with a raised stage for the band at one end (see figure 4.3). All sorts of speakers, amplifiers, trunks, and sound and lighting equipment surround the stage. Sound equipment may also be located some distance away from the stage, often on the other side of the main dance floor, and a disc jockey has usually set up a sound system of his own nearby. Some fans crowd around all the sides of the stage in order to listen or see better; these same people, especially those located on the sides (not immediately in front) of the stage, sometimes dance. Directly in front of the stage (and the sound and lighting equipment placed next to it) is the main dance floor, which is watched over by police; this is the area of the hall where people dance *la rueda* (see below). Small tables and chairs are set up along the three sides of the hall that are not occupied by the stage; this is where dancers can sit, rest, and enjoy their drinks. Way at the back of the hall, beyond all of the tables and chairs, one can find bathrooms and perhaps another bar; the bathrooms, which are commonly crowded, filthy, and not in proper working order, are often located on the side of the hall directly opposite and parallel to the stage. An entrance to an outside patio, if there is one, might be located on one of the sides of the hall as well. If the dance hall is a gymnasium, basketball hoops can be seen in the areas where the tables and chairs are located. Windows, which are normally located near the ceiling, may be broken or may not close properly.

Dance halls are often decorated, even if a special occasion is not being celebrated. Streamers, balloons, and flags with the names of *cuarteto* groups might be hanging from the ceiling (see figure 4.4). Posters of *cuarteto* bands and ads of sponsors might be put up on the walls, and a special on-stage set design might have the name of the group that will be performing on it (see figure 4.5). Motifs in line with the season (flowers for spring, Christmas trees during the holiday season) or well-known songs that are acted out are also seen on stage. A spider might be lowered during a song that is sung about a spider, or a chicken might run across stage when a chicken is mentioned, for example. In cases of special launching ceremonies, elaborate set designs may be changed during the

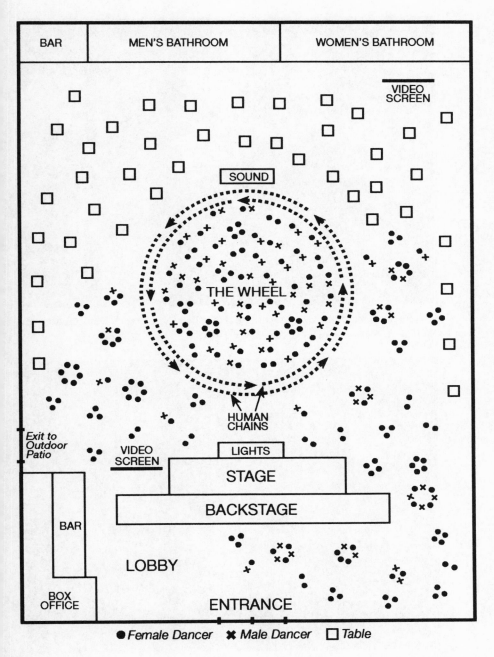

BAR | MEN'S BATHROOM | WOMEN'S BATHROOM

VIDEO SCREEN

SOUND

THE WHEEL

HUMAN CHAINS

Exit to Outdoor Patio

VIDEO SCREEN

LIGHTS

STAGE

BACKSTAGE

BAR

LOBBY

BOX OFFICE

ENTRANCE

● Female Dancer ✖ Male Dancer ☐ Table

4.3. Typical layout of a large dance hall and *la rueda*. Artwork by John de Vries, 2000.

4.4. Streamers used to decorate a small dance hall for Mother's Day. Photograph by Jane L. Florine, Córdoba, Argentina, 1994.

4.5. Chébere performing in front of a stage set having a cave and the band's logo at La Vieja Usina. Photograph by Jane L. Florine, Córdoba, Argentina, 1994.

course of an evening. Colored, flashing lights and smoke machines constantly draw attention to the activity on stage, but the rest of the hall is dark and noisy. Video screens, like those used in discos, may be located at opposite ends of the hall in order to be able to show special video clips during breaks or what is happening on stage all evening.

Waiting for the Dance to Start

If one gets to a hall early, before the band begins to play, one sees that many people have already arrived (see figure 4.6). Box office administrators have long been prepared to take in money, and police and security guards are ready and waiting to begin their jobs. Many other people are still busy trying to get everything ready for the dance, so all sorts of

4.6. The entrance of Gerónimo, a small dance hall, and the area where chairs and tables are placed, before the dance begins. Photograph by Jane L. Florine, Córdoba, Argentina, 1994.

activity is going on. Although the lights, sound equipment, and instruments have been set up much earlier, sound and lighting tests might still be going on. Musicians might be checking their microphones and tuning their instruments as well. If the action on stage is going to be projected on large video screens, the people who man the cameras are also setting up their equipment. Dance hall personnel, bartenders, and waiters are setting up the bar, and the fire used to barbecue sausages (if *choripán* is to be sold) is just being lit.

The tables and chairs located around the sides of the hall are often in place early, but they might still be in the process of being set up. The tables are usually about three feet square, made out of metal or wood, and not very sturdy; they are often old and have many dents in them as well. Chairs can either be made out of wood or metal, but are normally of the folding type; if they are wooden, it is easy for girls to snag their stockings on their splinters. Solid plastic chairs may be seen at locales in the interior, however. At this point in the evening, the hall looks clean, orderly, and fairly empty.

The disc jockey for the dance, who is usually someone who hosts a *cuarteto* radio show, arrives fairly early as well. Even before he gets to the dance, loud, recorded music is played nonstop on the sound system as background music; discs of *cuarteto* music performed by assorted bands are normally played, but other types of pop music might be used as well. Before the dance, during the three intermissions, and for a short time after the dance, fans talk with the disc jockey, who is down on the dance floor, and request that he play their favorite tunes.

Photographers and other vendors often come early so as to do more business. Photographers, who may work freelance or in conjunction with a particular band, are paid by fans to take pictures of them alongside band members. At the time a photo is taken, the photographer asks the client for a deposit; he collects the remainder upon giving the photograph to this same person at a future dance. Since photographers have photographs to deliver and money to collect, they come early to look for their clients. They also try to sell pictures they have taken of the band that is performing and key chains and necklaces with pictures of band members on them (see figure 4.7). Other vendors usually sell items with the group's and/or the solo singer's name on them: felt cowboy hats, tied in a bow on the top, which have a singer's face printed on the sides; felt or cloth headbands; baseball-type caps; and other assorted souvenirs (see

4.7. A vendor
displays his wares.
Photograph by
Jane L. Florine,
Córdoba, Argen-
tina, 1998.

figure 4.8). Not many fans either buy or wear these items in the dances;
they are usually sold and used only at dances performed by Carlos
Jiménez, Gary, and Tru-la-lá. It is the private vendors who keep all of the
money from these sales—not the bands.

Some *cuarteto* fans purposely go to dances early in order to claim a
table and some chairs; since there are not enough to go around, they
want to make sure that they will not have to stand up the entire evening,
as the great majority of dancers must do. They "reserve" tables and
chairs by putting personal items on them, dragging them over near the
stage, or by folding up the chairs and resting them on a table to signal
that they are "taken." After doing so, they sit around talking and smoking
as they wait for the dance to begin. (Most *cuarteto* fans smoke nonstop
the entire evening, even while they are dancing, as is seen in figure 4.15.
A person must ventilate his clothes upon returning home because al-

4.8. Fans wearing Gary hats at a dance. Photograph by Jane L. Florine, Buenos Aires, Argentina, 1995.

most everyone inside of dance halls smokes so much.) When the musicians start to come in, they chat with fans before they go backstage to change their clothes.

What Happens during a Dance

A standard format is followed during a typical *cuarteto* dance. If a group has two singers, the *moderno* one starts off the dance by singing for about 45 minutes (the normal length of a set). After a 15- to 20-minute break (the normal length of an intermission), the *tropical* singer comes on for about 45 minutes. Another break is then taken, after which the *moderno* singer returns for his second and last set. At the end of this set, the *moderno* singer often sings a slow, solo number without the *tunga-tunga;* the lights are focused on him, many people stop dancing to listen, and yet others dance in a non-*cuarteto* style. After the ensuing break, the *tropical* singer returns with a set of upbeat tunes to round out the evening. Some groups have a standard signature tune with which they either begin and/or end their dances.

Carlos Jiménez is one of the few solo singers who does not trade off with another singer (see figure 5.10). Since he does not divide his songs into *moderno* and *tropical* sets, he does not always sing for 45 minutes at a time; he may decide to have only three sets on a particular evening or to take a very long break, for example. Jiménez also does many other things that other singers do not do. At times, he stays out on stage all by himself, after the band has left, chanting and singing on his own. Even while the band is on stage, he jumps, gets down on his knees, and gyrates his body; on occasion he has climbed on top of sound or video equipment and has stood on it. He is famous for doing *la mano* (the hand), a gesture in which he rapidly turns his hand so that it alternately faces palm-down and palm-up as he simultaneously extends and retracts his arm. (Although *la mano* has no real significance, it is thought to be vulgar in some circles.) Sometimes he asks the crowd to sing for him (many fans normally know his song lyrics but not everyone sings while dancing); if they do not sing loudly enough, he suddenly stops and reprimands everybody. At times Jiménez invites fans to get up on stage and sing his solos, even if he does not know who they are. He occasionally asks special visitors—visiting rock groups, for example—to come up on stage either to talk or to perform with him. Even his way of dressing sets him apart from other singers: he wears tight, brightly colored, Elvis Presley–inspired outfits complete with sequins, stripes, feathers, and matching boots, all of which are made by his wife (Jiménez Rufino 1994).

Before each tune is performed, the announcer gives its title to the crowd. Girls scream loudly when the names of their favorite songs are announced. Between tunes, the announcer reads aloud the greetings and well-wishings that are passed to him on scraps of paper and makes jokes nonstop so as to leave no "holes" in the show (see figure 5.4); he sometimes reports that "lost" personal documents have been turned in. Musicians and singers, except for drum set and conga players, perform standing up. They do not move around much, but may occasionally do some choreographed steps together in time to the music while certain lyrics are being sung. Singers usually move more than musicians, and each one has his own particular style. Everyone in the band is normally dressed in the same uniform, but solo singers occasionally put on whatever they want to. Uniforms usually consist of a combination of matching dress slacks, blazers or suit jackets, vests, shirts, and sometimes neckties or bowties (see figure 4.9). Each group has several different sets of uniforms, which it updates frequently.

Band members are required to get down from the stage during breaks

4.9. Several members of the Jiménez band pose in uniform in the bar at Atenas. Back row, from left to right: Mario Salinas, a former band member, Ricardo Verón, and Bam Bam Miranda. Front row, from left to right: José Concha, an unidentified friend of the band, Tino Quinteros, and Tito Avedaño. Photograph by Jane L. Florine, Córdoba, Argentina, 1995.

and to socialize with the public; they must "sell" themselves and their groups (*venderse*). Although they might go to the bar to get a drink during breaks, band members are still "working" while they are not performing. It is their job to remember "regulars" and to recall when they have last seen them at dances. They pose for photographs, talk with the girls who are waiting for them by the stage door and the bar, and, in the case of one group, dance with fans during one of the breaks. Many band members have met their current girlfriends or wives while they were "selling themselves" at dances.

During breaks, dancers crowd the areas where drinks are sold, go outside to get some air or a *choripán* in the adjoining patio, and talk with the band members. If there is a patio, it is part of the dance hall; one does not go out the front door to get there. People do not actually leave the hall unless they do not plan to return to the dance, either. This is the time to sit at one's table and rest a bit if possible, and this is also when most of the drinking at the dance occurs. By the time the second and third breaks roll around, the dance hall has become almost too crowded for one to be able to get to the bar.

As the evening progresses, it becomes more and more obvious from the types of behavior that begin to occur both during and between breaks that people have become intoxicated. Men begin to approach girls more often in order to ask them to dance and to compliment them; telephone numbers are also exchanged more frequently. If fights occur, police and security guards immediately grab the guilty parties by the hair, lift them up off the floor if need be, and carry and/or drag them out of the hall within the space of a few seconds. Some of these fights might occur between women (prostitutes) over men. In extreme cases, bottles may be thrown in the back of the hall as the night wears on. Disturbances of this kind do not occur very often.

There are certain other types of things that one can expect to experience at a dance. Large prizes might be given away in breaks at special dances (cars, houses), and hordes of people from the media will be present at important launching ceremonies. At Chébere dances, young girls get up on stage and dance, whereas at Tru-la-lá dances, young boys are up on stage singing. It is common, especially at the dances of Carlos Jiménez, to see fans unexpectedly rush up on the stage in order to touch him; they are sometimes pulled away by guards, but are often allowed to remain. At Jiménez's dances, male fans often climb up on the shoulders of other people, take off their shirts, and wave them around in circles in time to the music. It is also common for them to sing along loudly with songs and to chant "Mona, dale dale Mona" ("Mona, come on; come on, Mona") in order to get Jiménez to come out on stage (Jiménez has had the nickname of "La Mona," which means "The Female Monkey [Chimpanzee]," since his childhood). During the last set, mostly at Jiménez dances, young women get up on stage and dance; these young ladies are often loudly dressed and may be "offering" themselves for the evening (some are prostitutes). After the dance is over, many people rush up on stage and mob Jiménez; his personal valet helps him out through a back door and into his nearby band bus so that he can escape from the crowd.

After the Dance

When the dance is over, the dance hall is in a shambles; some of the tables and chairs are turned over, many are strewn with empty cups and bottles, and others are wet from drinks having been spilled on them. Drinks have also been spilled all over the floor, which is littered with cups, paper, and bottles. Some people leave the hall quickly, but others mill around exchanging phone numbers. A few girls wait around for band members to see if they might be able to accompany them to a nearby hotel. Band members leave as soon as they have collected their money and have perhaps changed their clothes; in Córdoba they do not have to rely on the band bus to get home. Box office employees stick around until much later in order to finish up their work, and *plomos* and sound and lighting personnel must take down and store all of the equipment before they are free to leave.

After they leave the dance hall, most of the dancers have to find a way to get home; few own cars. If dancers cannot walk home, they have several choices. It might be possible to take a taxi, but taxi drivers often do not want to pick up clients outside of dance halls right after performances are over; drunks can get unruly, refuse to pay, or even vomit in one's vehicle. People may double up with *barra* members, a policewoman, or the disc jockey if a taxi can be found; each person is then dropped off, one by one. Since public transportation does not begin running until later in the morning, some people might wait until they can catch a bus home. Others might get on privately owned buses of the school bus type, called *piratas*, which are sometimes operated on nights of dances. *Piratas* can be taken for a peso or so to central locations such as the bus terminal, but passengers must put up with unruliness, drunkenness, and yelling. The most common time for fights and unruly behavior to occur is outside dance halls after dances are over.

How to Dance

There is not just one way to dance to *cuarteto* music. For example, young people often dance with older people, women often dance with other women, dancing can be done in couples or in a group, and men have different ways in which they can dance with women. One of the few "rules" in *cuarteto* dancing is that men do not dance together, either in couples or in a group, unless women also dance with them. In addition, *cuarteto* dancing is always done in a counterclockwise direction. There are many individual variations on basic steps, since a person does what he feels while dancing. No one truly takes lessons; rather, one learns by attending dances, watching dancers, and just trying to dance. Within these individual variations, certain basic steps and styles of dancing can be identified; for this reason, circle dancing, couple dancing, and dancing in *la rueda* (the wheel) will be described below. Basic steps and moves common to all three ways of dancing will be identified in the section on circle dancing.

Circle Dancing

At *cuarteto* dances, it is very common to see small groups of people dancing in circles or rings; these groups range in size from three to as many as eight or ten people. Quite often, these circles are made up entirely of women (from the same *barra*), who keep dancing in this fashion for an entire evening (see figure 4.10). If men dance in a circle, at least one woman must also be dancing with them. Since it takes up quite a bit of space, circle dancing is normally done around the edges of the stage or out in the lobby (when the dance hall is very full and there is not space for everyone inside). It is rarely done between tables or in the back of the dance hall, but it can be done, in a modified way, while dancing in *la rueda* (see below).

In order to form the circle or ring, dancers, with their arms hanging loosely at their sides, join hands with the people on each side of them; they all face toward the inside of the circle. Dancers' bodies do not touch while they are dancing; instead, they remain about an arm's length apart. As they hold hands and do the standard *tunga-tunga* step (see below), all of the dancers circle in a counterclockwise direction.

During certain sets of song lyrics, dancers all raise their arms straight up over their heads, as high as possible, without letting go of their hands; while these same lyrics are sung, they might do special movements, such as knee bends or kicks, instead of the basic *tunga-tunga* step. These moves have sometimes been initiated by band members on stage and have later been adopted by dancers. At times, however, these movements have been created by *barras* on their own. It should be noted that special movements, such as these arm lifts, are used very sparingly during an evening.

The Basic Step

When doing the basic *tunga-tunga* step, mainly the feet and the hips are moved; the upper part of the body is held almost immobile, and the arms

4.10. Young women doing circle dancing. Photograph by Jane L. Florine, Córdoba, Argentina, 1995.

are not often used (except to hold hands with other dancers or to encircle another dancer's body). Although *cuarteto* music is notated in cut time, the *tunga-tunga* step will be explained by referring to the four quarter notes contained in each measure (as if it were notated in 4/4 time): *tun* corresponds to the first and third quarter notes of each measure, and *ga* to the second and fourth quarter notes of each bar. A drawing that depicts the execution of the basic step (as it is used in circle dancing) is provided in figure 4.11; the numbers placed inside the footprints should be followed.

To begin, the feet should be somewhat spread apart and parallel, with the heels a bit closer together than the toes are. Only when the lyrics of the song start to be sung does one begin doing the steps. On the first quarter note of the measure, *tun,* weight is put on the balls of both feet, but with more on the left one than the right one. On the second quarter note of the bar, *ga,* the heel of the right foot is moved inwards, in a swivel fashion, as if it were drawing a 45-degree arc along the edge of a circle,

4.11. The basic *tunga-tunga* step (in circle dancing). The numbers placed inside the footprints should be followed, and foot movements should be made on the appropriate "*tun*" or "*ga*" syllables, as indicated. Footprints shown with dotted lines are performed by swiveling the heel in the direction indicated while keeping the ball of the foot on the floor. Weight is placed on the balls of both feet during step #1 of the sequence. Artwork by John de Vries, 2000.

toward the empty space between both feet; the right foot is lifted only slightly off the floor and is moved to the right as it is swiveled as well. While the right foot is being swiveled inward and moved to the right, the ball of the left foot is pushed against the floor and the left heel thus turns slightly to the left; this push helps the body to move over to the right. At the same time, the left hip is swiveled to the left, the hips and legs being moved from the waist down. The weight of the body is kept close to the ground, and the feet are more slid to the right or shuffled than lifted; no jumps are made. The swiveling of the hips, done while keeping the torso erect, looks very much like African dancing and may be a carryover from the region's African past.

On the third quarter note of the bar, *tun,* weight is put on the ball of the right foot as it meets the floor; it has been moved to the right during the *ga* syllable and is now set down to complete the step to the right. Next, on *ga,* the last quarter note of the measure, the left heel is swiveled to the inside (just as the right foot was previously swiveled to the inside, but now in the opposite direction) as it is simultaneously lifted ever so slightly off the floor and moved to the right. While this is happening, the right hip is swiveled to the right, moving from the waist down. On the first quarter note of the next measure, which is a *tun* syllable, the ball of the left foot is set down, with weight put upon it (weight is not put on the ball of the right foot this time), on the floor a bit to the right of where it had been placed during the previous bar, thus completing the step to the right initiated with the left heel on *ga* on the last quarter note of the previous measure. From here on, the pattern just described is repeated with the same foot and body movements occurring on the same counts of each bar (except that weight is put on the balls of both feet on just the very first "*tun*" step of the dance; weight is placed on the ball of the left foot only for the first count of each measure thereafter).

The standard *tunga-tunga* step is adapted to the speed and the character of the music that it is being danced to. When slower *moderno* tunes are performed, for example, the basic step is turned into a "rock" one; the same steps are used, but they become more elegant than before. In fast *tropical* songs, although the same steps are used, the feet must be used in a more brusque and agitated fashion. If one experiments by dancing to music played by different bands, he will discover that some groups play all of their repertoire much more slowly than do others. It will also become evident to him that some bands perform every tune at a different speed, whereas other groups play almost everything at the same tempo. In addition, he will find out that the *tunga-tunga* accompaniment pattern is much more prominently played by some bands than it is by others. When the *tunga-tunga* is played loudly and securely, the music is easy to dance to; when it is altered or hidden, a dancer can easily become confused.

Pirouettes

When dancing in circles, *cuarteteros* can often be observed doing a special type of turn, or pirouette. (In figures 4.12a and 4.12b, photographs of couples doing the arm sequence involved in executing pirouettes are provided; one photograph showing pirouettes being done while circle dancing, figure 4.13, is given. Although doing pirouettes in couples is somewhat different from doing them in a circle formation, it should be helpful to refer to all of these photographs while reading this section.) No matter how many people are dancing in a circle, only two dancers can ever be involved in performing a pirouette at any one time; dancers must take turns in doing them. Before a pirouette sequence is initiated, everyone in the circle is holding hands with the people on either side, as usual. If Person A decides that he wants to initiate a pirouette sequence (doing pirouettes is a spontaneous occurrence), he uses his right hand to draw the person to his right, Person B, in front of him (in this description, it will be assumed that Person A is male and that Person B is female); Person A's right hand remains holding Person B's left hand at all times during the pirouette sequence. (Person A's left hand continues to hold the right hand of the person to his left while the pirouette is carried out, and Person B's right hand continues to hold the left hand of the person to her right while the pirouette is executed; this is an aspect of doing pirouettes in a circle that cannot be seen in figure 4.12a, which in any case does show the initiation of a pirouette sequence done in a couple.) Once Person A has slid Person B over in front of him (they continue to face in the same direction as before, both looking toward the empty center of the circle; Person A ends up looking at Person B's back, so they are not facing each other), Person B's left arm is then lifted by Person A's right arm and hand so that it goes over her own head; it is then lowered in front of her body so that it is waist-high and parallel to the floor (it thus looks like her left arm is encircling the front half of her waist and that Person A's right arm is encircling the right side of her waist, as is seen in figure 4.12b). Person A and Person B both hold this position for a few bars or so; there is no set period of time in which a pirouette must be executed. When he decides that the time is right, Person A uses his right arm and hand to help Person B lift her left arm back over her head; he then has her move over to his right and shift into her original place in the circle. When the pirouette has been completed, Person A is still holding Person B's left hand with his right hand, and his left hand is

4.12a. Initiation of a pirouette sequence (couple dancing) by two Gypsies on December 8. Photograph by Jane L. Florine, Córdoba, Argentina, 1994.

4.12b. Ending the pirouette sequence (couple dancing); the arms will next be brought down to waist level. Photograph by Jane L. Florine, Córdoba, Argentina, 1998.

4.13. Pirouettes being done while circle dancing. Photograph by Jane L. Florine, Córdoba, Argentina, 1995.

still holding the right hand of the person on his left. Person B has contin-ued to hold the left hand of the person on her right with her own right hand during the entire maneuver (in figure 4.13 only the middle of the pirouette sequence done while circle dancing is seen).

All the while that this pirouette sequence is going on, the dancers keep moving counterclockwise and doing the standard *tunga-tunga* step with their feet and hips. During the time that the pirouette is being carried out, at the point that Person B's head has already passed under her left arm and this same arm is encircled around the front of her waist (and Person A's right arm is encircled around the right side of her waist), she is in truth in the center of the empty circle and the other dancers are dancing around her. This type of formation, with solo dancing in the center of a circle of other people, may have African roots (Carámbula 1995:68–81).

In a pirouette sequence, it is common that "Person A" be male and

"Person B" be female; men initiate pirouette sequences with women much more often than women initiate pirouette sequences with men. It is also quite common that both parties involved be female. Although there is not a set plan for when pirouettes should be initiated or which people in a circle should perform them, one common type of format is followed in circles that are arranged in a boy-girl-boy-girl order. In this type of arrangement, the fellows generally take turns doing pirouettes with the girls to their right. One young man (Male Dancer #1) does a pirouette with the girl on his right; at that point, Male Dancer #2, the fellow who is two people to Male Dancer #1's right, does a pirouette with the girl on his own right. Male Dancer #3 and Male Dancer #4, who are located four people and six people to the right of Male Dancer #1 (if there are eight people in the circle, four are male, and the order is boy-girl-boy-girl) then do the same thing with the girls on their right when their own turns come up.

Other Steps

When *cumbia* tunes are performed, circle dancers try to adapt the *tunga-tunga* step to the rhythm. As this is hard to do, they usually invent footwork that fits with the music while holding hands in their usual circle formation and revolving counterclockwise. When *melódico* songs without the *tunga-tunga* are performed, circle dancers listen and refrain from dancing.

Couple Dancing

When two people dance *cuarteto*-style together, be it two girls or a mixed couple, most of that just described regarding circle dancing still applies. Couple dancing is normally done in the same areas where circle dancing is carried out; it is very commonly done in *la rueda* as well, but in a modified way (see the section on *La Rueda*).

The arm position used in couple dancing can be much like that used in circle dancing, except that the two parties face each other (see figure 4.14 for hand, arm, and body positions). In one style of couple dancing, the partners hold hands (Dancer #1's right hand holds Dancer #2's left hand, and Dancer #1's left hand holds Dancer #2's right hand), dance with outstretched arms, and stay an arm's length apart; this type of couple dancing, in which there is no body contact except for the hands, is seen in figure 4.14. It is also possible that two dancers

4.14. Couple dancing next to the side of the stage at the Estadio del Centro: arm and body positions. One dancer wears a head-band promoting the Talleres Athletic Club's soccer team, which she roots for. Photograph by Jane L. Florine, Córdoba, Argentina, 1998.

might embrace each other while dancing, even if they are using the basic *tunga-tunga* step. In this type of dancing, their arms rest on each other's waists and shoulders, and their chests touch. When slow tunes without the *tunga-tunga* accompaniment are sung, couples adopt this latter type of arm position (close dancing) while they dance, whether they are mixed couples or not. Just as occurs in circle dancing, it is quite common for couples to raise their hands over their heads (figure 4.15), but with Dancer #1's right palm either flat against Dancer #2's left palm and Dancer #1's left palm flat against Dancer #2's right palm, or just holding hands, to accompany certain sets of lyrics. Couples

4.15. Couple dancing with raised arms (while smoking). Photograph by Jane L. Florine, Córdoba, Argentina, 1994.

also do the knee bends and/or leg kicks that might correspond to these same words.

In couple dancing, the basic *tunga-tunga* step described above is used, and the couple turns counterclockwise on its own axis starting when the lyrics begin; it is as though the two partners were dancing in a "circle" with only two people in it (whether they dance in an embrace or at an arm's length apart). When couples dance in *la rueda*, the basic *tunga-tunga* step must be somewhat modified; this will be discussed below. If *cumbia* music is played, they move their feet in any way possible that fits to the music, but continue to turn on their own axis in a counterclockwise direction.

It is quite common for couples (mixed or otherwise) to do pirouettes (see figures 4.12a and 4.12b for photographs of couples doing pirouettes). Although the pirouette sequence done by couples is similar to that described above for circle dancing, it is not quite the same. In this case, assuming that Person A is male and Person B is female, both parties are facing each other when they begin the move; Person A's right hand is holding Person B's left hand, and his left hand is holding her right hand as well. Since both dancers start by facing each other, instead of Person A just drawing Person B over to the left with his right hand and arm so that she is in front of him, he must use his right hand and arm to get her to turn a 180-degree angle to her left before she can pass her head under her left arm. Since Person A is holding Person B's right hand with his left hand, when he has her do the 180-degree turn, her right arm comes to rest across the part of her waist directly above her abdomen, and his left arm encircles the left side of her waist. After Person B's head has gone under her left arm, and her left arm and the right arm of Person A (the hands of these two arms are being held together) have together been lowered to the level of her waist, she in truth is caught in an embrace: her arms are crisscrossed over the front part of her waist, and Person A's arms are encircled around her back and are resting on her right and left sides. Instead of facing each other, the two dancers are now both facing in the same direction; Person B has her back to Person A.

When it is time to "get out" of the pirouette (the couple maintains the "encircled" position for a few measures or so), Person A uses his right hand and arm to lift Person B's left arm; she then passes her head underneath her arm once again, in the opposite direction from before, doing a 180-degree turn to her right. In this fashion, she ends up in her starting position. All the while, both dancers keep doing the basic *tunga-tunga* step as best they can and rotate counterclockwise on their own axis.

La Rueda

La rueda, which is sometimes called *la ronda,* translates as "the wheel" (see figure 4.16). This is the type of "circle" dancing that is done by both couples and circle dancers in a circular area out on the huge dance floor that lies in front of the band. When *la rueda* is done, from up above it looks like everyone out on the dance floor forms part of a solid disc of humanity (people are packed together as tightly as pin heads on a pin cushion) that revolves counterclockwise in the fashion that a plate revolves inside a microwave oven. This type of dancing or formation may be derived from African *candombe,* which was formerly danced in the area (Carámbula 1995:68–81). The dancers normally stand still during a song's introduction; it is only when the vocalist begins to sing the lyrics that they begin to revolve. Since many people, especially young men, stand around the rim of *la rueda* and watch those who are dancing, police are constantly nearby to prevent them from interfering with the dancers. The police also keep the dance floor clear for those who want to dance; if someone walks into the area where people are trying to dance *la rueda,* and is not dancing himself, he is pulled away. Although the thousands of people in *la rueda* are quite tightly packed together, they do not bump into each other, due to the special way the basic *tunga-tunga* step is used in this type of dancing.

When couples dance in *la rueda,* they use the same arm positions that have been described above; they also do pirouettes. They must adapt the *tunga-tunga* step so that they can revolve counterclockwise around the entire dance floor, however; they cannot revolve around in a small "circle." Since the partners are facing each other while they dance, this is done by having one person "lead," by advancing forward in the direction the mass of humanity is moving, and by having the other "follow," by doing his or her dance steps backward (see figure 4.17 for dance steps; the numbers placed inside the footprints should be followed). If a mixed couple is dancing, it is the fellow who leads and the girl who follows.

In the following description of the modified *tunga-tunga* step used in *la rueda,* only the female's "follower" steps will be described; her partner's steps would mimic hers, but would go in the opposite direction. This description will be based on that given earlier; only changes in the basic steps will be pointed out. The girl begins with her feet in the normal *tunga-tunga* starting position. On the first quarter note of the measure, *tun,* she puts pressure on the balls of both feet. On the second quarter note of the measure, *ga,* she swivels her right heel to the inside, just as before, and slightly lifts it off the floor as well, but she moves this foot straight backward as she slides it—not to the right. On this same *ga* syllable, the ball of the left foot is used to help push the right foot backward. The hips move from the waist, in the appropriate direction, as before. On the third quarter note of the measure, *tun,* the ball of the right foot is set down as the step taken with the right foot backward is com-

4.16. *La rueda* (photograph taken from the back of the dance floor at Atenas). Photograph by Jane L. Florine, Córdoba, Argentina, 1994.

pleted. On the fourth quarter note of the bar, *ga,* the left heel is swiveled to the inside and simultaneously slid straight backward (not to the right). At the same time, the ball of the right foot is used to help propel the left foot backward. On the first quarter note of the next measure, the cycle is repeated—except that from here on, weight is placed on the ball of the left foot only on the first "*tun*" of each measure.

Those *barras* that do circle dancing in *la rueda* also adopt this modified *tunga-tunga* step. Instead of revolving in their own little circles, they go around the entire dance floor by having some members of the circle dance "backward," and others dance "forward," but while maintaining a ring formation. Members of the circle hold hands, just as before, but they appear to advance forward or backward en masse in a fixed circular-shaped formation, not to revolve in a small group.

At times, two circles of dancers, one inside the other, are formed around the circumference of *la rueda* as if they were two human chains; these two lines of dancers revolve in a counterclockwise fashion around the outside rim of *la rueda,* using the basic *tunga-tunga* step and holding

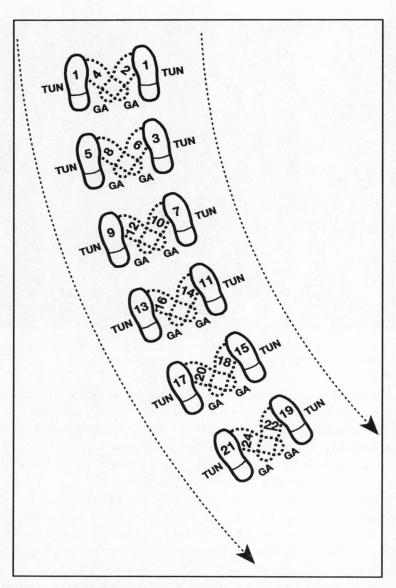

4.17. The modified *tunga-tunga* step done in *la rueda*. The numbers placed inside the footprints should be followed, and foot movements should be made on the appropriate "*tun*" or "*ga*" syllables, as indicated. Footprints shown with dotted lines are performed by swiveling the heel in the direction indicated while keeping the ball of the foot on the floor. Weight is placed on the balls of both feet during step #1. Artwork by John de Vries, 2000.

hands, as though they were two giant *barras* of circle dancers, one dancing inside of the other (see figure 4.3). These two chains of dancers separate the people dancing inside *la rueda* from the people who are watching them. At times, it appears that these chains of dancers begin "walking" in a disorderly fashion around the rim of *la rueda*, not dancing with the *tunga-tunga* step. Again, this type of dancing may have African roots (Carámbula 1995:68–81).

Dance Etiquette

Certain types of behavior, some of which have become unspoken rules of conduct, commonly occur in dance halls. The conventions discussed below regard the placement of dancers within a hall, the importance of *barras* at dances, the manner in which men approach women to ask them to dance, and reasons for not dancing. The topics discussed here are by no means a complete listing of the "rules" and conventions associated with *cuarteto* dancing; in order to provide such a detailed description of dance etiquette, extensive fieldwork would have to be carried out with *cuarteto* dancers.

Within a typical dance hall, the people who best know the band members and/or have some type of personal relationship with them will generally be those located close to the stage; the people who stay the farthest away from the stage are the dancers who least know the band members. Steady girlfriends and wives of band members, if they go to dances, normally stay on either of the short sides of the stage in plain view of the men with whom they have come. They might be seen holding their husband's or boyfriend's drink cup or bottle while he performs. If these women know each other, as they usually do, they often sit and/or circle dance with each other while the music is being performed; during breaks they are seen with the men that they "belong" to (as they put it). Girlfriends and wives of band members do not dance with any other men than their "own" unless they have gotten prior permission from them to do so.

"Regulars," girls who have crushes on band members, and personal friends of band members often crowd around both the front and the sides of the stage (and the stage door, through which the musicians must walk). If they plan to just listen and/or to watch, not to dance, they usually stand right in front of the stage. Those who are lucky might find an instrument or storage trunk, right next to the stage, on which to sit for the entire evening. Since they know the band members, they might ask them for permission to pile their belongings, such as coats, up on the stage.

Older people, who do not want to stand up all evening, usually occupy the tables and chairs that surround the main dance floor, where *la rueda* is done. Although many different types of people dance in *la rueda*, it is common to find prostitutes there. The rowdy people at a dance are usually located in the back of the hall, near the bathrooms; trouble might also occur at areas between the tables. It is over the course of the evening, not at the beginning of the dance, that rowdy behavior might be observed; disturbances arise as people get increasingly intoxicated, the dance hall fills up, and dancers are forced to stand and dance much closer together. The people seen dancing out in the lobby are normally *cuarteto* followers who do not like to dance in crowded conditions; since the hall gets so packed as the evening wears on, they move to areas in which they have more space. Those who really like to dance get annoyed when halls are so crowded that people constantly bump into each other, their toes get stepped on by others dancing nearby, and they cannot freely revolve in their circles. This happens quite often while circle dancing; girls who wear shoes with block heels are the worst offenders.

The young women who do circle dancing in the areas around the sides of the stage dance with their *barras*, the friends with whom they have come to the dance. While all-female groups circle dance, the girls who are dancing are somewhat "offering" themselves; men are usually "looking them over" as they go around and around (see the photograph in figure 4.10, in which a young man is looking at a girl he is interested in). Although it is an unspoken rule that girls should not break into circles formed by other girls or by groups of people they do not know (*barras* can be mixed or made up of one sex only), there is no corresponding rule for men. Since men often come to dances unaccompanied or with their own all-male or mixed *barras*, they might be interested in finding a girl to dance with. If a young man sees a girl that he likes, he might break into her circle and place himself right next to her. His next step would then be to try to lure her out of her circle in order to couple-dance with her. If the man is drunk, or if the girl is not interested in him, she ignores him and keeps on dancing. If the girl accepts, they first couple-dance near her *barra*. As time goes on, the two might move to *la rueda* and spend the rest of the dance together. Near the end of the evening, the two parties might exchange telephone numbers so as to meet during the week or at another dance, or perhaps to spend the night together. If a woman is seen leaving a dance before it is over, it is usually assumed that she has left to sleep with a man she has met; dancers do not normally leave dances early.

Although some people go to dances only to listen and to watch, they are a small minority. There may be some reasons why a person might spend part or all of an evening without dancing, however. If for some reason a girl arrives at a dance and no one from her *barra* shows up, she usually spends the evening listening and watching. Since it is not proper to break into other *barras,* she normally does not try to do so. Besides this, as *barras* usually have their own special way of dancing with each other (steps they have invented together, for example), she would not feel comfortable dancing in another group anyway. The feeling of communion that one gets at a dance is normally lost if one is without his friends. If a person has just gotten off work, and is too tired to dance, he might sit and listen as well. Other people choose to dance only to the types of songs they most enjoy, for example, only to *tropical* tunes. It should be kept in mind that these cases are exceptions, since *cuarteto* music is first and foremost for dancing.

The Ritual Function of *Cuarteto*

Social dances are not normally scheduled on a regular basis or fit to the yearly calendar, but in the case of *cuarteto,* events have a fixed schedule and follow established conventions; they have primary yet hidden functions (Shay 1971:55). *Cuarteto* dances are in truth rituals in which participants are transported to another world beyond that of reality; ritual space, ritual objects, ritual time, ritual sound and language, ritual identity, and ritual action are all a part of them. An atmosphere of affective security is provided, since most aspects of dances are predictable and thus become comfortable (Hanna 1979:27).[1]

Regarding the ritual use of space, all dance halls are laid out in a similar fashion and become transformed only on the repeated, fixed instances that *cuarteto* dances are held in them. The part of the hall a person occupies depends on his relationship with the band members, fans pick the same locations to dance in from night to night, and each type of standard dance step is done in specific areas of the dance floor as well. As for ritual objects associated with *cuarteto* dances, felt hats, alcoholic beverages, headbands, smoke machines, and *choripán* are all standard fare. In addition, the sequined and feathered Elvis-style outfits worn by Carlos Jiménez are almost sacred. An otherworldly, nonclock type of ritual time is created by the fixed chronology of events that occurs every evening, and the small, repeated units of the *tunga-tunga* create a cyclic type of time that prevents the music from "going anywhere" (Middleton 1990:220). The ritual use of time is also manifested in the fact that dances are played on fixed evenings, are held at standardized times, and are all of the same length (four hours).

Sound and language are also used in established and predictable ways at dances: bands play three standard styles of music, the *tunga-tunga* is found in almost all tunes, recorded *cuarteto* music is put on during breaks, and disc jockeys and announcers use conventional words and ways of speaking. The coordination of thousands of people while dancing (i.e., the wheel), the joint participation of all those present, the reading of greetings, and the fraternization of dancers with band members all help to establish a ritual kind of identity and feelings of solidarity and communion (Shay 1971:46–47). Dancers may also come to identify with singers, who become star or cult figures.

As some people in the *cuarteto* world put it, attending dances frequently fulfills a function much like that of going to mass; all participants are in communion with each other. The "family" climate, which is created by the announcer's reading of greetings, and the opportunity to socialize with band members in breaks, are both important parts of this process of sharing. Dancers also go to dance halls in order to meet with their personal groups of friends (*barras*) and to "communicate" with those up on stage, who are almost "worshiped." This feeling of communion and identification is enhanced by having many familiar people in the dance hall; empty halls are avoided by attending only "sure" dances of important groups.

Dance events are also therapeutic for fans, since they serve as an outlet and release from the cares of everyday life (Shay 1971:64). After four hours of consuming alcoholic beverages, listening and dancing to the *tunga-tunga,* and moving in a hypnotic, counterclockwise fashion, dancers feel refreshed. More specifically, extreme repetition of short rhythmic and/or harmonic units, such as those found in the *tunga-*

tunga, can lead to feelings of euphoria, transcendence, collective dying, or merging with the universe via the heightened right-brain activity which occurs as a result (Middleton 1990:255–58, 281–91; Schechner 1994:638). Fast, repetitive dancing—the constant counterclockwise movements used in *cuarteto* dancing, for example—can produce the same effects (Hanna 1979:14–15, 28, 66). Even movement (dancing) itself can help to bring about spiritual renewal, release of tension, and dissipation of weariness and depression (Hanna 1979:66–69).

Going to dances is a way to get "high"; by dancing away for four hours, one can forget about his troubles and leave feeling renovated. Since the same format or order is basically followed at every dance, and dancers are familiar with this structure, it is not necessary to think (i.e., "work") at dance events. The "new" elements introduced periodically (gimmicks, updated repertoire, and decorations) help participants to forget about their routine daily lives and to enjoy a little bit of excitement.

In summary, *cuarteteros* attend dances mainly in order to have fun (experience *alegría*), to escape from the worries of daily life in a time and space apart from reality, and to feel a sense of solidarity and communion in a ritualized setting. Although fans do not realize it, *cuarteto* events allow them to energize themselves in an atmosphere of play while maintaining connections with others like themselves in an urban world in which they are outsiders. As long as *cuarteto* continues to satisfy these needs, the phenomenon will continue to attract a large following.

The *Bailantas*

Although many groups from Córdoba have stopped playing in the *bailantas* of Buenos Aires, a few bands still perform in them from time to time. Since what band members encounter at *bailantas* is not the same as what they experience at dance halls in Córdoba, it is important to understand what happens at dances in Buenos Aires. Generally speaking, it is the format of the evening and how fans behave that differ markedly from what groups are accustomed to seeing back in Córdoba.

Before describing what happens at a typical *bailanta,* it is important to state that the remarks made below are based on what was experienced during three different evenings in Buenos Aires with the band named Gary. On each of these three evenings, Gary performed at two different *bailantas;* he no longer sings in more than two per night. Since it was necessary for me to travel and remain with the group during the course of each evening, the comments made here will be from the perspective of the band members (what they experience and must do each night). For this same reason, it was not possible to observe a crowd in a *bailanta* over the course of an entire evening or to listen to other groups than Gary perform.

Physical Appearance and Layout

Upon arriving outside a *bailanta,* a person will not have any trouble realizing that he is not outside a dance hall in Córdoba. Instead of encountering an old, run-down structure, he will see a modern, contemporarily designed building that is well-lit outside; some *bailantas* have cost millions of dollars to construct. The name of the hall will be over the front door, but it will be spelled out in large, well-designed, contemporarily shaped letters across the top of the locale; it will not appear on a hand-painted sign or in neon lights. The names of the groups to perform that evening will be artistically painted in fluorescent colors on the side of the building that faces the street; the dates of other dances to be held at the same locale, and the names of the groups that will be performing at them, will also be painted there. A short line of people will normally be standing in line on the sidewalk in front of the box office; a railing might run along the area where they are lined up. Since several different bands play in the same *bailanta* one after the other on the same evening, a group might already be performing (or have finished performing) by the time a person arrives. Dances begin approximately at midnight and end at about 7:00 A.M.

Flags with the name of the *bailanta* on them can sometimes be seen hanging from flagpoles that horizontally protrude from the top of the wall of the building that faces the street, and other flags, which are hung on vertical flagpoles that run along the sidewalk in front of the *bailanta,* might also be seen; one almost has the impression that he is outside the entrance of a fancy hotel. Next to the main entrance is a small door through which the musicians will pass when they arrive; it leads straight to the backstage area of the hall. It is through this same door that the *plomos* enter the building both to set up the band's equipment and later remove it.

Inside, halls have a long, rectangular shape, and have two different levels (upstairs and downstairs); the upstairs area is really a big balcony, complete with hand railings, that runs around the three sides of the locale that are not occupied by the stage. The stage occupies one of the short sides of the rectangle. At each one of the short sides of the rectangle are located video screens on which the band's performance during the evening is projected live. All sorts of small, colored light bulbs are placed around the locale, especially along hand railings and the structures that separate the two levels from each other. Chrome, glass, and mirrors are seen everywhere. A mural that fits the name of the *bailanta* (a city skyline is painted on one wall of the club named Metrópolis, for example) might be part of the decor, and the name of the *bailanta* is prominently and artistically displayed over the stage. The lighting used to illuminate the stage consists of a series of spectacular colored laser lights and strobe lights; smoke machines are used to change the lighting effects as well. While the stage is illuminated during a performance, the rest of the hall is very dark.

Downstairs, there are no tables or chairs on the dance floor; only a few, which are made out of chrome or plastic and are of a contemporary design, are located upstairs in the balcony areas. What this means is that everyone in the crowd downstairs, which looks like a solid mass of bodies from upstairs, must stand up for the entire evening. People have access to only a part of this balcony area upstairs, where the bar is often located, and can check their coats downstairs. The passageways that go behind and alongside the stage, which is very small, can be used only by band personnel and *bailanta* employees; these "off-limits" passageways connect with the small backstage area, which does not contain much more than a dressing room and a bathroom for the solo singer and his entourage.

A Typical Evening

When Gary performs in Buenos Aires (usually Friday and Saturday nights), his group leaves Córdoba by bus on Thursday and arrives in Buenos Aires early on Friday; the band always goes to the same hotel. Since Gary, his wife Karina, and his manager all travel by plane, they arrive at the hotel much later, around 10:00 P.M. The band members normally eat lunch and dinner together at a Chinese restaurant near the hotel (see figure 3.8).

At approximately 11:00 P.M., the *plomos* leave the hotel with one of the band buses in order to go to the first *bailanta* at which the group will perform. About an hour later, the performers meet in the lobby to wait for their own bus; they have already changed into their uniforms. The men wear dress pants and blazers, and the two women wear cream-colored hot pants, matching sleeveless midriff tops, long black vests, and tall, black boots. While everybody is waiting down in the lobby, girls from Gary's fan club, dressed in blue and white caps and T-shirts, sometimes come to talk with them.

The bus comes by the hotel just in time to get the performers to the first *bailanta* engagement; Gary, Karina, and Gary's manager also ride along. When the bus gets to the *bailanta,* everybody gets off and enters the building through the special door that takes them backstage. Since the *plomos* have arrived earlier with the equipment and have already set it up, it is time to begin the show (the *plomos* might have had to wait until a prior group finished performing before they set up). A special disc jockey who works with the *bailanta* might introduce the group; if not, Gary's announcer does so. Once Gary begins singing, his announcer does not do much besides give the name of each song; greetings to audience members are seldom read. Gary, who is dressed in jeans and a shirt, sings all of the tunes himself; he sings for almost an hour, nonstop, mixing up *moderno, tropical,* and *melódico* songs in an order that will please the crowd. When he sings at four-hour dances in Córdoba, he divides them into four sets and takes turns with a singer who does the *tropical* part.

While Gary sings, especially when he does his signature tunes without the *tunga-tunga* or holds out long, high notes, the girls go wild: they scream, fling items of clothing up to him so that he will pick them up and toss them back to their owners, and throw love letters pinned to stuffed animals up on stage. Since a "show" or recital format is followed in the *bailantas,* the people down below listen to Gary instead of dancing. There are only a scattered few who try to dance at the back of the hall, which is packed so tightly that one can barely breathe; those who attempt to dance do not usually know how to dance *cuarteto*-style. A vendor usually wanders through the crowd selling "Gary" hats, of the felt cowboy type with a bow on top, which many people wear while all of this is going on (see figure 4.8). When Gary finishes singing, he slips out the back door into the band bus. The other band members also leave the *bailanta* as quickly as possible and get into the bus. As soon as the *plomos* have removed all of the band's equipment out through the back door and have stored it on their bus, the group is ready to drive to the next *bailanta* where it will be performing. As soon as Gary and his crew leave this first *bailanta*, recorded music is put on by a disc jockey there. Audience members dance to these recordings while they wait for the next live group to get set up; they only listen when live groups perform.

After the band members arrive at the second *bailanta*, they often have a long wait before they will perform. The *plomos* carry all of the equipment backstage, but the rest of the band waits in the bus or goes to nearby bars or cafes to pass the time. Some people just stand out on the sidewalk in front of the *bailanta*, where the bus is parked, and talk. Others might buy a hot dog from a vendor on the sidewalk. When the time comes to perform, they repeat the procedure that they followed earlier in the evening. After Gary finishes singing at this second *bailanta*, he once again escapes into the bus. In order to get back to the hotel, he leaves the bus through its emergency door and gets into a car that is waiting for him right next to it. Many girls, thinking that Gary is inside the bus, beat on the windows and ask for his autograph. When all is safe, the driver opens the bus door to show them that Gary is not there. Once the band members get to the hotel, they have breakfast and go to bed. The next evening, they all repeat the routine that they have just gone through. Immediately after the last performance is over, they get into the buses and head back to Córdoba.

Performing *Cuarteto* Music in Buenos Aires

Members of *cuarteto* groups often say they do not like to perform in Buenos Aires; they prefer the familiar atmosphere of the dances back home and are anxious to return to Córdoba. Since they have no real opportunities to get to know the fans in Buenos Aires (except for girls who come looking for them at the hotel or out on the sidewalk of the *bailantas*), they do not really know who the "regulars" are and cannot form many personal relationships with their admirers. They also find it difficult that audiences in Buenos Aires do not dance. For many of them, when *cuarteto* music has been isolated from its dance component and is no longer performed in a communal fashion—as happens in Buenos Aires—performing is not fun; in a way, *cuarteto* music performed in Buenos Aires is not really *cuarteto* at all.

The comments of these performers only serve to underscore the function of *cuarteto* music in Córdoba. For *cuarteteros,* true *cuarteto* is much more than a series of musical notes and/or tunes that are performed for them to listen to; instead, it fulfills various types of personal needs and cannot be separated from its context. Dancing, dance halls, and *cuarteto* music all go together.

5

Power, Decision-Making, and Innovation
in the Evolution of Musical Style

According to the anthropologist Ward Goodenough (1981:90–100; 1978:79–86), people today must learn how to interact in a number of the different social groups or networks of interaction (microcultures) that comprise their cultures. Since it is individuals who learn and come to "share" a society's public culture, the study of the processes involved in arriving at this "sharing," as well as those regarding cultural change, must begin with the individual (1978:81). Small differences observed from group to group also become important. Because individuals compete and attempt to pursue or further their own interests in these processes of group interaction, issues of power and access to decision-making must be considered when studying culture and cultural change as well (1981:84, 86).

According to Goodenough (1981:109–113), every individual is a unique product of three different types of learning that together make up his or her personal outlook, or propriospect: what he has learned about his own culture, what he has learned about other cultures, and what he has learned completely on his own. The sum of the individual propriospects in a given culture, which is a society's "culture pool," or "reservoir of resources and skills," could be illustrated as follows (1981:112):

1. $p_1 = (A_1: a_1, b_1, —, d_1, —, \ldots) + (K_1, —, —, \ldots) + x_1$

2. $p_2 = (A_2: a_2, b_2, c_2, —, —, \ldots) + (—, —, —, \ldots) + x_2$

3. $p_3 = (A_3: a_3, b_3, c_3, —, —, \ldots) + (—, L_3, —, \ldots) + x_3$

4. $p_4 = (A_4: a_4, b_4, —, d_4, e_4, \ldots) + (K_4, L_4, —, \ldots) + x_4$

5. $p_5 = (A_5: a_5, b_5, —, d_5, —, \ldots) + (—, —, M_5, \ldots) + x_5$

6. $p_6 = (A_6: a_6, b_6, c_6, —, —, \ldots) + (—, —, —, \ldots) + x_6$

7. $p_7 = (A_7: a_7, b_7, —, d_7, —, \ldots) + (K_7, —, —, \ldots) + x_7$

8. $p_8 = (A_8: a_8, b_8, c_8, —, e_8, \ldots) + (K_8, —, —, \ldots) + x_8$

9. $p_9 = (A_9: a_9, b_9, —, —, —, \ldots) + (—, —, —, \ldots) + x_9$

. . . .

n. $p_n = (A_n: a_n, b_n \ldots \ldots \ldots) + (\ldots \ldots \ldots) + x_n$

(Goodenough 1981:112)

In this model, the numbers (1, 2, etc.) represent the individuals who belong to a society with Culture A; the "p" following each initial number refers to that individual's propriospect. Each individual's version of Culture A, and the various traditions of Culture A that he is competent in (a, b, c, d, e) are shown in small letters within the first parentheses. His knowledge of other cultures (K, L, M) is shown within the second parentheses, and his knowledge gained completely on his own is represented by the letter x. From this hypothetical model, it can be seen that all of the individuals listed share some elements from their own culture (Culture A), but have different versions of both their own culture and other cultures. The x element in the propriospect of each individual also varies. In other words, each person contributes unique elements to the culture pool (1981:112).

This concept of the culture pool is related to cultural change of various kinds. Over time, contents of a culture pool may be lost or changed through cultural drift, especially if the members who possess certain types of knowledge die before they pass it on (1981:113–14), and new elements are constantly fed into it through inventions, private discoveries, and contact with members of other cultures (1981:116–19). Because certain elements of the culture pool gain and/or lose status over time, decision-making and power relationships are implicated (1978:84; 1981:117).When studying cultural change, it is thus important to examine both the processes that govern the content of culture pools and those that govern the selective use that people make of the contents of their own society's culture pool (1978:119; 1981:84–86).

Real social power, says Goodenough (1978:84), is the extent to which people are in a position to facilitate or impede the gratification of one another's wants. Unequal power relationships exist in all human societies, and are compounded by "individual differences in knowledge and skills and in physical and personal attractiveness" (1978:84). In addition, since groups already in power wish to maintain their privileged status, "differential access to and knowledge of the various microcultures in macrocultural systems is a significant aspect of power relationships in all societies" (1978:86); acquisition of knowledge and skills that could lead to competence in a microculture is manipulated, and situations in which this competence might be demonstrated are controlled. Because the decisions made by those in power eventually lead to cultural change and difference, the impact of individual elements from a society's culture pool is thus related to a person's hierarchy in the power structure and his access to processes of decision-making (1978:83–86; 1981:118–19).

In this chapter, Goodenough's ideas regarding cultural change are applied to musical change in *cuarteto*. More specifically, the role of individuals in the decision-making processes that have led to musical evolution (innovation) in the bands Chébere, La Banda del "Negro" Videla, Tru-la-lá, Gary, Santamarina, and Carlitos "La Mona" Jiménez, and the power relationships involved, are analyzed and compared. Each band is thought of as a separate microculture, or network of group interaction, in which hierarchies of power are present and access to musical decision-making is unequal. For this reason, a complete synopsis of the unique "culture" of each band is presented separately before discussing the differences and similarities found among the six groups. Musical decision-making is taken to mean opportunities of band members to contribute individual musical knowledge to a group's sound, repertoire, compositional processes, making of arrangements, rehearsals, and/or manner of recording.

It is shown here that stylistic differences, i.e., the musical style of each band, depends upon the amount of power that is possessed by group owners, arrangers, singers, musicians (instrumentalists), and announcers. Hierarchical power relationships, which differ from group to group, limit the contributions (access to decision-making power) of some band members as well. By discussing each band individually, it is also clearly demonstrated that the culture pools of the six groups are all different and are not drawn upon equally. By putting the bands into this comparative context, it will become evident why the group culture of Carlos Jiménez, the band to be studied in detail in the next chapter, is quite different from that of all the others. The description of his group's musical operations will lay the foundation for understanding the processes that were involved in the changes and innovations made in his musical style during 1994 and 1995.

Elements included in the individual description of each band's culture are as follows: group history (including instrumentation and styles performed), the band as it exists and operates today, group processes that concern musical decision-making (style, instrumentation, repertoire, composition, making of arrangements, use of written-out parts, rehearsals, and recording), and the personal background of band members (age, education, musical training, prior experience with or interest in *cuarteto,* and preferred musical genres). Following the discussion of the six bands, general conclusions are drawn regarding power relationships and access to decision-making in *cuarteto* groups.

Chébere

Group History

Chébere, which dates back to 1974, when it was formed to make a recording for the Venezuelan market which was never released (SADAIC 1992:32), is the oldest active band in the city. Although it has always been a symbol of change and modernity, Chébere started out with the typical formation of early *cuarteto* groups (SADAIC 1992:32). From the beginning, however, it was unlike other bands: its young members performed for the love of music, admired the Beatles, liked rock, wore bright clothing, and had long hair (SADAIC 1992:32–33). At their dances, they played with their pianist standing up, used a bass guitar instead of an acoustic string bass, and all sang with microphones (Hepp 1988:88; SADAIC 1992:32–33). Early on they began adapting *melódico* tunes to the *cuarteto* performance style as well ("Chébere: veinte años" 1994:1). These early innovations, and many others made over time, have been widely imitated by other *cuarteto* groups (Hepp 1988:78, 92).

For the first couple of years after it was created, Chébere was not a successful band. Its members played filler with a women's group, the Chichí, for approximately one and one half years in order to make ends meet. The group's first singer, Sebastián, had left immediately after the recording to be marketed in Venezuela was made, so Julio Manzur, a friend of some of the band members, had taken his place. It was in 1976, with a song called "Vestido Blanco, Corazón Negro" ("White Dress, Black Heart"; FRANCO—VALDÉZ), that Chébere made it big. On this successful recording, the band introduced the idea of using *moderno* and *melódico* repertoire to which the *tunga-tunga* had been added (Chébere: veinte años: 1994:1–2). In 1978, when the group recorded its third long play, the accordion was replaced by synthesizers; Julio Manzur had left the group by this time (he returned for a short time later on, however), so the recording was done with the singer Leo Fraga (Lugones 1995:1). By this time, organ, *clavinet*, and a female chorus had also been added to the group ("Chébere: veinte años" 1994:2). Since Leo Fraga was not successful with the band, in 1978 he was replaced with the singer Pelusa, who was renowned for his melodious style of singing and who stayed with the group until 1983 ("Chébere: veinte años" 1994:2; Lugones 1995:2). While Pelusa sang with Chébere, several major changes occurred: drum set was added in 1978, two trumpets replaced the female chorus in 1979, and electric guitar and saxophone were added in 1983 (Hepp 1988:90–91). The tradition of having two singers alternate *moderno* and *tropical* sets was also "invented" during this time. Up until 1980, it had been customary for Ángel Videla, the group's keyboard player and arranger, to jokingly sing a few *tropical* tunes during dances to allow the band's singer to rest. After a *tropical* tune Videla recorded on a Chébere long play in 1980 became a hit, he "officially" began to sing sets of *tropical* repertoire in dances, one side of each Chébere long play began to be devoted to *tropical* music, and the two-singer tradition in *cuarteto* bands was launched ("Chébere: veinte años" 1994:3; Lugones 1995:2; SADAIC 1992:33).

With the arrival of the singer Fernando in 1984, Chébere took on much more of a *moderno* and rock flavor; a trombone was also added to the group. In 1987, Fernando was replaced by Jorge Quevedo, who remains with the band, and in 1990 the saxophone was replaced by a second trombone. When Ángel Videla left the group in 1990, both a pianist and a *tropical* singer were hired to replace him, and a Latin percussionist (*timbales*) was added to the band ("Chébere: veinte años" 1994:3–4). The *tropical* singer who replaced Videla, Rubens Da Silva, is Brazilian; he was still with the band in 1994. His hit tune "Giro Giro" (VILLARREAL—PIZZICHINI), sung in both Portuguese and Spanish, allowed the band to enter the disco scene and to update its *tropical* style (SADAIC 1992:33; Ábalos 18 November 1994:2–3).

With these many changes that have taken place over the years, Chébere has become a thirteen-member band. It now has two trumpets, two trombones, synthesizer, electric piano, electric guitar, bass guitar, drum set, *timbales*/percussion, a *moderno* singer, a *tropical* singer, and an announcer ("Chébere: veinte años" 1994:4). Although the group continues to follow a strict division of the *moderno* and *tropical* styles, the *moderno* repertoire includes *melódico* selections; one slow number without the *tunga-tunga* is also sung per evening. The "evolved" style of Chébere, especially the occasional disappearance of the *tunga-tunga* in its music, has moved many people to say that it is no longer a *cuarteto* group (Waisman 1993:5).

Over the years, Chébere has continued to introduce innovations. It was the first group to use scenery and smoke machines up on stage, and in 1993 it became the first *cuarteto* band to record in the United States (Hollywood, California). In 1994 it won a Premio A.C.E. (the equivalent of a Grammy) for being the best *tropical* group in Argentina and signed a contract which would make it the first *cuarteto* band to distribute its recordings in the U.S. Latin market ("Chébere: veinte años" 1994:4; Ábalos 18 November 1994:2–3).

The Group Today

Of the original six owners of Chébere (the first six members were all partners), only three remain: Alberto "Beto" Guillén (bass), Alberto Pizzichini (synthesizer), and Eduardo "Pato" Lugones (announcer). These three joint owners, who continue to perform with the band, have divided up management duties: Guillén is in charge of musical matters, Pizzichini handles group administration, and Lugones, who is the most visible owner due to his duties, is responsible for public relations (see figure 5.1). Lugones, a highly respected and gentlemanly figure in the *cuarteto* world, compiles historical data about the band, gives out all official information regarding Chébere, and meets with people who have

5.1. Eduardo "Pato" Lugones at the El Padrino Bar. Photograph by Jane L. Florine, Córdoba, Argentina, 1998.

questions about the group. Other band personnel include an arranger named Osvaldo Ferri, two sound technicians, four assistants, three administrators, and two drivers ("Chébere: veinte años" 1994:4). Almost everyone who works for Chébere has full employee status and paid vacations. A stable group, most of the band members have been with the ensemble for at least five years.

Chébere does its own recording and distribution under the Clave Records label and maintains an office in downtown Córdoba. On weekends the group performs mostly in the city itself, in locales such as La Vieja Usina, Villa Retiro, and La Sociedad Belgrano, but during the week, it travels in its two buses to nearby locations in the province to perform. Its style attracts a university crowd that frequents both dance halls and discos (Hepp 1988:92), and many fans come just to listen. Two young girls, who are not officially part of the band, often dance on stage next to the singers.

Musical Decision-Making

Repertoire and Composition

All three owners have a say in picking out repertoire, which consists of a combination of cover tunes and original songs, during their weekly meetings. Although the owners often work with one local composer, who is given ideas for lyrics and is asked to write tunes, they also consider material submitted by other local composers and/or compose their own material (band members do not submit their own compositions but may suggest cover tunes). Their goal is to have quality songs, with interesting music and well-written, tasteful lyrics that fit the styles of their singers (some *tropical* possibilities are eliminated, since Da Silva cannot sing quickly in Spanish); making money for themselves in song royalties is not important.

Making of Arrangements

Osvaldo Ferri, who played trumpet with Chébere for seven years and did occasional arranging when Videla was with the group, took over the band's arranging duties and stopped performing upon Videla's departure (see figure 5.2). Although he got some musical training when he performed with a youth military band, he is for the most part self-taught. An avid fan of jazz and salsa, he incorporates elements from both genres into his arrangements. Currently a member of both the Córdoba Symphony Orchestra and the Municipal Band, he has experience playing many different styles of music.

More often than not, the owners assign Ferri two songs to arrange per week (one for each singer); he may suggest cover tunes. Although he is free to arrange the tunes as he wishes, the owners supervise the end product. After the owners give him a recording to arrange, he makes a complete score by hand, transcribing by ear; the vocal part, *tunga-tunga,* and percussion lines are not notated. He then copies off individual parts for everyone except the singers and the percussionists (the guitar, piano, and bass parts often consist of chord symbols).

Rehearsals

Ferri, who directs the weekly rehearsals held in a studio building owned by Chébere, has both singers arrive after the other band members have already rehearsed; the singers, who do not read music, have learned their

5.2. Osvaldo Ferri at a Chébere dance in La Sociedad Belgrano. Photograph by Jane L. Florine, Córdoba, Argentina, 1995.

parts from recordings and have transcribed their lyrics ahead of time. The brass players occasionally have sectionals (rehearsals for themselves only as a section) in order to rehearse difficult new parts before the rest of the musicians arrive. In order to be able to listen to his arrangements at home, make any necessary changes, and recopy the parts, Ferri often records just the instrumental parts of tunes during rehearsals.

While rehearsing, he makes indications regarding expression, dynamics, and timbre. Although each person is encouraged to be himself within the Chébere style, some musicians in the group have more freedom than others. The percussionists, for example, are asked to create rhythmic patterns that fit the style being performed (they have rock and *tropical* backgrounds); the guitarist, who plays by ear, is frequently given a certain number of bars during which he is to create his own solo, and the pianist, whose background is in jazz, is allowed to create his own steady, repeated, rhythmic chordal figures (used while comping) in *tropical* tunes. Although the brass players must play what is written, they work on ensemble playing outside of rehearsals and come up with their own choreography. The band members are allowed to point out ways to improve and/or correct arrangements and to suggest how original tunes should be "finished" (how to improve introductions and endings, for example).

Recording

Chébere normally records and does its sound mixing in Buenos Aires, but once did both in the United States. The band sometimes uses guest artists (musicians who perform with Phil Collins and Madonna recorded with the band in Los Angeles, California), female choruses, and sound effects on its recordings, but all of the group members record live ("Chébere: veinte años" 1994:4). Each of the two compact discs Chébere records per year consists of two halves: one with *tropical* selections, and the other with *moderno* ones. Within the *moderno* half, one tune without the *tunga-tunga* is recorded. All band members are listed individually on liner notes, and everyone—not just the owners—appears in photographs of Chébere on recordings or in print.

Personal Background of Band Members

Although all three of the owners are nearly fifty years old, the other members of Chébere range in age from twenty-six to thirty-eight; their average age, excluding the owners, is thirty. Very few of these men are true *cuarteteros*. Two did go to *cuarteto* dances to dance when they were young and another two went in their youth to perform, but the rest of the band members were not interested in *cuarteto* when they were growing up. In fact, six members of Chébere had neither attended a *cuarteto* dance nor had ever performed *cuarteto* music before they began working with the group. As for education, one band member has finished only primary school, three have begun but have not finished high school, three have finished high school, and seven have begun but have not finished university programs of study. Regarding musical training, two men have conservatory degrees, and one of the two has studied music at the university level. Two band members have had no musical training (one of these two is the announcer), and three cannot read music. The rest of the group members have learned music through an assortment of private lessons, jazz-school lessons, conservatory lessons, and youth military band instruction. When the members of the group (including Ferri) were asked to name the genre of music they would most like to play to earn their livings, they responded as follows: salsa (3 people), jazz (3 people), rock (2 people), salsa or jazz, classical music, *cumbia,* romantic music, heavy metal, and melodic instrumental music.

La Banda del "Negro" Videla

Group History

Ángel "Negro"Videla, one of the founding members of Chébere, left the band in 1990 after seventeen years of playing keyboards, arranging, composing, and singing with it; he decided to form his own group as a solo singer and to attempt a daring musical experiment. Besides having enjoyed the Beatles and rock music in his youth, Videla had listened to recordings of Cuban and Caribbean music loaned to him by a man his father had met. As a result, he had always enjoyed *tropical* music. By 1990, he had also studied music at both the conservatory and university levels in Argentina and had taken courses in arranging and music (computer) technology in the United States (at Berklee College of Music and the University of Miami); he wanted to try something "new." Videla wanted to perform "authentic" Caribbean music in Córdoba—without the addition of the *tunga-tunga*—by introducing Dominican merengue, which has much in common with *cuarteto.*

Prior to this, Videla toyed with the idea of living in the United States. In 1990, right after leaving Chébere, he made a recording of merengue in the States, *Con Todo Su Cariño,* using American musicians; the choruses, which were sung by Dominicans, were recorded in the Dominican Republic. In 1991, when he returned to Córdoba, he formed a merengue group with fourteen members: himself on piano and vocals, four percussionists (who played instruments such as *güira, tambora,* and drum set), two dancers who played *güiro,* two trumpets, trombone, tenor saxophone, keyboard, electric guitar, and bass guitar. Four of these band members were brought from the Dominican Republic. Sensing public disapproval of his musical experiment, after just four months Videla disbanded the group. Once he had eliminated the Dominicans and had added a percussionist, an announcer, and a *moderno* singer, he then went back to performing *cuarteto* with La Banda del "Negro" Videla.

During my stay in Córdoba, Videla was again making changes. When I first arrived, his group had the instrumentation that has just been described, but the trombone had recently been eliminated. Since several men were let go when their contracts had expired in December 1994, by January of 1995, most of the band's personnel had been changed. My interviews were carried out with the "old" group members (I could not find the drum set player or the trombonist, however), who knew Videla's working style, but the new band members were observed in a rehearsal and performances.

Videla named his "new" group Sazón (Seasoning), and introduced it to the public in a mysterious fashion in June 1995; he placed signs around the city with the word "Sazón" on them, and announced the significance of the word at the band's launching ceremony ("Basta de discriminación" 3 July 1995:C1). Having replaced the older musicians and the orchestra manager in order to create a more youthful image, his group is now made up of young men in their early twenties who are from the interior. When the band was restructured, Videla planned to feature the accordion and to perform many genres of music, such as *vallenato* (a type of popular music from Colombia that uses the accordion), rock, and rap ("Basta de discriminación" 3 July 1995:C1). At a dance observed in August 1995, however, he was following the familiar Chébere style and division of repertoire.

The Group Today

Videla and Emeterio Farías are both co-owners of Sazón (see figure 5.3). Farías, a longtime *cuarteto* promoter, runs the most important *cuarteto* advertising agency in the city and has invested most of what he has made from organizing dances into *cuarteto*-related activities: he rents out two large dance halls, has *cuarteto* video clips made for groups at his television station (Rango TV), and owns a radio station (Radio Suquía) that does *cuarteto* broadcasting. He also sponsors an important radio program that advertises *cuarteto* dances on LV2. Generally speaking, Farías tends only to the administrative, advertising, and financial needs of Sazón. For this reason, the band is run from Mejor Propaganda, his advertising agency, right downtown in the *cuarteto* district. Videla, who is the musical director, arranger, singer, and pianist of the group, also auditions and hires personnel. Although Videla and Farías have tried to enter the Córdoba dance hall circuit with Sazón, it continues to perform mostly in the interior except for a small dance hall in Córdoba; it no longer goes to Buenos Aires. When the band travels, Videla likes to go on his own.

5.3. Ángel "Negro" Videla and Emeterio Farías at Mejor Propaganda. Photograph by Jane L. Florine, Córdoba, Argentina, 1995.

Musical Decision-Making

Repertoire and Composition

Videla chooses Sazón's repertoire (with Farías's suggestions at times) and composes some of the songs the group records; Farías is occasionally listed as a coauthor. Although he does use material submitted by local composers, up to now he has been renowned for using cover tunes sent from abroad. Now that so many bands are imitating his idea of using Caribbean cover tunes, however, he has begun using more of his own material. His band members might suggest cover tunes to do, but they do not usually compose or make diskettes for the group. Videla is especially known for the playful *tropical* tunes, with spicy lyrics, that he sings.

Making of Arrangements

Videla, with few exceptions, does all of the arranging for the band with the electronic equipment he has in his home studio. He begins with a sketch, creating lines for trumpet, saxophone, keyboards, and bass after selecting the (cover) tune and the key. He then copies out the parts for the musicians by hand. Although Videla and the other singer both know how to read music, they follow the customary practice of learning songs and transcribing lyrics by ear. The percussionists, and sometimes the guitarist, are not given parts, either, but all of the other musicians play with music (the bass and keyboard players sometimes use chord symbols). Despite the fact that they all can read music, everyone plays by ear when cover tunes are imitated.

Rehearsals

Videla attempts to hold weekly rehearsals, which he directs and Farías does not attend, in an abandoned dance hall. When possible, he rehearses two new tunes per week, controlling even small details of interpretation and timbre. Although he is open to feedback, he is definitely the boss. The musicians say they contribute their own personal styles of playing to the group more than anything else, but that they can sometimes make suggestions regarding such things as introductions and endings when original material is being rehearsed for recordings.

The guitarist is allowed to play by ear in order to capture the original feeling of the tunes being performed, and the bass player is often allowed to vary the *tunga-tunga* much more than he would be allowed to in other *cuarteto* groups. Percussionists, whose work is much more controlled in this band than in others, are asked to imitate what they hear on a recording or diskette with sequences; only at times may they add additional rhythmic patterns that fit with the style. Before the creation of Sazón, one percussionist played an electronic instrument that imitated the *tambora*.

Recording

In the past Videla has recorded and mixed in Buenos Aires, but the compact disc released by Sazón was recorded in Buenos Aires and mixed in the United States. Since Videla does not perform much in Córdoba, he was currently doing only one new release a year. For this last recording, done with BMG, he prepared diskettes of the selections to be recorded and then removed almost all of the sequences on the diskettes, one by one, when he, the other singer, and most of his musicians recorded live in the studio. The vocal, accordion, guitar, bass, and Latin percussion parts were recorded live, whereas Videla did the keyboard and *timbales* parts electronically in his home studio.

Videla has normally recorded more *tropical* than *moderno* tunes on his releases; one *melódico* tune without the *tunga-tunga* has usually been recorded on each one also. Since Videla is the band's solo singer, he records more selections than the other singer does on each disc, and his face alone usually appears on albums and publicity material. He lists the band members in liner notes, though, and often includes their photographs there.

Background of Group Members

Even before he formed Sazón, Videla was much older than his other band members. (The information given here was collected from eleven members of La Banda del "Negro" Videla, not Sazón, and Farías is not included.) When the interviews were carried out, Videla was forty-eight and the other band members ranged in age from nineteen to forty-three (their average age was twenty-nine). Six of the men had attended *cuarteto* dances in their youth, and one had attended them only to perform. Of the four band members who had not gone to dances, one had played *cuarteto* for the first time upon working with La Banda del "Negro" Videla. As to education, one person had finished a university degree, three had begun or were still enrolled in university programs (one was studying music), four had finished high school, one had dropped out of high school, and one had attended only grade school. One man had a conservatory degree, and the announcer was the only person who did not know how to read music. The rest of the band members had received their musical training through either university courses, conservatory lessons, private lessons, jazz school lessons, and/or youth military band programs. When asked to name the kind of music they would most like to perform to earn their livings, the men responded as follows: jazz-rock (2 people), *boleros*/ballads (2 people), jazz (2 people), Argentine folk music (2 people), classical music, and rock.

Tru-la-lá

Group History

Tru-la-lá was formed in 1984 by Manolo Cánovas, its present owner, announcer, and *güiro* player (see figure 5.4), with economic support from Emeterio Farías. The band evolved out of an earlier *cuarteto* group, called Sucundín, also put together by Cánovas. Sucundín had the original *cuarteto* instrumentation, but performed both *moderno* and *cuarteto-cuarteto* tunes; Cánovas sang the *moderno* ones and a singer named

5.4. Tru-la-lá's announcer and owner, Manolo Cánovas, reading greetings at a dance. Photograph by Jane L. Florine, Córdoba, Argentina, 1998.

Marito did the others. When Sucundín floundered after a year or so of existence, it was restructured and named Tru-la-lá. Even before founding Sucundín, Cánovas had already formed other *cuarteto* groups, such as Los Guayaberos and Cuore, had played accordion and/or sung in many bands, and had become an experienced arranger and composer (SADAIC 1992:25; Ábalos 25 November 1994:2–3).

When Tru-la-lá was created, it had eight members: the original five members of Sucundín plus keyboard, *timbales,* and percussion. Marito was the group's only singer. The band acted as "filler" at dances performed by the more important groups in town until a hit tune, "Mi Tío es un Ají" ("My Uncle is a Pepper," a song not registered with SADAIC), boosted its popularity. Several months after Tru-la-lá's founding, the singer Gary was hired to do its *moderno* songs, leaving the *tropical* and *cuarteto-cuarteto* ones for Marito.

Tru-la-lá's early success did not last, so most of its members left the group in 1986. After a period of inactivity, the band was regrouped with

Gary singing the *moderno* repertoire and José Moyano doing the *tropical* selections. Then, in 1989, five members of the band left to form a group of their own, which they called Sandunga. As Moyano was one of the men who had to be replaced, Cánovas hired Javier "La Pepa" Brizuela, who became highly successful, as the band's *tropical* singer. When Gary left Tru-la-lá in 1990 in order to try it on his own as a solo singer, Cánovas chose Sandro Gómez, a folk music singer who remains with the group today, to replace him. A period of stability followed until 1994, when four men left to form La Barra ("Todo cuarteto es divisible" 26 September 1994:C1). Since La Pepa was among the four who left, Cánovas hired Jean Carlos Sánchez, one of the Dominicans who had been brought to Córdoba by Ángel Videla, as his *tropical* singer.

The reason that four band members left Tru-la-lá in 1994 had to do with the arrival of Víctor Scavuzzo, a professional arranger, composer, and pianist, on the scene (see figure 5.5). In 1992, Cánovas hired Scavuzzo to be the band's official arranger with the hope that Tru-la-lá's arrangements would thus become more sophisticated. Before Scavuzzo's arrival, all band members had discussed and changed around tunes in rehearsals, in part because Víctor Miranda, the former arranger, did not know how to read music (the three others who left had also performed by ear). When Scavuzzo began appearing at rehearsals with finished arrangements and parts for those who could read music, the participatory style of arranging ended and recording procedures changed. Although all band members still played live at dances (except for a drum machine), it became necessary for only a few band members to record in Buenos Aires, where they dubbed in their tracks on diskettes that had been prepared in Scavuzzo's home studio. The four men who formed La Barra were upset, feeling that these new work methods disallowed personal creativity; they had also lost power in the group (their compositions were not being used as frequently so they were losing money in song royalties).

Tru-la-lá has thirteen band members: three sets of keyboards, electric piano, bass guitar, electric guitar, accordion, drum set, *timbales*, congas, a *tropical* singer, a *moderno* singer, and an announcer–*güiro* player. Electronic keyboards (sequences) are used heavily, without emphasizing percussion, and the accordion, although present, is not very noticeable in arrangements. The group follows a strict division of *moderno* and *tropical* styles, but many of its *moderno* selections have a *tropical* flavor. Since the

5.5. Víctor Scavuzzo working in his home studio. Photograph by Jane L. Florine, Córdoba, Argentina, 1994.

arrival of Jean Carlos, who dances while he sings, some choreography has been used.

The Group Today

Tru-la-lá's office, located in the downtown *cuarteto* district, is run by two male assistants, who also program dances, act as orchestra managers, and man the box office. Cánovas controls every aspect of group operations and chooses the band members, most of whom have employee status. He has at times promoted *plomos* to the status of "musician" (making them percussionists who might later become keyboardists that play by ear) and has hired nonmusicians, assuming they will learn how to play by ear (see figure 5.6).

Tru-la-lá has a very heavy dance schedule, especially during the summer months, playing in Córdoba on weekends, in nearby areas during

5.6. A *plomo* promoted to musician plays congas with Tru-la-lá. Photograph by Jane L. Florine, Córdoba, Argentina, 1994.

the week, and occasionally in the *bailantas* of Buenos Aires. The band travels in two buses. Although there was a real drop in attendance at Tru-la-lá dances when La Barra was formed, *trulaleros* (Tru-la-lá fans) have continued to follow the group faithfully (see figure 3.6). For example, two sets of parents, who are avid *trulaleros* and hope their sons will become *cuarteto* singers someday, have their young boys sing onstage with the band. In general, *trulaleros* do not belong to the lowest economic sector, nor are they university students; they might sometimes attend Jiménez dances as well.

Musical Decision-Making

Repertoire and Composition

Cánovas picks the repertoire the band performs and/or records. Although he uses some of his own compositions and others by Scavuzzo, he often picks tunes composed by band members brought in on diskettes; almost all of the Tru-la-lá musicians and singers compose for the group. He might make small changes in songs brought to him, but he has

Scavuzzo help band members in polishing their arrangements. About half of Tru-la-lá's repertoire consists of cover tunes, and the other half comes from band members' compositions.

Making of Arrangements

Víctor Scavuzzo has a background in both popular and classical music. Although he played accordion in dance bands for many years, he has a conservatory diploma, plays trumpet, has studied music at the Escuela de Arte of the Universidad Nacional de Córdoba, and is a professor of piano at the Conservatorio Provincial. Before working with Tru-la-lá, he had played in at least one *cuarteto* group led by Cánovas and had done arranging and composing for many different *cuarteto* bands. He keeps up on all of the latest trends in popular music and music (computer) technology.

After Scavuzzo is given the tunes Cánovas wants him to arrange, he makes a sketch and works with the electronic keyboards he has in his private studio. The accordion player of the group, Roberto Domínguez, copies off the parts of the finished arrangements by hand (one part for the accordion and one for the bass and piano, which perform with chord symbols). The keyboardists use the accordion part as a guide and do not get their own copied-out parts.

Rehearsals

Rehearsals are normally held weekly, right before the band is going to perform at a dance, and in the same hall where the dance will be held. In the rehearsals, which Scavuzzo directs, only the singers and the percussionists do not read from parts. The keyboard players, who read the accordion part, modify it by playing a third above in some places, a sixth below in others, and so forth. The percussionists normally imitate what Scavuzzo has already recorded for them on a diskette, but they may sometimes add rhythms of their own. Everyone plays cover tunes by ear, and singers follow the usual practice of learning all selections ahead of time by ear, transcribing their lyrics.

The current members of Tru-la-lá can sometimes make suggestions regarding changes in introductions, breaks, and endings when new material is being rehearsed, and they add their own personal styles to the group's sound. Most of the band members, however, agree that their most important musical contribution to the group is the composition of new tunes.

Recording

Tru-la-lá records twice a year with BMG, doing its recording and mixing in Buenos Aires. Since Scavuzzo prepares diskettes of the new tunes in his home studio, only the two singers, the guitarist, and the accordion player go with him to record live in Buenos Aires over the electronic sequences. Although the names of the band members are not separately listed on liner notes, a photograph of the entire group often appears on Tru-la-lá's album covers. In fact, any photograph taken of Tru-la-lá normally shows the faces of all of the band members.

Background of Group Members

Manolo Cánovas, who was forty-five in 1994, is older than the rest of the group; their ages range from twenty-three to thirty-two, with the average age being twenty-five (not including Scavuzzo, who was forty-four in 1994). Six Tru-la-lá performers used to go to *cuarteto* dances when they were young, and two others attended them only to work. Of the six who did not attend dances, one played *cuarteto* for the first time upon working with Tru-la-lá. Regarding education, one man has earned a university degree, and seven have begun but have not finished university degree programs (not in music); five men have finished high school, and one dropped out before he finished. Although seven of the members of Tru-la-lá have terminal conservatory degrees, two have had no musical training at all (they cannot read music); the rest of the men have had mostly private and conservatory lessons. The genres of music the members of Tru-la-lá would most like to perform to earn their livings are as follows: classical music (3 people), *cuarteto* (3 people), salsa/merengue (2 people), Argentine folk music (2 people), tango, rock, *melódico*, and *cuarteto*-style *tropical* music.

Gary

Group History

Edgar "Gary" Fuentes, who has never had any musical training, says he has always wanted to be a singer; long a fan of slow, romantic music, he saw singing *cuarteto* as the only possible way to do so (see figure 5.7). Gary began his career with a group called Los Felinos y Demián at the age of seventeen or eighteen ("Gary es el boom" July 1991:56), and next performed with both Lito and Heraldo Bosio. After this, he formed a

5.7. Gary, informally dressed, sings at a dance in Unquillo. Photograph by Jane L. Florine, Unquillo, Argentina, 1994.

duo called Héctor y Gary (Ábalos 2 December 1994:3). It was in approximately 1986 that he asked Manolo Cánovas if he could sing with Tru-la-lá, telling Cánovas that he wanted to introduce a new singing style and repertoire to the group ("Gary es el boom" July 1991:56). In the five years that Gary spent with Tru-la-lá, he was very successful as a singer, arranger, and composer. When he left the group in 1990 to try it on his own as a solo singer, the band he founded had the same instrumentation he had become accustomed to hearing in Tru-la-lá: accordion, electric guitar, bass guitar, electric piano/keyboards, synthesizer/keyboards, drum set, a *moderno* singer (Gary), a *tropical* singer (José Moyano), and two announcers. Shortly after this, when he eliminated the accordion from the band, he added another set of keyboards and *timbales.* Another major change occurred in the group after he used two female chorus singers on a recording of the tune "Solo Tú, Solo Yo" ("Only You, Only Me"; TOTO COTUGNO). Because the song became so successful, he added two female backup singers to the band in order to be able to perform it at dances (see figure 5.7). His group is now made up of thirteen people: two sets of keyboards, piano, bass guitar, electric guitar, congas, *timbales,* drum set, a *moderno* singer (Gary), a *tropical* singer, two female chorus singers, and an announcer.

Although Gary had become a successful *cuarteto* singer even before he left Tru-la-lá, he was not satisfied; he had always wanted to be a slow ballad singer. For this reason, on one of the first discs he released as a solo singer, he recorded a slow tune, "Ángel" (GALLARDO), without the *tunga-tunga*. The song became an instant hit, Gary began to sing and record more songs of this type, and he eventually became renowned for his slow, romantic singing—even in Buenos Aires ("Ritmo cordobés en la plaza" 8 February 1995:2C). Gary may now sing as many as four or five slow numbers—with the crowd's approval—in a single evening. In the *bailantas*, he sings all of the band's repertoire himself, whereas in dances he and the *tropical* singer alternate sets.

When Gary sings, he uses a simple, informal approach: he wears a shirt and jeans, not an elaborate costume, as seen in figure 5.7 (the band members wear uniforms). He believes his success with his audience has been due to this simplicity and sincerity; after all, he began singing slow songs in order to be honest with the public about his taste, he says—not to look for a market. Since Gary's goal is to become an international recording artist, he hoped to launch a disc of slow songs to be recorded in Los Angeles, California, in 1996, in the Latin American market—besides doing *cuarteto* ("Un mensaje" 10 September 1994:C1).

The Group Today

Gary and his wife, Karina, are the owners of the band. Karina is in charge of all of the administrative and financial operations of the group and accompanies Gary when he travels. Eduardo "Pato" Lopez, who is in charge of promotion for the band, is usually in the group's office in downtown Córdoba only twice a week. Two secretaries handle business when the band is traveling, and a representative takes care of the group's affairs in Buenos Aires. When Gary decided to seek more of an international presence, his office was changed from a small, three-room apartment to a huge, luxurious one located in a former hotel with marble floors and staircases. This new office, which looks almost like an art gallery inside, is tastefully decorated.

Gary has been tremendously successful with his group. All of his releases have become either gold or platinum records, he sells more recordings than any other *cuarteto* artist does, and he has been awarded several trophies for his accomplishments ("Gary de Córdoba" December 1994:20; "Siempre hay lugar" 9 January 1995:C1). When he released the compact disc *Dalila* in December 1994, it was announced on LV2 that 50,000 units had been sold the same week of its release; *La Voz del Interior* reported total sales of 47,000 units, however, as of January 9, 1995 ("Siempre hay lugar" 9 January 1995:C1).

Gary attracts more of an upper-class following than do other *cuarteto* groups, and many families in the interior go to listen to him sing. Although he is tremendously successful throughout the country, he sings in the province of Córdoba one weekend a month at most ("Gary de Córdoba" December 1994:6–13). The band frequently performs in Buenos Aires, where Gary has had a fan club for three years, and is almost constantly on the road. Although Gary, Karina, and López fly when Gary performs in Buenos Aires or distant locations, the rest of the band travels in two buses.

The band members enjoy each other's company, express great satisfaction with Gary, and say they have no plans to leave the group (two people left the band during my research, but only because they moved abroad). They are all hired on a contract basis and receive from two to four weeks of unpaid vacation at the end of the year. Many of the musicians are seen at Gary's home on their days off, as if they were part of his family, and often ask Gary and Karina, who feel they deserve to be helped out, for loans to purchase property or cars.

Musical Decision-Making

Repertoire and Composition

Gary picks all of the band's repertoire "intuitively," he says. Some songs are his own, many are composed by his band members (he changes them to make them marketable), and others are composed by friends who perform with La Barra. When Gary uses cover tunes, they are normally of the *moderno* type (he has recorded one by Pink Floyd, for example). If they are originally in English, he might leave some of their words untranslated in order that their "feel" not be changed. Everyone is encouraged to contribute material, says Gary, because he feels that thirteen people can come up with better ideas together than can one person on his own. He even allows band members to use his home studio to compose electronically.

Augusto Bruchmann, the musical director, arranger, and head keyboard player of the group, helps Gary to compose and to pick out new band members (see figure 5.8). Bruchmann himself occasionally creates introductions and short instrumental sections in some tunes. Since Gary does not know how to read music, Bruchmann writes down his ideas for him, follows his suggestions of how to arrange them (Gary sings musical fragments to him and suggests which instruments could be used to play them), and helps Gary to draw on the unique talents of each individual band member. For example, since Gary likes the sound quality of his guitarist, who has a background in heavy metal, he gives this musician many solos.

Making of Arrangements

Bruchmann, who almost finished a degree in composition at the Universidad Nacional de Córdoba, has extensive musical training, especially in classical and early music. When he arranges a cover tune, he listens to the recording and writes out only two parts (one for the key-

5.8. Augusto Bruchmann waiting in the hotel lobby in Buenos Aires. Photograph by Jane L. Florine, Buenos Aires, Argentina, 1995.

boards and the other for the underlying accompaniment line, the *base*) with a pencil and staff paper. The singers and percussionists are not given written-out parts, but the percussionists might be told the number of bars in certain sections or where breaks will occur. The part for the underlying instruments (guitar, bass, and piano) often consists of chord symbols.

Rehearsals

Because the group is on the road so much, it rarely rehearses except for perhaps a hurried session held right before a dance to incorporate a new cover tune into the band's repertoire. The only other real rehearsing the group does is to prepare new material that must be recorded. In this case, band members might shut themselves in for a couple of weeks to rehearse the underlying accompaniment parts of the new tunes. Then, in the recording studio, portions of these tunes (their arrangements) are invented "live." In other words, instrumental and vocal parts do not always exist before the songs are actually recorded. Once songs have been "finished" in the studio in this fashion, the band performs them at dances in the same way they have been recorded.

If the group rehearses, it does so in a house Gary owns outside of Córdoba (in Unquillo) with Bruchmann in charge. If possible, the band members listen to a recording of the tunes to be rehearsed before they get to Unquillo. The underlying accompaniment parts are rehearsed first, and the percussion parts are then added. Once the vocal parts are ready, the whole band rehearses together. The percussionists are "directed" by the senior percussionist, who suggests rhythmic patterns they should play, but all of them have a lot of flexibility to do whatever they want. Bruchmann sings the guitar solos to the guitarist, who plays by ear and/or reads chord symbols. He might sing the vocal parts to the two women in the group as well, but the woman who sings the second vocal parts often comes up with them on her own. Once all of the parts have been "invented," there is no improvisation during performances.

Recording

Gary records once a year with BMG in Buenos Aires. Although everything on his recordings is done live, not all of his band members participate. At times the lead percussionist has recorded all of the percussion parts himself, for example, and two women from Buenos Aires have occasionally recorded the backup vocals—not the women in the band. Guest artists, playing instruments such as trumpet, violin, and violoncello, have also recorded with the group. When the band has later played these tunes in dances, the "extra" instrumental voices have been imitated with synthesizers. Since Gary is the group's solo singer, he records all of the songs on his compact discs, and his face and name alone appear on the bands's recordings and promotional material. Now that Gary is thinking internationally, the quality of photographs used on his recordings and promotional material has become quite professional. In order to portray his romantic singing style, red roses were shown on the front of his 1994 recording.

Background of Group Members

Since Gary looks for good human beings instead of focusing on the personal appearance of his band members, his musicians are somewhat older than the performers in other groups are: they range in age from twenty-one to forty-three, with thirty-two being the average age. Regarding the band members' experience with *cuarteto*, seven of them used to attend *cuarteto* dances in their youth. Of the six people who did not, two performed *cuarteto* for the first time when they began working with Gary. One member of the group has earned an official conservatory degree, and another (Bruchmann) almost finished a degree in composition. Five members of the band have had no musical training, however, and do not know how to read music; the rest have learned music by taking either private or music-school lessons. The overall educational level of the group members is very high: five have begun but have not finished university degrees (only one of them has studied music at the university level), and all of the rest have finished high school. Regarding the types of music they would prefer to perform in order to make their livings, the band members responded as follows: *cuarteto* (4 people), salsa (2 people), Latin American *melódico* music (2 people), heavy metal, Argentine folk music, classical music, rock, and jazz.

Santamarina

Group History

In 1982, the brothers Carlos and Rubén Bottalló created the band Santamarina, which they named after a train station they had seen in Chile ("Como ellos, no hay dos" 4 January 1991). Born into a musical family (their father is a local dance hall entrepreneur), the brothers earned conservatory degrees in accordion and percussion in their early teens. Although they were avid fans of the Beatles, in 1970 they formed an amateur group called the Cuarteto Royal, with the traditional *cuarteto* instrumentation. Some years later, they founded a group that included women (Tres Almas y Carlos Bottalló). When the military dictatorship came into power in 1976, they remained in Chile for a year and a half before returning to Argentina with the idea of finishing the degrees in law and chemistry they had begun before their departure. Instead of returning to school, the two men eventually went back into music and founded Santamarina (SADAIC 1992:28; "Como ellos, no hay dos" 4 January 1991).

Although Carlos and Rubén Bottalló were not real *cuarteteros* (they prefer ballads, *boleros,* and heavy metal even today), they knew that playing *cuarteto* was the only way to live as musicians in Córdoba in the 1980s. As a result, they formed Santamarina in the Chébere style that was then popular: with trumpets, but without an accordion (SADAIC 1992:28). The band's first singer was Coco, a vocalist they had met in Chile (Ábalos 16 December 1994:2), and the rest of the group's original instrumentation was as follows: piano, keyboard, bass guitar, two trumpets, drum set, *timbales,* and an announcer. In 1984, Coco was replaced with a singer named Sergio, and at approximately this same time, alto saxophone, tenor saxophone, and electric guitar were added to the group. Some of Santamarina's early recordings also used a female chorus, in the Chébere style, and later, a trombone was added. When Sergio left Santamarina in 1985, Julio Manzur, a former singer with Chébere, was asked to join the group (Ábalos 16 December 1994:2); Julio remains with Santamarina to this day, but is now the band's *moderno* singer. Since the late 1980s, when Carlos Bottalló began singing *tropical* selections with the group, Santamarina has divided its repertoire and sets into *moderno* and *tropical* categories. A *tropical* singer named Facundo was added to the band when Carlos retired from performing in 1991, and the saxophones were eventually eliminated.

During 1994 and 1995, the band's image was updated: some of the older musicians were replaced with younger ones, and the group's instrumentation was slightly changed (Ábalos 16 December 1994:2). In September 1994, the band's roster was as follows: two trumpets, trombone, piano, bass guitar, electric guitar, drum set, keyboards, a *tropical* singer who played *timbales,* a *moderno* singer who played congas, and an announcer. One of the trumpets was eliminated soon after, and the guitarist, the *tropical* singer, and the drum set player were then replaced. Since a drum machine was added at the same time, the new percussionist taken on was hired to play *timbales* and Latin percussion—not drum set. The new *tropical* singer, Landi, was asked to play *güiro,* and the announcer began playing congas. Since Julio Manzur is over forty, Landi, who is in his early twenties and has long hair, is being featured. Santamarina is now a ten-man band that does *tropical* and *moderno* selections. Although one trumpet and one trombone still remained in 1994, there was talk of eliminating them in the near future. Another change occurred in 1995, when Carlos Bottalló began arranging in more of a *cuarteto-cuarteto* style than before to try to win back followers who had been turned off by the refined arrangements he had been making.

The Group Today

Santamarina has four owners: Carlos and Rubén Bottalló, their brother Fernando, and Julio Manzur. Carlos handles all music-related matters, Rubén oversees promotion and office management, and Fernando is in charge of technical matters and personnel. Rubén and Fernando still perform with the group (bass and piano, respectively). Another brother, Hugo, handles publicity and travel arrangements, and Roberto Ramis, who is Santamarina's orchestra manager and box office supervisor, also helps out in the office. All band members have employee status, with the corresponding benefits, but the band does not take yearly vacations and performs on important holidays. Besides their work with Santamarina, the Bottalló brothers own and manage a car dealership, apartments, a construction company, and taxis.

Santamarina's office is located in the neighborhood of San Fernando —not in downtown Córdoba—in a building that includes a rehearsal area and a place to store the band bus. The group spends most of its weekends performing in the province of Córdoba and the neighboring provinces, and is especially popular with fans in the city of Villa del Rosario. Although Santamarina began going to the *bailantas* in 1989 and stopped performing in them in 1992–1993, the band was thinking about returning to the *bailanta* circuit in 1996. When the group travels, the owners go with the band bus.

Musical Decision-Making

Repertoire and Composition

Although he no longer sings or plays keyboards in the group, Carlos Bottalló is still the musical mind of Santamarina: he auditions and selects band members, composes many tunes, chooses repertoire, does all arranging, directs rehearsals, and supervises recordings (see figure 5.9). About half of Santamarina's repertoire consists of cover tunes (Ábalos 9 December 1994:2), and the other half is material composed by Carlos in conjunction with his brothers Rubén and Fernando. It is mostly Rubén and the singers who make suggestions of cover tunes, which are usually songs popular abroad or updated versions of early rock-and-roll hits. Although Carlos normally composes Santamarina's original material himself, he often lists Rubén and Fernando as coauthors in order that they share the song royalties with him. The group rarely performs tunes written by band members.

Making of Arrangements

Carlos Bottalló has training in classical music, but he has taken additional arranging courses and has kept up with the latest developments in musical technology and popular music. Although he does all of the band's arranging himself to control Santamarina's style, his friend Víctor Scavuzzo, who works in a similar fashion, did two tunes for him on a 1995 recording.

Carlos does his arranging with electronic keyboards in his home studio. He begins with a sketch and then creates the parts in the following order: trumpets, strings, bass, piano, and percussion. Once he is finished, he copies off the parts by hand. Although he tries to have two newly arranged cover tunes ready for each weekly rehearsal, original material is introduced only when the band is preparing for recording sessions.

Rehearsals

Almost all of Santamarina's musicians read off parts in rehearsals. The two singers, however, follow the common practice of listening to recordings and transcribing lyrics to learn the material. Although the percussionists usually imitate what they hear on demos and/or recordings, they are occasionally allowed to use additional rhythmic patterns. The guitar,

5.9. Carlos Bottalló at a Santamarina recording session in Buenos Aires. Photograph by Jane L. Florine, Buenos Aires, Argentina, 1995.

piano, and sometimes the bass play with chord symbols, but the guitarist has his solos sung to him. Because Carlos asks the musicians to play exactly how he wants them to (dynamics, expression, etc.), they have little input besides their tone, technique, and knowledge of musical styles. For this reason, some of Santamarina's musicians feel that their expertise is not being well used.

Recording

Carlos Bottalló prepares the diskettes that are taken to the recording studio in Buenos Aires twice a year, and then, in Buenos Aires, only the guitarist and the singers record live over what he has already prepared. On one 1995 recording, a professional trumpeter was hired to record live with the group instead of using the band's own trumpet player. In the past the group recorded with both CBS (1982 to 1988) and WEA (1988 to 1991), but it now has signed with Sony. Although the policy of the owners has always been to show only their own faces on album covers and publicity material, five faces appeared on Santamarina's June 1995 release: those of both singers, the two owners who still perform with the group, and the announcer.

Background of Band Members

The ages of the band members in December 1994, before the group was restructured, ranged from twenty-six to forty-two; Carlos Bottalló was thirty-eight. Only two of the band members had ever gone to *cuarteto* dances when they were young, but Rubén and Carlos had worked at dances with the Cuarteto Royal, and their brother Fernando had been exposed to *cuarteto* by having observed their activities. One person had attended a dance for the first time upon working with Santamarina. Three of the band members had earned conservatory degrees, two had gotten no musical training at all and did not know how to read music (the announcer and the *tropical* singer), and the rest had learned music through various kinds of private lessons and youth military band instruction. One band member was currently pursuing a conservatory degree on the side. As to general educational level, one man had earned a university degree, three had begun but had not finished university degrees, five had finished high school, and two had dropped out of high school. The kinds of music these men preferred to play were as follows: *cuarteto*, classical music, rock, country-western music, salsa and classical music, jazz, ballads, salsa, soft rock, heavy metal, and ballads and *tropical* music.

Carlitos "La Mona" Jiménez

Group History

Carlos "La Mona" Jiménez (see figure 5.10), who was born and grew up in a working-class neighborhood of Córdoba, was an early fan of the Beatles, tango, Argentine folk music, rock and roll, and *cuarteto* (Hepp 1988:84; Mero 1988:25). He attended many *cuarteto* dances because his uncle, Coquito Ramaló, worked in the box offices where the Cuarteto Leo performed and was a *cuarteto* singer (SADAIC 1992:20). Jiménez began singing professionally at the age of fifteen with the Cuarteto Berna (Hepp 1988:84; Mareco 9/6/92:7F), and in 1971, left

5.10. Carlos Jiménez performing at Atenas. Photograph by Jane L. Florine, Córdoba, Argentina, 1995.

Berna to sing in his Uncle Ramaló's Cuarteto de Oro (Hepp 1988:85; SADAIC 1992:21). In 1984, he and four other members of the Cuarteto de Oro left Ramaló to form their own band because they disagreed with many of Ramaló's policies (Hepp 1988:85). (See chapter 6 for a more complete personal biography of Jiménez and the history of his band.)

When Jiménez founded his group, Chébere and brass instruments were in vogue. Since he did not want to sound like Chébere and considered the accordion to be the heart of *cuarteto*, he kept it in his newly formed band (Mero 1988:38, 48). But since one of his goals upon leaving Ramaló was to update *cuarteto* (Mero 1988:35), he started his group with the following instrumentation: synthesizer (which imitated the sound of the violin), electric piano/keyboards, accordion, bass guitar, congas/bongo drums, percussion, an announcer who doubled on *timbales*, and himself doing the singing (Mero 1988:40–41, 48–49; Hepp 1988:85–86; Mareco 9/6/92:7F). Although the band did not have its own violinist, real violins were sometimes used when it recorded (Mero 1988:49). In addition, because La Mona had recently undergone an operation on his vocal chords, a *tropical* singer temporarily did one set before he began singing (Mero 1988:46, 49).

Jiménez is said to be the only remaining representative of the traditional *cuarteto-cuarteto* style, but the musical style of his band has changed noticeably since 1991, the year in which a Peruvian conga player began performing with his group and percussion began to be stressed in the band. In 1993, a Dominican *tambora* player who had come to Córdoba with Ángel Videla was also incorporated into the group, and in 1994, an Ecuadorian dancer who played percussion was added. The band's percussion section then began to stand in a horizontal line in front of the other musicians on stage and to do choreographed dance steps while it performed. In 1994, the group experimented with Afro-Caribbean rhythms and genres ("Carlitos Jiménez presenta" 18 September 1994:4C), but in 1995, it went back to the *cuarteto-cuarteto* style ("¿La Mona eternamente?" 24 July 1995:C1). In December 1994 the band's instrumentation was as follows: accordion, bass guitar, keyboards/drum machine, keyboards, electric piano/keyboards, five percussionists (*tambora*/bongo/*güira*, *güiro*/electric guitar, *timbales*, congas, and African dance/percussion), one singer, and two announcers.

The Group Today

Jiménez is the owner and solo singer of his group, but he does not like to call himself an "owner"; he says that all the band members are in fact "owners" (i.e., they all have a say in what happens in the group). His wife, Juana, who handles all of the administrative and financial concerns of the group, also makes his costumes. The band is run from Jiménez's house in Cerro de las Rosas, a wealthy neighborhood of Córdoba, where rehearsals are also held. One of the two buses the group travels in can often be seen parked outside Jiménez's home, where many of the band members are frequently found. The group plays in Córdoba on weekends and performs in the province of Córdoba and the neighboring provinces during the week, and since 1988, when Jiménez made his historic performance at the Cosquín Folk Festival, the band has gone to Buenos Aires once or twice a year to perform. Several staff members have accompanied the group loyally for years.

Jiménez's followers have the reputation of being from the lowest strata of the population (Mero 1988:50, 66, 86–87, 94). For them La Mona is not a singer, but an idol; he is one of their kind who has succeeded (Mero 1988:87). Jiménez entertains these fans by moving all over the stage, contorting himself into various unusual positions, and getting them to sing. His band members enjoy themselves as well, dressing up in costumes during Carnival season, for example (see figure 3.2).

Musical Decision-Making

Repertoire and Composition

Jiménez picks all of the repertoire for his band—which is almost entirely original material, not cover tunes—but does so after he has listened to everyone's suggestions. Tunes by local composers are used, but it is quite common for band members to contribute their own compositions. In fact, the men are expected to compose and to offer suggestions regarding how to adapt and/or arrange the group's repertoire; all ideas are welcomed, whether they be for dance steps, new rhythms, musical genres to perform, or anything else. Since Jiménez changes band members' tunes around to suit his own personal style, either he or his wife is often listed as being a joint songwriter on band members' songs.

Jiménez does not know how to read music, so he does his own tunes with the assistance of Luis Tapia, one of the keyboard players. When Jiménez gets an idea for a song (the words and music), he calls up Tapia, no matter what time it is, who records the tune on a tape recorder over the telephone. The two men later do the arrangement with electronic equipment in Luis's home studio.

Making of Arrangements

The Jiménez band is one of the few *cuarteto* groups that does not have an official arranger; instead, the group members work together in rehearsals to create the final arrangements. As some band members say, each person contributes "his grain of sand" to the final product—while respecting the composer's basic ideas brought in on a diskette. Since all of the Jiménez musicians play by ear, there is no need to transcribe or copy any parts, but when five string players from the local symphony played with the band on one occasion, parts were prepared for these guests. The men unanimously insist that playing by ear allows them to play with feeling ("from the heart") and to transmit their emotions to their audience—what musicians who play with music cannot do, they say.

Rehearsals

Because the Jiménez band travels and performs so much, rehearsals, which take place in a small house (*quincho*) located in back of the swimming pool at Jiménez's home, are held only to prepare for recording sessions. Since the men often work for ten to twelve hours a day for several days at a time, meals are served and snacks and drinks are set out on the table. When band members do not perform in a tune that is being rehearsed, they chat and drink *mate* as they wait.

The diskettes of the songs that have been selected are brought to the rehearsals, which are scheduled by two of the senior band members (the bass player and one of the keyboard players), and each composer normally directs the rehearsal of his own tune(s). Since Jiménez does not come to rehearsals until the basic parts have been put together, the composer of each song must also sing its melody line while his tune is rehearsed. Upon rehearsing, parts of each song are changed and turned around until all of the group members are satisfied with the final product. When Jiménez is present, he might ask band members to "invent" passages in a certain style he has in mind.

Recording

The band normally records twice a year, in studios located either in Buenos Aires or Córdoba, for the BMG label; it recently switched over from PolyGram in order to get national distribution (Ábalos 23 September 1994:21). In special cases, it might record live at a dance hall during a launching ceremony. As occurs during rehearsals, the musicians—not Jiménez—are in charge of setting up the recording schedule and supervising it. When the band cuts its recordings, each person records his part live, one by one, beginning with the keyboards and the instruments that play the *tunga-tunga*. The composer of each tune supervises the recording of his song(s) in the studio, singing the vocal line(s) to give the band members something to go by as they record their tracks. All of the musicians critique each other's performances, often asking for minute details to be rerecorded and subtleties of timbre, attacks, ensemble, and dynamics to be perfected. As the musicians wait their turns, they eat snacks and drink *mate*. Finally, after all the other parts have been recorded, Jiménez goes to the studio to record the lyrics. A picture of Jiménez is always on the front of his recordings (he appears alone in all of his publicity shots as well), but the names of all the people who have participated in making the recordings are listed in his liner notes.

Background of Group Members

Since Jiménez prefers to work with loyal, experienced musicians, and does not worry about their appearance or age, the men in his group are a bit older than those of most *cuarteto* groups: they range in age from twenty-two to forty-three, with the average age being thirty-four, and many of them have been with the band for years. Two of the men have four-year conservatory degrees and many have taken private lessons; five have not studied music at all. Regarding the educational background of the band members, four have finished high school, four have dropped out of high school programs, and five have finished only elementary school. As for the types of music these men would most like to play in order to earn their livings, their answers were as follows: *cuarteto* (4 people), *moderno,* Latin jazz, Argentine pop music, rock, romantic music, lyric string music, merengue, salsa/merengue, and salsa/classical music.

Conclusions

General Observations

Reflecting upon these six "cultures," it is possible to draw certain conclusions about the role of power relationships, access to musical decision-making, individual involvement, and culture pools in the formation of musical style in *cuarteto* groups. Musically speaking, the most powerful individuals in *cuarteto* bands are normally their owners, who usually choose repertoire (often their own), pick and supervise the arranger, hire band members, and determine recording procedures. If an owner also fulfills musical functions in his band, such as composing, arranging, directing rehearsals, performing (especially as a solo singer), and putting sequences on diskettes for compact discs, his musical preferences become imposed on the band. For this reason, an owner's face may often come to represent his group. Since all owners generally have the same musical roles and duties, they belong to a special microtradition within the *cuarteto* world.

The actions and attitudes of owners determine the access their band members have to musical decision-making and to what extent a band's culture pool will be drawn upon. If a prominent owner-employee division is present, the skills and talents of band members are not a big factor in a group's musical style; instead, it becomes a reflection of the owner's taste and background. When an owner relinquishes some of his power, perhaps because he must depend on others to assist him, such as arrangers, and groups are run more democratically (Jiménez's band, in particular), individual contributions to the culture pool become more significant.

From the description of the six groups given above, it can be seen that the amount of musical power possessed by other members of *cuarteto* bands falls into the following order (those with the most power are listed first): arrangers, singers, musicians (instrumentalists), and announcers. Even if he is not an owner, an arranger is musically powerful because he is in charge of orchestration (his musical background and taste are therefore influential), directs rehearsals, and may prepare diskettes for recordings. If he is also a composer, or if the owner relies heavily on his musical expertise, his power and access to decision-making increase. Singers have more influence and access to decision-making than musicians do because a band's repertoire must often be planned around their personal styles. Anytime singers and musicians are allowed to contribute their own compositions, factors in their personal backgrounds (propriospects) can be influential, as also occurs when musicians perform by ear and/or with chord symbols. Musically speaking, unless announcers are owners, they contribute little to their bands besides performing percussion instruments and perhaps suggesting repertoire. In summary, it is hard for individuals at the lower end of the power continuum to contribute to group processes if they are not owners or allowed access to musical decision-making.

Just as owners of *cuarteto* bands all belong to a special microtradition, so do arrangers, singers, musicians, and announcers each belong to their own separate microtraditions that span the entire *cuarteto* world. These distinct microtraditions have their own general levels of power in *cuarteto* groups, but power relationships vary from band to band because membership in microtraditions may overlap. When a person belongs to more than one *cuarteto* microtradition, his power and access to musical decision-making increase, especially if the microtraditions he belongs to are at the top of the power continuum. For example, an owner who is also an arranger, (solo) singer, and instrumentalist in his own group would be extremely powerful, since he would belong to the four highest microtraditions on the *cuarteto* power continuum. An owner who acts as his band's announcer would belong to only two microtraditions, one of which is the lowest on the power continuum, thus having less influence than the other hypothetical owner just mentioned.

Within each of these separate microtraditions of *cuarteto* personnel exist many other smaller mini-microtraditions, each with a distinct level of musical power and access to musical decision-making. For example, arrangers vary in power and access to musical decision-making depending on the duties they carry out; an arranger whose diskettes become his band's recordings is much more powerful than one who does not make diskettes. As a result, it could be said that this type of arranger belongs to a special mini-microtradition within the arrangers' microtradition. An arranger who composes for his group is more powerful than one who does not, so arrangers who compose belong to a special arrangers' mini-microtradition as well.

Various types of mini-microtraditions, which vary in power and access to decision-making, can easily be found within the musician category as well. Percussionists, for example, have more freedom to impose their personal styles than many other musicians do because they play by ear and often create their own parts. Guitarists, who belong to their own mini-microtradition (they all come from rock backgrounds), are often allowed to create their own solos, and some instrumentalists (bass and piano), who are allowed to create their own ostinato/*tunga-tunga* patterns by looking at chord symbols, belong to another. Brass players, who belong to a mini-microtradition with little access to power because they play off written parts, have often learned how to play their instruments in youth military bands.

Conclusions Regarding the Six Groups

In the following summary of how power relationships, access to decision-making, and culture pools are used in the six groups included in the
study, it will become evident that Carlos Jiménez's band is quite unlike
the others. His democratic management style allows the musicians in his
group almost unlimited access to processes of musical decision-making,
and as a result, to make personal contributions and innovations that can
lead to changes in musical style—a situation that does not occur to the
same degree in the other bands. Put on a comparative power continuum,
his band members have much more musical influence and freedom (to
innovate) than do the members of the other groups. It is because individual elements from the Jiménez culture pool are so heavily drawn upon
in the group's processes of musical decision-making that the propriospects and personal contributions of each Jiménez band member, as well
as individual participation in the "stories" of *Raza Negra* and "Penita,"
are described in detail in the following chapter. There it will also be seen
that Jiménez's special personality and ideals, not just his democratic
management style, have always played a major role in the evolution of
the band's musical style.

As will be shown below, the six bands in this study can be placed in an
order which shows the range of power exercised by band owners. Before
providing a diagram of this phenomenon, the features which allow the
groups to be so ordered will be discussed. The analysis will begin with
the bands in which the owners have the most power and access to decision-making and will proceed in order down to those in which they have
relinquished these same privileges to the greatest degree.

Santamarina

The most powerful musical figure in Santamarina is Carlos Bottalló,
who is in charge of all its musical activities (composing, arranging,
rehearsing, and recording) and can change the group's style without
consulting anyone, as he did in 1995 when he took on elements of the
cuarteto-cuarteto style in his arrangements. Before he retired from playing
keyboards and singing with the band, his power was even greater. Although some of the other owners share in song royalties and make suggestions to him, most of the other group members have little access to
musical decision-making or innovation besides pointing out wrong notes
in parts, changing around arrangements in rehearsals, and contributing

their personal interpretations. The few musicians who record live, play with chord symbols, and/or sometimes play by ear, have a bit more input than those who do not, and the singers, who have a say in repertoire choice, have a bit more influence than do the musicians. Only one band member chose *cuarteto* as his preferred genre to perform, and few of the band members had ever had any real involvement with *cuarteto*. In any case, Santamarina's culture pool is minimally drawn upon. The words "owner" and "employee" are used quite frequently by all Santamarina personnel, thus showing that there is an important hierarchical structure in this group.

Videla

Ángel Videla, like Carlos Bottalló, is a powerful figure: he selects band members, composes, chooses repertoire, arranges, directs rehearsals, sings and plays keyboards with the group, and prepares parts of diskettes for recordings. He makes stylistic decisions, such as doing merengue or changing his group's focus as he has with Sazón, on his own. The members of his band apparently have more input and access to musical decision-making than the members of Santamarina do because they occasionally play by ear (for cover tunes) and almost all record live, but they have little opportunity to contribute their own songs, suggest repertoire, or participate in other musical decision-making or innovative processes. As in Santamarina, those who play without parts and/or by ear somewhat make individual contributions, as does the *moderno* singer, who is allowed to choose repertoire suited to his personal style. Since Videla allows his men a bit more access to decision-making than does Bottalló, his band's culture pool affects the group's final product more than does Santamarina's. No one in Videla's group chose *cuarteto* as the music he would most like to play, and few band members had any background in *cuarteto*.

Tru-la-lá and Chébere

Certain similarities are evident in the musical power structures of Tru-la-lá and Chébere: the owners still perform with their bands and compose (this is much more important in Tru-la-lá than in Chébere), and each band has a separate arranger who is neither an owner nor a performer (power is delegated to arrangers, but their work is supervised). Although Scavuzzo and Ferri both make arrangements and direct rehearsals, Scavuzzo is more powerful than Ferri is, since he composes and prepares diskettes for recordings.

The access of singers and musicians to decision-making in both groups differs as well. In Tru-la-lá, most musicians do not record live but are allowed to submit their own compositions and cover tunes; although most rehearse with music, parts are changed by ear, and all cover tunes are learned by ear. The singers, who help choose appropriate repertoire, also compose. In Chébere, to the contrary, all members record live and suggest cover tunes, but do not compose. A few Chébere musicians play by ear, use chord symbols, and/or are asked to create short solos, giving them a chance to be creative, but in no case is the entire band ever asked to play by ear. Repertoire is planned around Chébere's singers, but neither one composes.

It would appear that the musicians of Tru-la-lá, because they are allowed to compose, make a bigger individual contribution to their group than the musicians of Chébere do to theirs (although Chébere members record live, whereas all Tru-la-lá musicians do not). It is interesting to point out that Tru-la-lá has the most highly trained musicians of the six groups studied, but four of its members chose *cuarteto* as their favorite music to play. Chébere is unique, since a large number of its musicians had never gone to *cuarteto* dances before having joined the band (the group has a wide-reaching culture pool) and the fact that not a single band member chose *cuarteto* as the music he would most like to perform.

Gary

Although Gary owns his group, he relies heavily on his arranger since he does not read music and needs assistance to compose his own tunes. Although Gary does make the final repertoire selection and chooses the musicians, he consults with Bruchmann regarding these types of matters as well. In a way, Bruchmann has more power than many arrangers do because his work is not heavily supervised. He does not compose or prepare diskettes for recordings, but he "invents" much of what appears on compact discs in the studio and makes suggestions to instrumentalists and backup singers.

Gary allows musicians and vocalists certain access to decision-making and musical power by recording their compositions and suggested cover tunes, letting them create their own parts, allowing them to compose in his home studio, and recording live (although some of them do not record at all). Most of the musicians play by ear and/or use chord symbols, which gives them a say in the total musical product. Musical power is delegated to experienced performers (to the head percussionist, for example), and the group's culture pool is intentionally drawn upon (the guitarist's tone quality for solos, the women's ability to create second voices, etc.). With such access to decision-making, the backgrounds of individual members are important in the band's overall sound and style. Although this group has the highest educational level of the six bands studied, four members chose *cuarteto* as their favorite genre, and many had attended *cuarteto* dances in their youth.

Carlos Jiménez

Although Jiménez is the owner of his group and is supposedly in charge of all its concerns, almost everyone, except the announcers, plays an important role in musical decision-making. Jiménez makes the final decisions regarding hiring of band members and repertoire, but many of the other musical functions in the group are fulfilled by his musicians. All of the band members compose and arrange their own tunes for the group, directing them in rehearsals (there is no designated arranger), and everyone is expected to bring forth new ideas of any kind in a type of brainstorming process. The ideas and talents of all the musicians, whom Jiménez calls "owners," are also capitalized upon, since they play by ear, supervise and coordinate rehearsals and recording sessions without Jiménez being present, record live, and critique each other's performances. In this type of band, in which the culture pool is heavily drawn upon, individual propriospects are very significant.

Jiménez's band is unusual among *cuarteto* groups for several reasons. To begin with, it has three foreign musicians. Secondly, his band members are older than those of the other five groups studied. Thirdly, his band members have had less formal schooling and less formal training in music than the members of the other five groups in the study have had. Lastly, all of the members of the Jiménez band, except the three foreigners, have backgrounds in *cuarteto*. In fact, five men chose *cuarteto* as the genre they would most like to play, more than in any other group.

Power Continuum

The power continuum just discussed can be depicted horizontally, as it is on the diagram below. The farther left one goes on the diagram, the more power the group owners have, and the less access to decision-making power the other band members have. As one goes to the right on the diagram, the power exercised by owners decreases, and the access to musical decision-making enjoyed by group members increases:

least access   most access

Santamarina   Videla   Chébere/Tru-la-lá   Gary   Jiménez

Final Reflections

As an afterthought, it is interesting to note that Santamarina and La Banda del "Negro" Videla, the two bands farthest to the left on this diagram, are the most intellectually and hierarchically run of the six groups as well as the two bands of the six that attract the smallest number of followers. The groups on the left side of the diagram are also, for the most part, the ones in which band members do not have backgrounds in *cuarteto*, have a great amount of formal musical training, and would prefer to play genres other than *cuarteto*. Those farthest to the right are the bands in which group decision-making processes are evident, the degree of formal musical training is low, and intuition is considered to be important in performance (versus reading music). These same groups (on the right) are also the ones in which members have the most background in *cuarteto* and most often choose it as their favorite musical genre. And lastly, the groups to the right side of the diagram are both the ones that draw the biggest audiences and the ones in which band members openly express satisfaction with their owners and their ability to be creative.

It would appear that group cohesion and contentment in *cuarteto* bands are the result of a democratic management style, the power to be able to contribute and create in one's band, and a love of performing *cuarteto* music. Since traditional *cuarteto* audiences are intuitive, not intellectual, it may be in part this feeling of group cohesion and contentment that leads *cuarteteros* to choose one band over another in their search for *alegría* (happiness).

Carlos Jiménez and the
Process of Musical "Change" (Innovation)

When I arrived in Córdoba in September 1994, Carlos Jiménez and his group were about ready to launch *Raza Negra*. Every *cuarteto* fan I met was talking about the upcoming launching, and the disc was constantly being mentioned in the media. From what I could tell, it appeared that *Raza Negra* was going to be a landmark recording: Jiménez, the traditionalist of *cuarteto* artists, was going to make radical "changes" in the genre by fusing Afro-Caribbean rhythms and musics with it—a first in Córdoba. The launching ceremony was set for Saturday, 24 September, at La Vieja Usina (Ábalos 23 September 1994:21).

Raza Negra and *El Marginal:* The Setting

Raza Negra was first available for purchase on 21 September, which is Student's Day and the first day of spring in Argentina. Many fans had reserved and paid for their copies of the disc in advance; others began lining up outside the record stores in downtown Córdoba early on the morning of September 21 in order to buy one. On this very same day, 10,000 units were sold, 2,000 of which were sold by one key store that specializes in *cuarteto* music. This quantity of sales was unusually high for Córdoba; it was commented by some record store owners that they normally needed an entire month to sell 2,000 units of any single genre of music (Ábalos 23 September 1994:21).

There were several reasons why people were so anxious to get a copy of *Raza Negra,* besides the fact that it was supposedly a drastic experiment. First of all, Jiménez had not released a disc for a year. Secondly, he had spent two months in Buenos Aires recording and perfecting *Raza Negra,* an unusually long time, and had spent the equivalent of U.S. $80,000 of his own money to do so. After the recording was finished, he had offered it to BMG (he had been recording with PolyGram up to this time). Luckily—for Jiménez—BMG accepted the disc and reimbursed him for his recording costs. Lastly, only five of the tunes on *Raza Negra* had ever been performed at dances; the other eleven were to be performed for the first time at the launching ceremony, and fans wanted to learn all of the new song lyrics before that day (Ábalos 23 September 1994:21). Starting on 21 September, *Raza Negra* was heard all over the city.

Although very little is ever published regarding *cuarteto* in the newspapers of Córdoba, comments about *Raza Negra* began to appear in *La Voz del Interior,* the city's major newspaper, long before the record launching and continued to be made for months after. Some common themes that appeared in most of these articles were Jiménez's motivation for having made the recording, the risk involved in combining Afro-Caribbean rhythms with *cuarteto,* and the issue of change and innovation in *cuarteto* music. From what was written, it appeared that Jiménez had made a conscious effort to combine Afro-Caribbean genres and rhythmic patterns with *cuarteto* to offer a tribute to the black race; by recording *Raza Negra,* he was also acknowledging the importance of African music in the world.

The authors of the articles, for the most part, made it seem that Jiménez was also consciously introducing change in *cuarteto* in order to better compete with other groups, to keep up with the times, and to make his repertoire more interesting—despite the risks involved. Jiménez was generally complimented for paving the way for future evolution in *cuarteto* music as well. In yet other articles, Jiménez was quoted as saying that he was not trying to "change" *cuarteto* music at all, that he was only adding some extra rhythms to it while maintaining its basic elements. As a result, it was not possible to tell if he was really going out on a limb to "change" *cuarteto* music or not.

The first reference made to *Raza Negra* in *La Voz* appeared on 24 July 1994 (C1), in a full-page article written by Luis Gregoratti and Germán

Arrascaeta; both the motivation behind the creation of *Raza Negra* and the concept of change in *cuarteto* were mentioned. Jiménez was quoted as saying that the African race has always been marginalized, and that as a result, has always expressed itself in music, song, and dance. He also said that African music has long been influential in both the Caribbean and in Argentina, but that he and other Argentines had not dared to make innovations based upon it until people like Juan Luis Guerra and Wilfredo Vargas had given them the courage to try out new ideas and fusions.

Regarding change in *cuarteto,* one musician in the Jiménez band was quoted in the article as saying that the music in *Raza Negra* included "true innovations" and that it was "thousands of kilometers beyond everything that had been done (or tried)" up to that point. Jiménez himself had the following to say regarding change: "Just as Chébere did when it imposed a kind of evolution [in *cuarteto* music] via its recordings (on each new recording it included a new instrument), I have to base change in my music upon that which is familiar. [I have to change], especially if you keep in mind the fact that I release two albums a year. The [group's] repertoire has to be modified every six months. If not, people would get tired of listening to the same tunes every Thursday, Friday, Saturday, and Sunday" (Gregoratti and Arrascaeta 25 July 1994:C1).

The week of the launching, two articles appeared about *Raza Negra:* an unsigned one in *La Voz* ("Carlitos Jiménez presenta" 18 September 1994:4C) and another, by Gabriel Ábalos, in *A diario* (23 September 1994:21). Details of the genres used in *Raza Negra* were mentioned only in the *La Voz* article (*guaguancó, bomba, mozambique, son,* pop, merengue, rap, and *cuarteto*), but the reason for making the recording and the idea of renovation (change) were emphasized in both newspapers. According to *La Voz, Raza Negra* was supposedly a "tribute to the black race" and an attempt to show that "music is transmitted viscerally." Its content was something new and "stylistically avant garde" that would permit Jiménez to keep up with the competition. Since he had carried traditional *cuarteto* about as far as it could go, Jiménez was ready to do something novel with a renovated sound, said the unidentified author. This same person continued as follows:

> For many people, this recording will sound as if all the rhythms that Pérez Prado, Tito Puente, Wilfredo Vargas, and the Cuarteto Leo

played have been been put together in a blender. The singer defines this mixture as a "*pasodoble, cumbia,* merengue, conga, and mambo cocktail." But what is unique about the disc is the risk involved in giving up the [*cuarteto*] rhythm and getting carried away by black music.

Everyone talks about modernizing *cuarteto* and making it a more important genre of music, but how does a person renovate it? In the first place, one should not ignore the influence of Afro-Caribbean music. The members of Jiménez's band say that "Jiménez understands that popular dance is linked to visceral matters, that reasoning is not involved in dancing, and that people will keep on dancing if they are offered colorful music."

Carlos Jiménez has his own concept of what change is. "A person can have thousands of ideas and might want to do lots of new things, but it is difficult to change; it is a decision that can separate you from the audience." The singer from Córdoba always listens to the comments of his followers, and knows that his music is pleasing. However, it is because of this same attitude of wanting to please that he wants to offer something different, and to play with other rhythms. "Sooner or later a person gets tired of performing the same [tunes]. Worse yet, you have to keep in mind that we do this four times a week and for four hours without stopping."

"Many times desire pushes you to [jump into] a swimming pool without any water in it. Or else, you put so much effort and speed into things that you end up driving a flying saucer instead of getting the rhythm to the people."

"Many kinds of things can be done with *cuarteto* music, but it must always be possible to dance to it." ("Carlitos Jiménez presenta" 18 September 1994:4C)

What Ábalos wrote in *A diario* about the meaning behind *Raza Negra* was similar to what had appeared in *La Voz*. Jiménez told Ábalos that ever since the time that three foreigners had joined his band (a Peruvian, a Dominican, and an Ecuadorian), they had all been wanting to do a tune in honor of the African slaves, who were the real creators of most percussion patterns. Regarding the topic of change, however, what Jiménez told

Ábalos had not appeared in *La Voz:* he said that *Raza Negra* had been done with some new rhythmic ideas, but that it respected the basic *cuarteto* rhythm. In other words, despite the addition of the foreign band members and their new ideas, the *tunga-tunga* was still being performed. "As long as the dancers can still keep the beat and their way of dancing, you can change the rhythmic patterns [if you want to].You can never go so far that people have to change their way of dancing though," explained Jiménez (Ábalos 23 September 1994:21).

Immediately after the launching ceremony, a six-page featured cover story about the evening, as well as a huge poster of Jiménez, appeared in the fan magazine *Alegría* (Soria 1994:4–9). Although most of the article was devoted to a description of the event (television stations from all over the country covered the launching, 11,000 people got inside the dance hall, and 2,000 people were forced to remain outside because of lack of space inside the hall), Jiménez was asked to explain why he had done the recording.This time, his answer was as follows: "*Raza Negra* is a tribute to the Africans who put up with slavery. Their influence, still seen today, is reflected in the greater part of popular music all over the world and especially America." When he was asked about the changes that he was making to *cuarteto,* he replied as follows: "I'm not changing [*cuarteto* music], that's just not so. I am basically doing the same *cuarteto* music as ever. The difference now is that it is fused with Peruvian and Dominican rhythms" (Soria 1994:9).

Immediately after the launching, an article appeared in *La Voz* about the ceremony (27 September 1994:3C). In this article, Luis Gregoratti, the author, gave his opinions about the event; the comments of four celebrities regarding *Raza Negra* were also published. The four men expressed their surprise with Jiménez's risk taking, imagination, and creativity, congratulated him, and said it is good to modify one's work without losing one's identity. Gregoratti emphasized the risk involved with the whole endeavor of *Raza Negra,* especially since Jiménez had made the recording with his own money before obtaining a label. He also wrote about the "never before experienced moments" in the history of *cuarteto* that had occurred at the launching ceremony, a three-tiered set complete with a cornfield, a scarecrow, and a windmill, for example. In Gregoratti's opinion, Jiménez, who was responsible for the latest innovations in *cuarteto* music, was in a "new period" of his career; with *Raza Negra,* he had proved that "any type of evolution" is possible in *cuarteto.*

On 9 January 1995 (*La Voz*, p. 2C), in a summary of important developments that had occurred in popular music during 1994, Gregoratti was still talking about the impact of *Raza Negra:*

Carlitos Jiménez made the most alternative and risky disc of his career. Having made the decision to unite *cuarteto,* merengue and other Caribbean dance steps, he gave an example to his new recording company regarding his interest to move forward and to show himself as a *cuartetero* who is different from the rest. At the same time, his recording company understood and played along with his move, thus making *Raza Negra* into one of the [biggest] happenings of the year regarding the regional music of Córdoba.

It was not just the release of this disc that was noteworthy—it was put out in the worst month of the year for sales, September, but even so, fans had reserved their albums by paying for them in advance—but the launching ceremony of the disc as well.

Although this may well be a first attempt to enrich the original rhythm of the *cuarteto,* the move made by Jiménez was later imitated by other local bands, who, speculating about their own futures, decided that their evolution would also depend upon trying their luck with *tropical* music. (Gregoratti 9 January 1995:2C)

On 11 March 1995 (*La Voz*, p. 2C), Gregoratti mentioned the importance of *Raza Negra* yet again. In this article, he discussed how competition among *cuarteto* groups was elevating the quality of *cuarteto* music being produced and singled out the importance of *Raza Negra:* "Carlitos Jiménez made a disc that, with excellent sales, marked a turning point in his career." Gregoratti also gave his own opinion about change: "the future of the genre is tied up with change. This is unavoidable."

After all these months of hearing about the new stage of *cuarteto* music ushered in with *Raza Negra,* the article that appeared in *La Voz* after Jiménez released his next compact disc, *El Marginal,* must have surprised many fans. On 24 July 1995, two days after the launching ceremony of *El Marginal,* a full-page unsigned article about Jiménez, entitled "¿La Mona eternamente?" ("Is La Mona Eternal?") was published. The launching ceremony and the disc itself were described as follows:

Last Saturday, the singer presented his latest album live. Starting with the title, the new work sums up his own beginnings and his fight to maintain his position in the Argentine music market: *The Marginal Man*.

New clothes, but the same music as ever. As occurs in all the presentations of new albums, last Saturday the musicians of Carlitos Jiménez showed off new uniforms. But the repertoire of the disc they presented reunited the singer with the old rhythm of the *cuarteto*. "While everybody else now fuses styles, I try to make myself different from the rest by doing something more traditional." The disc uses the basic rhythmic pattern that was typical of the [*cuarteto*] movement in its earliest years, includes a tune with the North American musicologist Jane Florine on flute, and connects his career to the fight of many people to survive within society. The principal tune and the disc itself are called *El Marginal* (JIMÉNEZ—TAPIA—BRITOS). (*LaVoz* 24 September 1995:C1)

With the release of *El Marginal*, Jiménez turned his back on all of the innovations he had made in *Raza Negra* and returned to his traditional *cuarteto* roots. Considering the events of just a few months before, this sudden reversal makes one wonder how and why such a process of change occurred over such a short period of time. Based on the information cited above, it would appear that Jiménez made changes (in both *Raza Negra* and *El Marginal*) in order to better compete with other *cuarteto* groups in Córdoba and to ensure that his fans and band members would not become bored. According to these same sources, *Raza Negra* was a planned tribute to the black race, black slaves, and black culture, and *El Marginal* was a conscious expression of the marginality he had always felt while trying to survive in the *cuarteto* world. Since Jiménez "returned" to the traditional *cuarteto* style with *El Marginal*, the fact that he had told the media he was not trying to "change" *cuarteto* at all, even with *Raza Negra,* comes to mind. Despite what the critics all had to say, he had apparently meant exactly that.

In this chapter, a closer look will be taken at how and why these stylistic changes in *Raza Negra* and *El Marginal* occurred by focusing upon the individuals who were involved in the corresponding decision-making and innovative processes. To begin with, each man in the Jiménez group is introduced in the form of a short personal biography; the propriospects that make up the band's culture pool are described. The five percussionists are introduced first (beginning with the three foreigners), followed by the keyboardists, the other musicians, the announcers, and Jiménez. Each man's comments regarding his own musical role in the band, the contribution of group members in processes of musical decision-making, and the concept of musical change are also given. Before examining the events and the individual contributions that led to the recording of both *Raza Negra* and *El Marginal*, a detailed explanation of why Jiménez and four other men left the Cuarteto de Oro in 1984 is provided. Since the band's founding principles and ideals have set a precedent for individual contributions in its processes of musical decision-making, group operations, and current stylistic innovations, it is important to understand what these men hoped to accomplish when they formed their own group.

After the individual biographies and this contextual information have been presented, the true story behind the creation of *Raza Negra*, including how processes of musical decision-making and personal contributions of band members were involved in its conception and stylistic innovations, is told in a semi-narrative style by quoting Jiménez at length. Although part of the story of how the stylistic changes in *El Marginal* came to be is also told through the eyes of Jiménez, most of the discussion regarding this compact disc is focused on the tune "Penita," which I rehearsed, performed, and recorded with the band. Since I was personally involved in the production of the recording, and both observed and participated in the processes of musical decision-making that were involved in its conception, the individual musical contributions and group processes that led the band to return to the traditional *cuarteto* style are described through my own eyes. After these biographies and "stories" have been presented, conclusions are drawn regarding individual innovation in the decision-making processes that led to stylistic changes in *Raza Negra* and *El Marginal*, and observations are made regarding musical change (innovation) that arises from within a culture.

The Members of the Group

Bam Bam Miranda

"Bam Bam" Miranda (Miguel Antonio Miranda Matienzo), who was thirty-eight in 1994, was born in Lima, Peru (see figure 4.9 for a photograph of Bam Bam, whose nickname comes from the Bam Bam character of the Flintstones). Bam Bam was born into a musical family that specialized in popular music, and he was exposed to all sorts of music in his home: black folk music, jazz, *tropical*, and classical music, for example. Although he has almost always played by ear, he did get some rudiments of musical training at school, where he briefly played several different instruments (flügelhorn, bass, drum set, French horn, and harpsichord) in school ensembles. Bam Bam studied petrochemical administration after he graduated from high school, but dropped out of the program to become a full-time musician. He eventually devoted himself exclusively to percussion instruments, congas and *cajón* (a "big box" played as though it were a drum) in particular, and to the performance of popular music. Before he was brought to Argentina in 1985 by the singer Alejandro Lerner, Bam Bam had played with groups as famous as Machito. In Argentina, he later performed with other famous singers, such as Teresa Parodi, before he began playing with Jiménez and company in 1991.

Bam Bam has enjoyed being a part of the Jiménez group because the work that the band members do is "creative"; they are more successful than most other groups because they are allowed to work with total freedom and are highly intuitive, he says. "Thanks to our restlessness, we are renovating all the time; Carlos Jiménez is an enlightened man," he explains. Bam Bam also thinks that this creativity is evident in the fact that the band has five percussionists (an unusually large number, he feels) and stays away from doing cover tunes: instead of doing "disarrangements" of cover tunes, they lead the way for other groups by doing original material, he says. According to Bam Bam, osmosis and tone color are important factors in the group's work; "osmosis is one's genetic memory; true creation ended centuries ago," he insists. For example, in his own case, Bam Bam says that his musical ideas come from what he listens to: jazz, salsa, ethnic music, black music, and other genres. His favorite music is Latin-jazz, but he does like *cuarteto*. He agrees that the band members want to help *cuarteto* evolve, but says their goal is not to break basic structures or to change *cuarteto* into something else.

Bam Bam thinks that he has contributed to the evolution of *cuarteto* because he has added polyrhythms to it. He tries out new rhythmic patterns on Jiménez, who accepts them as long as he can dance to them; Jiménez then proceeds to show dancers how to dance to these added rhythms by using them while he sings. Jiménez never turns down an opportunity to listen to a new idea, says Bam Bam, and has never rejected a single one of his suggestions. Bam Bam feels that more could be done rhythmically with *cuarteto* if it were not for the fact that so many solo singers—unlike Jiménez—have "star" complexes. Besides adding new rhythms to the band's repertoire, Bam Bam says that he contributes musically by composing ("Cuarte Conga"), singing choruses, and giving lessons to and guiding the other Jiménez percussionists. He listens to as much music as he can (to get new ideas), practices every day, and plans to be a percussionist no matter what (Miranda Matienzo 1994; Miranda Matienzo 1995).

Abraham Vásquez-Martínez

AbrahamVásquez-Martínez, whose nickname is "El Dominicano" (The Dominican), is another one of the three foreign members of the Jiménez clan (see figure 7.1b). Age twenty-six in 1994, Abraham was born in Santo Domingo, in the Dominican Republic, and came to Argentina with ÁngelVidela in 1991. He began in the Jiménez band in 1993, after having played with many of the other *cuarteto* groups in Córdoba. Abraham's basic function is now to play *tambora,* but he also plays *güira*, sings choruses, and dances. He knows how to play congas, bongo drums, and *timbales* should the need arise. Abraham got his start in music at the age of four, when a relative gave him a *tambora,* but from the age of fifteen until he finished high school, he quit playing the instrument. After he decided to take up *tambora* again, he began playing merengue, the genre that he still prefers to listen to and perform, with several groups. Abraham is quick to point out that *cuarteto* and merengue are similar (they share the same underlying bass pattern) and that much of what he plays with Jiménez is *cuarteto* music based on merengue. Although Abraham has some long-term musical goals (he would like to learn how to read music and how to play bass guitar and drum set), he hopes to return to live in the Dominican Republic someday. At that time, he will most likely give up music. In fact, Abraham's true hope is that playing *cuarteto* will help him to reach some of his material goals.

Abraham says that all of the musicians in the Jiménez group have all the liberty in the world to do whatever they want to musically. He emphasizes the fact that everyone in the band loves to do *cuarteto;* they do not do it just to earn money. In addition, they are all allowed to be creative, which is a special feature of the group:

Here I have the liberty to create as an individual. I believe that this is good for me because I now feel a bit more professional than before. I try experimenting with things that are going to turn out better in the future but that are already pretty good right now, too. Really, in my country, I did not have the freedom I now have. That is, in my country, I was more restricted than I have been here. This is because here I have the opportunity to develop things instinctively. Here, when I think up something for the group, they support and encourage me. Back home, they think that some people know a lot and others don't. When the people who supposedly know a lot want something to be done in a certain way, you have to do what they say there.

Abraham also feels that he and the other musicians have developed mentally and have grown to new heights of musical innovation because they are not bound to written-out parts. Although the band members all add innovations to the band's repertoire, they are careful not to go beyond the taste of the public in order to impose what they like, he says.

Regarding the individual contributions he has made to the group, Abraham insists that neither he nor Bam Bam Miranda has tried to change anything that the band was doing; although they have added foreign musical ideas to the group's repertoire, what they have really added is their "good vibrations," he says. According to Abraham, he has contributed to the group musically by having composed tunes (with the assistance of Pupi, one of the keyboardists who has his own electronic equipment), by having introduced merengue steps on stage, and by having taught the Watusi (i.e., the percussion section) choreographed dance steps (Vásquez-Martínez 1994; Vásquez-Martínez 1995).

Byron

Byron, "El Ecuatoriano" (The Ecuadorian), was born in the city of Esmerald, Ecuador, one of the most African regions of that country; he is of African descent. At age twenty-two, Byron was the youngest member of the Jiménez group in 1994. Although he has had no formal musical training, he became fascinated with African dance at an early age; he dreamed of performing in a dance troupe and of having his own dance group someday. When Byron was young, he also listened to salsa and merengue—the music he prefers to this day. He did some courses in mechanics after he had finished high school, but he cut his studies short in order to go on a tour of several countries in South America (Venezuela, Colombia, Peru, Chile, and Argentina) with a folklore troupe that he had begun dancing with. Although the tour began approximately in 1990, it was only in October 1993 that the group got to Argentina, where Byron decided to stay. He eventually joined the Jiménez band in 1994, after a trial period of a month. Although he was hired to do African dance and play mostly maracas and *güira* with the group, he also knows how to play *tambora, timbales,* bongo drums, congas, cowbell, and other small hand percussion (but not drum set). Byron says he plans to go back to Ecuador to start a dance troupe someday, but that meanwhile, despite the fact that he had never heard of *cuarteto* music before he arrived in Argentina, he is enjoying his work.

Byron feels that there is a lot of freedom in the Jiménez group: members contribute freely, state their opinions, and listen to each other's comments. A person offers what he knows, band members are very accepting of new ideas, and everyone has a role in the arranging of tunes, he says, but it is Jiménez who makes the final decisions after everyone has had his say. He feels that his main contribution to the group has been to show the public that it is possible to dance to *cuarteto* music in many ways—not just *cuarteto* style. As a result, Byron has taken his "teaching" of dance outside the dance hall: he gives lessons in salsa, merengue, and African ritual dancing in a cultural center in downtown Córdoba (Byron R.M.A. 1994, Byron R.M.A. 1995).

Conejo Rivarola

Héctor Omar "Conejo" (Rabbit) Rivarola, who was born in Córdoba and was twenty-six in 1994, had been playing *timbales* with the group for about six years at that time (see figure 7.1a). He plays tambourine, sings choruses with the band occasionally, and makes sure that the proper song lyrics are in place on a stand next to Jiménez's microphone before every tune is sung as well. According to Conejo, he became a *timbales* player because that is what his father did; he learned by watching him. From an early age he attended *cuarteto* dances to watch his father perform, but he did some dancing at them as well. He says that he now listens to both *cuarteto* and *melódico,* but that *cuarteto* is still his favorite kind of music. Since Conejo began playing in *cuarteto* groups when he was just ten or eleven, he finished only elementary school; he did not have time to finish the conservatory program he began when he was eighteen or nineteen. As a result, he still plays by ear (he would like to learn how to read music). His first playing job was with an all-female group. It was the owner of the second band he played with who recommended him for his present position, which he hopes to keep indefinitely, because he enjoys working with Jiménez. Conejo says he plays with pleasure, since he does so to support his family.

As far as Conejo is concerned, everyone in the band has great freedom to be creative and to give musical opinions. He and his colleagues are all intentionally trying to improve *cuarteto* music by adding little things to it he says, but they are definitely not trying to change the genre, he insists. All that has really happened in the group's evolution, he explains, is that they "have added a little more percussion, which has perhaps changed the flavor of the music a bit." It is precisely because he is one of the band's percussionists that Conejo feels he has been able to make an individual contribution in the group's musical evolution. He says that he has made another type of personal contribution to the band, however, since he composes and arranges for the group. Instead of using electronic equipment to make diskettes with sequences, he composes by playing on a keyboard and singing for his colleagues (Rivarola 1994; Rivarola 1995).

Tribilín (L.M.A.)

L.M.A., who is nicknamed "Tribilín," or "Tribi" for short, was thirty-seven in 1994 (Tribilín is a fictitious Disney character with big boots); he is one of the musicians who has been with the group since its founding in 1984. Although Tribi had been an amateur rock musician in a group called Años Luz and had never played either *cuarteto* music or percussion when he was hired in 1984 (he was working in a factory at the time), Jiménez gave him a chance on congas. He now plays *güiro* and electric guitar and sings choruses with the group. Tribi, who was born in Salta, moved to Córdoba with his family when he was very young. Among the amateur musicians in his family were his father, who sang tango, and some relatives of his in Salta who did *cumbia.* When he was young, he was mainly a Beatles fan; he also listened to *cuarteto* some but rarely went to *cuarteto* dances. At one point, he did sing *melódico* for a while, but rock has always been his favorite music. He now listens to *moderno* (by a pop group called Los Enanitos Verdes) and Luis Miguel among other things. Tribi learned to play by ear, but took just enough private lessons to get his *carnet de músico* (musical work credential). Since he has now been performing for so long, he says that the day Jiménez retires, he will retire from performing as well.

Tribi feels that the band members have become more demanding on themselves over the years; they force themselves to produce more and more and to constantly improve what they offer to the public. It is true that they want to sharpen the audience's ears by offering them better repertoire, better sound quality, and better choruses, he says, but he emphasizes the fact that this must all be done without changing the underlying *tunga-tunga*. As far as his own contribution to the group goes, he says that his humor has been his most important offering—despite the fact that he composes for the band; his *cuarteto* version of the rock tune "¿Quién Se Tomó Todo El Vino?" ("Who Drank Up All of the Wine?"; C. JIMÉNEZ—M. ALTAMIRANO—J. CUETO) has been one of the band's biggest hits. Tribi does at times add his rock expertise to the "salad of things" the group does, he admits (Tribilín 1994; Tribilín 1995).

Pupi Rojo

Eduardo "Pupi" Rojo has played synthesizer/keyboards with the group since the time of its founding in 1984; he moved to the city of Córdoba (he was born in the province of Córdoba) after Carlos contacted him and asked him to join the band (see figure 3.2). Jiménez knew about him because he had heard him playing with some smaller groups in the area. Pupi, who was thirty-one in 1994, is from a musical family. In fact, since his father ran a dance hall at their home, he remembers having listened to *cuarteto* music from his bedroom when he was just four years old. He learned music on his own at first, by ear, and taught himself how to play the accordion. Pupi likes to tell the story of how he used his self-taught accordion technique to teach a Franciscan priest how to play the organ. Later on, he studied in a conservatory for four years and earned a degree as a professor of sightsinging and theory. Since he began working in *cuarteto* groups when he was eleven, he chose not to begin high school.

When Pupi talks about how the Jiménez group functions, he says that all of the band members support the idea of adding new elements to *cuarteto* music, of being on the cutting edge, but without overstepping the bounds of the genre. He is grateful that they all add new elements to the music on purpose: "Music is no longer music if it does not progress; if it stops evolving, it becomes something else," he comments. Pupi feels that the Jiménez group differs from the rest because all of the band members are constantly trying to come up with innovations. He thinks that everyone has ample opportunities to contribute personal knowledge and to work comfortably. The band members have made a great effort to keep up with modern technology and have used it to enhance *cuarteto*, he says. As far as he is concerned, they have used synthesizers in a positive way, to create a bigger and/or thicker sound and to support and enrich keyboard parts, for example.

Regarding his individual contribution to the group, Pupi does a lot of arranging and composing for the band, especially with his computer. He says that he has taken new harmonic and musical elements from other genres he has listened to and that he has intentionally added them to the band's tunes (his own compositions in particular). Since he is an avid salsa fan (his dream is to play just one tune with any famous salsa group), his intensive listening to that type of music has helped him to impose elements of salsa on the *cuarteto* style; for example, he has consciously imitated brass parts and quartal harmonies, he says. Pupi stresses the importance of listening to non-*cuarteto* types of music and the absorption of outside influences on the creation process: "When you are composing or arranging, all of a sudden parts of music that you have been listening to just come to you. Your brain recalls what you have heard, part of an arrangement, timbres, or a tune that you have listened to, and relates to it; it becomes activated. It could be timbres or voicings that [one's brain] relates to. Anyway, that's how the connection and combination of elements occur."

Pupi says that outside listening and absorption of new musical elements are critical in a group like theirs, in which everyone plays by ear (they might make "guides" to program the proper number of measures for the electronic instruments, but do not write out "parts"); he does feel that it is also necessary to study music formally, though. He confesses that he could never play in a group in which he would be "limited" by having to read music or by being told what kinds of timbres to play (Rojo 1994; Rojo 1995).

Tino Quinteros

Mario "Tino" Quinteros, who was born in Cruz del Eje, Córdoba, and was twenty-seven in 1994, had been with the Jiménez group for about six years at that same point (see figure 4.9); he plays keyboards and drum machine in the group. Tino began working as a musician when he was thirteen, so when Jiménez asked him to join the band, he had already played in many different *cuarteto* groups. He got interested in music by listening to his father play the accordion and went on to study at the conservatory in Cruz del Eje for five years. He began high school in Cruz del Eje as well, but was forced to drop out of both the conservatory and the high school when his family moved. Tino says that he often went to *cuarteto* dances when he was young, both to listen to the music and to dance, and that *cuarteto* is still his favorite kind of music. Despite this fact, he now listens to everything he can get his hands on. Looking back, Tino feels that he was asked to join the Jiménez group because he was young at the time—not a seasoned veteran—and could be trained in the band's work methods. He now dreams of ending his musical career with this very same group.

Tino says that everyone in the band contributes ideas and suggestions in order to improve the material they arrange and perform. Although they make every effort to respect the arrangements that composers bring to them and to work with the composers themselves, each person adds his own little contributions, or "grains of sand," to the final arrangements, he explains. A person is not able to make changes to arrangements on his own, says Tino; instead, it is the joint effort of all the band members in the making of arrangements that allows their "great clan" to be able to continue. He emphasizes the fact that the small contributions made to improve their arrangements are not made in order to "change" *cuarteto;* to the contrary, the genre's basic essence must be maintained: "It's not that the music has to change. It's just that it should evolve so as to please the public. We try to see what they like. A person tries to listen to other kinds of music in order to see what he might be able to get out of them. And, well, we always try to make the music evolve in a way that suits the taste of the people."

Tino modestly says that he adds his own little "grains of sand" (ideas that are often inspired by music he listens to on the side) to the band's arrangements; since he does not compose a lot, this is the most important type of musical contribution that he makes to the group, he feels.

Although he is not a prolific songwriter, Tino is listed as being a co-composer of one tune on *Raza Negra* (Quinteros 1994; Quinteros 1995).

Luis Tapia

Manuel Luis "Tehuelche" (a type of Patagonian Indian) Tapia, who plays keyboards/piano and sings choruses in the group, was twenty-eight in 1994 (see figure 7.1b). Luis, who was born in Córdoba, has many musical brothers and sisters; his father, who loved folk music, arranged for all of them to take private lessons, which included theory and harmony. Since his father liked folk music so much, guitar (*guitarra criolla*) was the first instrument that Luis learned how to play. Although his early background was in folk music, he began playing with *cuarteto* groups when he was fifteen in order to pay for his music lessons; he had not really gone to *cuarteto* dances before this time. As a result of his work schedule, he dropped out of high school. Before he began playing with Jiménez, which happened soon after La Mona founded his band in 1984, Luis had played with three other *cuarteto* groups. Since one of these bands, Los Gitanos, was a group of young musicians sponsored by Jiménez, Carlos knew of Luis's work. Nowadays, Luis enjoys listening to all sorts of music (classical, salsa, and merengue, for example), but he has a passion for instrumental string music by Johann Strauss. After Jiménez retires, Luis hopes to become an arranger and a composer because earning his living as a *cuarteto* musician has been a hard kind of life to lead.

According to Luis, there are many creative people in the Jiménez group. He thinks that all of the band members feel a need to come up with new ideas and new material because they get suffocated by any kind of routine. He says that the band members have always felt this need to be creative, and that they have always tried to make their repertoire evolve musically, but that they managed to change their style noticeably only after the foreign musicians had arrived: "They brought their ways of playing to us. They brought us their ideas. They are creative men as well. But besides this, we have to adjust to them; if they are to fulfill a role, we have to compose based on what that role is. I have composed things I never even imagined that I was going to compose, even a salsa tune."

Although Luis has always composed and arranged for the group (he uses electronic equipment to make diskettes and also helps Jiménez to record and arrange Carlos's own compositions), he says that the arrival of the foreigners to the band has inspired him to create nonstandard rhythms on the drum machine and to then ask Bam Bam to learn how to play them. Although Bam Bam has not been able to understand where Luis has gotten these rhythms from, Luis is sure they have been inspired by ideas the three foreign musicians in the band have brought. In fact, Luis thinks that his biggest individual musical contribution to the group has been his musical ideas—no matter in what fashion they have been inspired. He describes himself as being an idea person who creates spontaneously, by jumping from one idea to the next, and says that it is impossible for him to remember all of the melodies that constantly run through his head—there are just too many of them. Often, since he is ahead of the times musically, he says, he must wait in order to be able to try out some of these ideas (Tapia 1994; Tapia 1995).

José Concha

José "Cabezón" ("Big Head") Concha is one of the musicians that left the Cuarteto de Oro with Jiménez in 1984; he plays accordion in the group, but also knows how to play keyboards (see figure 4.9). Age thirty-seven in 1994, he was born in Malagueño, a town near the city of Córdoba. Although there were not any musicians in his family, José's father sent him to take private lessons, at the age of eight, when he noticed that his son was making toy accordions out of boxes he played with. He eventually earned a four-year teaching degree in music. When José was small, he listened to *cuarteto* music and went to *cuarteto* dances to dance. Later, at the age of fifteen, he dropped out of high school and started his own *cuarteto* group, Los Universals. After his group folded, he played with Coquito Ramaló for three years before leaving the Cuarteto de Oro with Jiménez. Although the *moderno* style of *cuarteto* music is his favorite musical style, José now listens to peaceful music—not *cuarteto*— when he is at home. He says that the day Jiménez retires, he is not going to play with a lesser group. In any case, he wants to do some sort of activity that is much less hectic than playing *cuarteto* music is; he wants to be able to have his weekends free.

José feels that the band had evolved musically before the arrival of the three foreign percussionists, but that these new men have inspired considerable musical change in the group. "Before we couldn't do so much," he says, "but now we do more merengue, lots of merengue, and all of those things." He insists that the two basic elements of *cuarteto*, the accordion and the *tunga-tunga*, must remain despite any type of musical evolution that may occur in the genre. Regarding his own musical contributions in the group, José mentions the fact that he has composed original tunes for the band (he does not make diskettes with sequences). He emphasizes the fact, however, that his recent ideas have been inspired by their new percussion section, the Watusi. He also feels the fact he plays accordion, which is not used as much or in the same way as it was in the days of early *cuarteto*, limits his chances of contributing musically to the group (Concha 1994; Concha 1995).

Ricardo Verón

Ricardo Verón, who was forty-one in 1994, and Carlos Jiménez have been friends since they worked together in the Cuarteto de Oro; Verón is also a founding member of the present group (see figures 4.9 and 7.1a). Ricardo now plays bass guitar with the band, sings choruses, checks out the sound equipment for Jiménez, spontaneously chooses the order of the tunes that are performed each evening, calls out the names of the tunes that he has chosen to the musicians as the dance progresses, and arranges rehearsal and recording schedules. In the early days of the group, he also acted as the band's announcer when its true announcer played *timbales* in *tropical* selections. Jiménez often jokes by saying that he knows Verón better than he knows his own wife.

Ricardo, who was born in Córdoba, finished only primary school; since his mother died when he was very young and he had to help his father to take care of his siblings, he could not continue with his schooling. For as long as he can remember, he has liked music. For example, when he was five, he already sang, recited, and danced at school. Ricardo also has recollections of having gone to *cuarteto* dances to "study" the performers. Later on, after he had become a Beatles fan, he began playing the guitar. He switched to bass guitar at some point and also played percussion for a while. Ricardo eventually took some private lessons in order to be able to pass the exam that would allow him to get a *carnet de músico*. Then, at the age of seventeen or eighteen, he began playing *cuarteto* music to earn a living. By the time he started in the Cuarteto de Oro as a substitute performer, he had already played with several other groups. Although Ricardo now listens to various kinds of music (merengue, salsa, and Luis Miguel, for example), he prefers to listen to music that is slow and romantic.

According to Ricardo, everyone in the Jiménez group works together in order to come up with new musical ideas: "We have had the same way of working for a long time. We think that it is very beneficial for us to come up with a lot of ideas—all of us working together. We achieve a lot of things that way. I believe that ten people can think better together than can one mind alone. There are groups in which just one person, an arranger, decides everything—an arranger. Well, OK. We always contribute a lot of things individually, instead. Carlos accepts our ideas because that is also typical of the way our group works. Here, in spite of the fact that the Mona Jiménez is a solo singer, we do more ensemble work, as a group, than anything else."

Besides contributing ideas for arrangements, the band members all put their personal stamp on tunes that have been brought to them, says Ricardo. For example, since many songs are brought in as demos that have been recorded on electronic keyboards, the touch of the person who programs the sequences on the keyboards cannot be copied by the musicians who later have to copy the sequences with their instruments. "It is not the same to play a part on my bass as it is to play the same part on a keyboard," says Verón. "I cannot play like the keyboardist [who programs the sequences]," he adds. As a result, says Ricardo, each musician always adds small things to arrangements that are typical of his own way of playing.

According to Ricardo, everyone in the band wants to keep up with the times when they do new arrangements; however, no matter what many people think, they are not intentionally trying to "change" *cuarteto*: "Because we have enriched this music and have helped it to grow, people have gotten the wrong idea about us. They think that just because we have added certain things to the music, we want to change it. People need to be informed of the truth. This is a good opportunity to inform people that we are enriching the music that we do, not changing it. We always want there to be something new from 'La Mona.' We do not want the music to get monotonous and to have people say to us someday, 'Hey, you're doing the same thing that you did twenty years ago.' We want people to say, 'Hey, what you are doing is nice. It has rhythm and you keep changing small things.'" What the Jiménez group does, says Verón, is to maintain the basic *cuarteto* foundation, above which any "changes" are made. It is true that the forms, figures, and rhythmic patterns of his bass parts have evolved somewhat from the days of early *cuarteto*, he says, but the basic elements of the genre (the *tunga-tunga* and the accordion), despite having been enriched, remain in the band's music, he insists.

Regarding his individual musical contribution to the group, Ricardo points out that he composes many tunes for the band by using a friend's computer and that he gets many of his musical ideas by consciously listening to lots of music. "One learns a lot and is nourished by listening to a lot of new music," he says. He feels that his individual contribution to the group as a bass player has also been very important: "One of the secrets of playing the bass is to be precise and to play with good tone. Precision is important. In other words, I believe that every percussionist [should understand the function of the bass]. . . . Despite being a string instrument, the bass has a percussive sound. Since the bass forms the foundation upon which the rest of the music is built, you need to be very precise when you play it, and you need to have a special talent for controlling the speed [of the *tunga-tunga*]. The foundation has to be well constructed."

Ricardo hopes be a producer, composer, and arranger when he retires from performing so as to put the knowledge he has gained with Jiménez to good use. Since he currently produces a group of young men getting started in *cuarteto*, he has begun to move toward his goal (Verón 1994a; Verón 1994b).

Tito Avedaño

Pedro "Tito" Avedaño, one of Jiménez's two announcers, was forty-three in 1994 (see figure 4.9). Although Tito, who was born in Córdoba, has never had any formal training in either announcing or in music, he has listened to music since the time that he was small: first to the *orquestas características* and later to *cuarteto*, his preferred style. Since he began working when he was in his teens, he dropped out of high school. Although he was also a Beatles and a Sandro fan, he has been professionally involved with *cuarteto* music since he was young. In his youth, Tito lived near La Sociedad Belgrano, where many *cuarteto* dances were held. Instead of actually going to the dances, he and a friend did publicity for some of the vendors outside the locale, just for fun. One day, at Carnival time, Alberto Tosas suddenly needed an announcer for his group. When he heard Tito "working" outside the dance hall, he asked him to help out. Tito did, and ended up staying with the group, which basically did a *moderno* style of music, until Ramaló asked him to work with the Cuarteto de Oro. At the time Jiménez left the Cuarteto de Oro, Tito went with him to be his announcer.

When Jiménez first went on his own, Tito played *timbales* on the group's *tropical* numbers. Besides this temporary musical role he formerly had with the band, Tito feels that his musical contribution to the group has been very limited. Instead, he says, his job has always been to do public relations. For example, he has long had an FM radio program on which the band's music is mentioned. Although his involvement in the group's musical matters is minimal, Tito says that the band members work very hard and try to do their best musically. He feels that the style of the group has changed quite abruptly with the arrival of the foreign percussionists but that people still keep coming to Jiménez dances anyway. Tito is not sure, but he might go into radio work when he retires (Avedaño 1994; Avedaño 1995).

Mario Salinas

Mario Salinas, who is nicknamed both "El Lagarto" (The Lizard) and "El Matador" (The Killer), is the other Jiménez announcer (see figure 4.9). Mario, age thirty-eight in 1994, was born in Córdoba. Although there were no musicians or announcers in his family, he and a friend began acting as announcers at shows and parties when they were both young. Before going into *cuarteto*, he also worked as a disc jockey at a disco. (Mario has always liked both disco music and *cuarteto;* he now listens to updated versions of the same music by groups such as Los Enanitos Verdes and Los Fabulosos Cadillacs.) He has been working as a *cuarteto* announcer for approximately twenty years now (he has worked with Berna, the Doble Cuarteto, and Ariel Ferrari), ten of which have been with Jiménez. Mario assumes that he will do FM radio work the day he is no longer with the Jiménez group, although he did finish high school and is a certified typist. He had wanted to study at the university level, but his father's death forced him to change his plans.

Mario says that his individual musical contributions to the group are extremely limited. He does occasionally sing in fun with the band at Carnival time and may sing along unofficially at times with choruses, but his role as an announcer does not permit him to be innovative; instead, since Jiménez is a solo singer and cannot be overshadowed, he must fit into what has normally been planned for performances, he says. Mario likes to compose song lyrics and tunes, but says that his original material is not used by the Jiménez band. He feels that if he were a musician in the group, his musical contribution would be much greater (Salinas 1995a; Salinas 1995b).

Carlos Jiménez

Juan Carlos Jiménez Rufino (see figure 5.10) is the full name of Carlitos "La Mona" Jiménez (Hepp 1988:83), the symbol of *cuarteto* music. The singer, who was born in 1951, got his nickname of "La Mona" ("The Female Monkey" [in this case meaning Chimpanzee]) at the age of seven. When he and his young friends used to play in their treehouse, they liked to pretend that they were Tarzan. Jiménez's friends decided that he looked more like "*la mona Chita*" (Chita, the female monkey) than Tarzan, so they gave him the nickname he still has today (SADAIC 1992:20). Jiménez, who never liked being called Chita, would run home to his mother, who would tell him that yes, he really was like Tarzan (Mareco 6 September 1992:7F).

Carlos Jiménez's curly black hair, facial features, and skin color (it is darker than white) would seem to indicate that he is the product of a mixed racial background. When asked about his heritage, Jiménez says that he is a *mestizo* with no African blood; he is a descendant of the *comechingones* and *tobas* (two Indian groups from the region), one of his grandmothers was from Catamarca (in northern Argentina), and he had some Spanish ancestors (Jiménez Rufino 1994). Because of his physical appearance, some people might put him into the category of *cabecita negra* or *negro*. His band members and followers exhibit similar physical characteristics and skin color, and a few of his band members speak of their Indian or *mestizo* heritage. As has been stated above, for example, Luis Tapia goes by the nickname of Tehuelche.

La Mona was born and grew up in a blue-collar area of Córdoba, his father being an EPEC (Empresa Pública de Energía de Córdoba) employee. He finished elementary school (sixth grade), but his numerous absences resulted in his dismissal from secondary school (Hepp 1988: 83). From the very beginning, he was exposed to many kinds of music. His father, for example, played guitar and harmonica for Carlos and his brother when they were small (SADAIC 1992:20). Since the brothers' uncle, Coquito Ramaló, worked in the box offices of the dance halls in which the Cuarteto Leo performed and was also a *cuarteto* singer, La Mona became an early *cuarteto* fan as well (SADAIC 1992:20). Carlos danced at *cuarteto* dances (he also danced folk styles, tango, and rock and roll very well) and loved nightlife right from the start (Hepp 1988:84); he often climbed in through a window during the wee hours of the morning so that his father would not know that he had been out having a good time (SADAIC 1992:20). Besides enjoying *cuarteto,* Carlos and his brother listened to Beatles' music when they were young (Hepp 1988: 84; Mareco 6 September 1992:7F). After Carlos's brother had a motorcycle accident (the two had been given motorcycles), their father gave Carlos an electric guitar and his brother a drum set in order to deter them from riding their motorcycles anymore; Carlos was fifteen at the time. As a result, the two boys played rock music for fun (Mero 1988:24–25; Mareco 6 September 1992:7F). At one point, Carlos even sang tango in a club—illegally, since he was a minor at the time (Hepp 1988:84).

Jiménez, who has had no musical or vocal training of any kind, began his professional singing career at the age of fifteen. This happened when his Uncle Ramaló encouraged him to enter a singing contest; a new group, the Cuarteto Berna, was being formed, and it was having a contest to select a singer (SADAIC 1992:20–21). La Mona won the contest due to his great ability to imitate José Sosa Mendieta, the singer of the Cuarteto Leo (Mareco 6 September 1992:7F). In 1972, Jiménez left Berna to work in the Cuarteto de Oro, which belonged to his Uncle Ramaló, and in 1984, he left Ramaló in order to form the group that he still has today (Hepp 1988:85). Immediately before he left the Cuarteto de Oro, Carlos had an operation to remove some polyps from his throat (Mero 1988:46). While he spent two months recuperating, he was covered by a singer named Piruchio and by some men who had entered a contest that Ramaló had sponsored in order to find the person who could best imitate Carlos.

Jiménez's individual contributions to *cuarteto* go far beyond what he does in his own group (see chapter 7 for detailed information on Jiménez, his personality, his overall importance to his fans, and his lasting role in *cuarteto*). Loved by all, and famous as being a Robin Hood figure who gives away money, cars, and houses to the poor, it has even been suggested that he run for political office (Barei 1993:55; Mero 1988:68, 162–64). Many working-class people see him as a symbol of one of their kind who has made it to the top but without having turned his back on them (Hepp 1988:18–23). His fans idolize him for what he represents—not for his singing voice. In fact, Jiménez says that his job is to make people happy. He is not a true singer, he insists, but does sing from the heart and with feeling (SADAIC 1992:20).

Jiménez is the symbol of traditional *cuarteto,* yet he is also an innovator who has paved the way for many other *cuarteto* musicians (Gregoratti and Arrascaeta 24 July 1995:C1). He brought the genre to the whole country as a result of his 1988 Cosquín appearance and opened doors for fusions with *Raza Negra* in 1994 (Lewin 1994:223; "Carlitos Jiménez presenta" 18 September 1994:4C). He could have been the first *cuarteto* artist to have launched the genre in the United States, since in 1989 or 1990 a Mexican entrepreneur offered to promote him there. He turned down the offer because his band members, who would not have been playing at dances while they were in the United States with him, would have lost all their income earned from dances during the month or so they would have been outside Argentina. Since Jiménez has always felt that his band members are friends and colleagues, and that he is merely a person who gives them work, he is worried about what will happen to the men when he retires; he does not like thinking ahead or about their future. As he has no real education or musical training himself, he has no idea what he will be able to do after he stops singing, either (Jiménez Rufino 1994).

Within his own group, Jiménez makes many individual musical con-tributions. Being the solo singer of the band he makes all of the final decisions about what repertoire will be recorded and performed, yet he makes many of his choices after having consulted with all of the band members. As Jiménez sees it, he is not more important than anyone else in the group. He also hires the band personnel and has been known to take on certain men in order to help them out financially—not because he has needed them. Although he composes and helps with arranging as well, he leaves much up to the individual musicians; everyone is ex-pected to contribute freely in the group (as though they were all owners), musical decision-making is delegated, and creativity is encouraged. Jiménez makes an effort to listen to all different types of music in order to get new ideas for his band's style. Since he is very open-minded, spontaneous, and intuitive, many of his decisions are made as a result of whatever happens to come up or is available. He jumps from one idea to the next, soaking up suggestions and new opportunities. As has been described in chapter 5, Luis Tapia assists him in capturing his ideas for songs and putting together demos.

Setting the Scene: The Departure from the Cuarteto de Oro

When Carlos Jiménez left the Cuarteto Berna to join the Cuarteto de Oro, which was directed by his uncle, Coquito Ramaló, it was for personal reasons. In Berna, he had been forced to sing rigidly in front of a microphone and had not been allowed to dance or move around so as not to overshadow Berna Bevilaqua, the "star" of the group (Mareco 6 September 1992:7F). (Jiménez has always been famous for his dancing on stage; for many years he was banned on television because his dancing was thought to have been pornographic.) Since he had not been able to act like himself with such management policies and was not making much money with Berna, Jiménez moved on to the Cuarteto de Oro when his uncle offered him a job (SADAIC 1992:21).

When Jiménez left the Cuarteto de Oro to form his own group, the band that he still has today, in 1984, it was for much more serious reasons. Four of the members of the Cuarteto de Oro left with him as well despite the fact that Ramaló had left them with nothing: they did not even have their own instruments (Mero 1988:45). When these men founded their group, it was because they had serious problems with some of Ramaló's policies; they wanted to work in a different way. Since these founding principles are still manifested in the group's musical style, processes of musical decision-making, and general operations today, it is very important to understand both the reasons why these men left Ramaló's group and the actions they took as a consequence—in order to "rectify" what they were dissatisfied with—when they formed their own band.

First of all, the men who left Ramaló did so because they did not like his management style or personality. One man put it as follows: "At that time, the criteria by which we worked were very different from those that we now live by. We were directed by Ramaló, who ran the group like a drill sergeant, and who put a great amount of distance between himself and the band members. He even distanced himself from the audience" (Mero 1988:35–36).

The men decided to leave with Carlos, which was a huge risk, because his personality was completely the opposite of Ramaló's and since he had good rapport with audiences:

"The reaction of the audience was always different with Jiménez [than it was with Ramaló]," remembers [José] Concha. "Carlos was always an idol to his fans, and he responded to them appropriately. This was quite different from their reaction to Ramaló, who was a very rude and distant guy. It is for these reasons that when it came time to leave the group, we decided to continue on with Jiménez. We perhaps did so because he had never turned his back on his old neighborhood [and friends]. We believed that with [Carlos], we could go forward. That's why it was that we left with him, despite the odds against us, in 1984." (Mero 1988:37)

From the start, the Jiménez clan was thus a group that did not want to be run in a hierarchical fashion. The four members of the Cuarteto de Oro who left to join Jiménez, Ricardo Verón (bass), José Concha (accordion), Luis Gómez (piano), and Tito Avedaño (announcer), were joined by Ramaló's sound man, Mario Carnero, and his handlers. Carnero was asked to play percussion, as was Tribilín, a former rock performer. Pupi Rojo was brought in to play keyboards (no violinists were available, so he was hired to simulate the violin part), and "Negro" Elías was hired to sing one *tropical* set before Carlos began singing (Mero 1988:48–49).

The men who left Ramaló had not been happy with his manner of doing recordings, either (Mero 1988:40). To record one entire album, for example, Ramaló would give them only five days. The work was boring, the arrangements were not good (only a couple of new ones were added on each recording), new repertoire was not included (nor were new composers drawn upon), and the group sounded just as the Cuarteto Leo had many years before: "We were aware that this was not right," recalls Verón. "We went to record knowing that we had a set time limit in which to finish. They also told us what we had to do. Now we take as much time as we need, even if we do not sleep or eat, in order to do things well" (Mero 1988:40).

Another problem that came up with Ramaló was that instead of singing half of the tunes per dance, as he should have, he had begun to make Jiménez sing for almost the entire evening alone. "Go on out and sing. I'm tired," he would say to Carlos (Mero 1988:48). In the end, Ramaló was singing only four or five songs during an entire evening. Instead of singing, he had begun to act like an accountant running a business (Mero 1988:48).

The biggest gripe the men had with Ramaló, however, was that the Cuarteto de Oro was not keeping up with the times musically. Young people had stopped coming to the dances because they could not identify with either the repertoire or the instrumentation that was being used in the group. According to Verón, the world had evolved, but Ramaló's music had remained ten years behind what people wanted (Mero 1988: 38); in the thirteen years that some of the men (Jiménez, for example) had been with the Cuarteto de Oro, there had been no changes of any kind made in it. It was for this reason that Jiménez came up with the idea of founding and leading his own group, one with "another style, another mentality" (Mero 1988:38).

In a personal interview, Jiménez explained that young people had stopped coming to the dances because they did not know how to dance to the "old" music that was being performed by the Cuarteto de Oro (*pasodobles*, foxtrots, rumbas, etc.). A change was definitely needed: "We could not keep on playing *pasodobles* and *rancheras* and *tarantelas* because the young people [didn't want us to]. . . . it was only people who were over fifty who were coming to dance with us. The young people didn't come to dance with us because they didn't want to sing 'da da da tum.' They didn't want to dance *tarantelas* and *pasodobles*. They wanted to dance to what they were listening to on the radio, instead. What happens is that the world changes and you have to change along with it. You can't use the same dresses today that your great-grandmother used to wear" (Jiménez Rufino 1994).

In order to remedy the situation, Carlos tried to make some changes in the group's repertoire. Unfortunately, his efforts were not received favorably:

The first conflict [with Ramaló] came about when I decided to sing "Amor de Compra y Venta" ("Love That Is Bought and Sold"; D.R.), a song by a Spanish group called Los Chichos that a friend of mine who came to visit from Spain had brought to me. I changed it around and arranged it so that it would sound like *cuarteto*, going by the fact that it has the structure of a *pasodoble*. I showed it to Ramaló, who told me that it was a song for prostitutes. I said that wasn't true, that people would dance to it, and that it wasn't for prostitutes. Despite all of this, I sang it. In addition, I have sung it at every dance that I have performed at since 1980, the date when this happened. (Jiménez, quoted in Mero 1988:47)

There were additional frustrations and irreconcilable differences that finally led Jiménez to leave Ramaló:

I left [the Cuarteto de Oro] because I thought it had reached the end of its cycle. . . . No progress was being made, we didn't have the necessary equipment, and the sound system was bad. I was singing with a microphone that was falling apart, that was coming to pieces. I had to tie it together with a string. I was fed up. . . .

It had always been like this. After I was operated on to remove seven polyps that I had in my throat, I was practically speechless for two months. I couldn't talk and my head was spinning around. I decided that if I were going to have to return [to a group] without proper sound [equipment], without lights, and without any of the basics that a band must have, it would be better to never sing again. I'll go carry bags in the Abastos market instead [if I need to find work], I thought.

I met with Ramaló and told him that I wanted to change, that I wanted to do things in another way. I offered him the possibility to do it, but he didn't want to. He said what for, if everything was fine as it was. I told him that I had to leave then. Those two months after the operation were very sad, wondering what was going to happen to me. (Jiménez, quoted in Mero 1988:46)

Because leaving Ramaló was such a big step, the five men who left the group planned for one year before they called it quits. According to Ricardo Verón, the last album that they did with Ramaló was in fact "theirs" (Verón 1994a; Verón 1994b). At Verón's suggestion, they arranged everything on their last long play differently and started to change the repertoire that was being used in Ramaló's group. When they finally did leave, they were thus ready to fend for themselves. The instrumentation they came up with for their band was unique for the time: bass guitar, keyboards (to replace the violin), electric piano, accordion, *timbales*, and congas (Verón 1994a; Verón 1994b). Since Jiménez had undergone an operation and could not sing for an entire four hours, a different singer did a *tropical* set before La Mona came on (Mero 1988:49).

When they founded their group, the five men were advised to get rid of the accordion. Since at that time it was all the rage to imitate a Caribbean or Central American style of ensemble, which had brass and wind instruments, people thought they were foolish not to go along with the crowd. As Verón put it, "nobody wanted to pick up an accordion anymore or to do the *tunga-tunga*. Instead, they were trying to do another kind of music" (Mero 1988:38). Jiménez never considered copying that style, because among other things, he thought it was an imitation of "Central American" music—not *cuarteto* (Mero 1988:38). On top of that, since Chébere had added these instruments, he could not imitate its sound; he had to "bring out the difference between the styles and conserve the *cuarteto* tradition" (Mareco 6 September 1992:7F).

To Jiménez, it was impossible even to think of eliminating the accordion from the group. As he puts it, "The accordion is the spirit of Córdoba, of *cuarteto* music. It is a symbol" (Jiménez Rufino 1994). All of the men who formed the band agreed that the accordion was important to them as an identity symbol. If they had formed a group without it, and had added wind instruments instead, their identity would have been lost, says Ricardo Verón: "'No, we are going to keep the accordion until we die,' we said. 'We have an identifying trademark.' As we have always said, our group is like Coca Cola. That is, we have always believed that over time we have had good results. Something can be mediocre, good, or bad. If it is original, however, it helps to establish an identity. Yes, it is important to have one's own identity. We are original and we are the manufacturers of our own product" (Verón 1994a; Verón 1994b).

The men decided to use the traditional *cuarteto* instrumentation, based around the accordion, but with an updated, youthful sound in their new group. Part of this meant adding strings, like more violins and violoncellos, and electronic keyboards (Mareco 6 September 1992:7F). The strings could often be used only on recordings (two men from the local symphony orchestra usually recorded with them, and in April 1985, five string players from the symphony performed with the group; Mero 1988:108), and most of the time had to be simulated with keyboards; due to circumstances beyond his control, Jiménez had to adapt his idea of how a *cuarteto* group should ideally be put together:

A *cuarteto* group must have a bass, a piano, and an accordion. I don't have a violin, but I have keyboards that [imitate] violins. This happened because it is only recently that violinists are appearing,

young boys. At the time I created my group, there weren't any. . . .
At that time, the youngest violinist around was sixty years old.
There weren't any violinists who were thirty or twenty-eight. There
just weren't any. I had to go out and look for a keyboard player to
replace the violin. In a recording, on a record, I used a viola, a cello
. . . that is, five string players from the symphony. It was spectacular.
You have no idea what that *cuarteto* group was like. It was wonderful. That is my dream . . . I love strings. (Jiménez Rufino 1994)

The result of the new instrumentation and repertoire was very positive
for the band. On its first recording, the song "La Flaca La Gasta" (C.
JIMÉNEZ—R. VERÓN—E. GÓMEZ) became a big hit (Mero 1988:
48). As a result, most of the other groups once again added accordions
to their bands; only a few of them kept trumpets. "The rest returned,
with changes, to the basic elements" (Mero 1988:48). The audience
reaction was also very good: "The fans reacted favorably to the independence of Jiménez in 1984 . . . because they felt they were now being
represented. New tunes, new instruments, and new lyrics were incorporated that attracted a new, younger audience" (Mero 1988:35–36).

What the Jiménez band members say should be remembered about
this whole process of updating and modernizing *cuarteto* is that they have
always been trying to "improve" it, not "change" it; the *tunga-tunga* must
remain in the bass and the piano parts and the sound of the accordion
must be present. Instead of using the word "change," which implies that
cuarteto music might become unrecognizable or even turn into something else, they prefer to use the word "evolve." As Jiménez has stated,
cuarteto is in a continual process of evolution: "I am sure that our music
is constantly evolving. In our group, we maintain a certain format inherent to *cuarteto*, using the keyboards and the bass, but in each new recording we achieve a new sound. While we are doing this, we are always trying
not to lose the connection that exists between young people and my
music" (Gregoratti 24 May 1993:1C).

As has been stated above, the 1984 group had two Latin percussion
instruments: *timbales* and congas. From the start, says Verón, all of the
band members were interested in doing Caribbean music; for this reason, they recorded one pseudo-salsa number on their first album.
"Tiremos la Casa por la Ventana" ("Let's Throw the House Out the
Window"; R. VERÓN—J. DELSERI—DON FILINTO), a different
salsa-style tune they were advised not to record, became the hit tune on

one long play they did shortly after that. Although the song became popular, Verón insisted it did not have enough percussion. He also predicted that one day the group would have really good percussionists and that the band members would see that more percussion could be successfully added to *cuarteto*.

According to Verón, from the beginning, all of the men realized that the percussionists in their group could play only basic rhythms in a very square fashion. They did the best they could until the three foreigners from Peru, the Dominican Republic, and Ecuador joined the band:

> There was a whole series of things we could not do because we did not have the percussion players that we needed. So as time passed, and we got these fellows (the Peruvian, the Dominican) we could get where we wanted to. . . . For example, the other day we were rehearsing while we were traveling. We were . . . singing a tune that we had wanted to do in 1987 or 1988, sometime around then, but could not do at the time because we did not have the necessary percussionists. We had always had this idea [of adding more percussion]. We had rhythms that . . . although we did not have a [good] conga player, for example, we put them together. . . . I now put together a lot of rhythms on the drum machine—a ton of rhythms that Bam Bam plays for me. I set them up for him on the drum machine. I bring them to him all put together. Afterwards, they all get erased [they are played live—not with the drum machine—in dances] once he has learned them, of course. (Verón 1994b)

It is Verón's feeling that if Bam Bam had not arrived to play congas, someone else would have; the desire to add percussion was always there in the band. After Bam Bam joined the group, Tribi was moved to *güiro* and electric guitar.

Verón also feels that the music of Juan Luis Guerra has had an important influence on the group's style; it has encouraged them to add percussion instruments to their music and has changed the way in which these instruments are used in the band. Although salsa has long been listened to in Argentina, says Verón, Guerra was the source of a merengue craze in the country; he became successful in Argentina because he promoted himself intelligently and launched his campaign from Europe. Verón insists that Guerra "educated" all of the Jiménez band members:

"He educated us because, for example, on this latest compact disc [*Raza Negra*], I have managed to accomplish a few things. They are technical things. I said to the guys, 'Look, I would like the high frequencies of the percussion instruments to sound like the ones that Juan Luis Guerra uses.' On this recording, we have achieved this . . . with the *güira* and the sound of the *tambora*" (Verón 1994b).

In 1984, yet another precedent was set in the group that would reappear in later years: Jiménez hired someone to perform in the band almost exclusively because the man needed a job. Not only that, this person was hired to play an instrument he had never before played:

> One day I was in downtown Córdoba and Tribilín appeared. That is, [L.M.A.], a member of the rock group Años Luz, a friend of Freddy Zaveley from the rock recitals that were held in La Falda. Tribilín said that he was without work and that he would like to come and play with us. I was putting the group together just then. I knew that I was up against two months of postoperative recuperation and that I had to come up with something from one minute to the next. I asked him how he thought he was going to play *cuarteto* if he was a rock musician and played electric guitar—especially since I did not have an electric guitar in my group. He started to tease me and to say that, well, it was a challenge, and he came home with me. I tried him out on percussion and he worked out. (Jiménez, quoted in Mero 1988:49)

In conclusion, many of the musical policies and principles that are followed by the group of Carlos Jiménez today, as well as some of his "new" ideas, were already in place when the band was founded in 1984. From the start, the band has operated as a group in which there is no distance between Jiménez and the band members or between the band members and the public; individuals have always pooled their ideas and resources and have stated their own opinions. For example, it was Verón, not Jiménez, who suggested that they might begin to update the Cuarteto de Oro's arrangements in order to prepare themselves for their 1984 departure. Verón was also the person who first pointed out that they could use more percussion in the band as well. The band members work as many hours as are necessary in order that both they and their followers will be satisfied with the final product. From the start, their mission has been to renovate *cuarteto* music so as to keep it up with the times, regarding instrumentation, sound, and repertoire, but while simultaneously maintaining the traditional *cuarteto* identity and being original. The group has always been interested in Caribbean music and the addition of percussion instruments as a way of "improving" *cuarteto* music as well. And, lastly, Carlos Jiménez has always shown a great personal concern for his band members; he has treated them more like friends than employees from the very beginning.

The Truth behind *Raza Negra*

Upon reading the newspaper and magazine articles that were published about *Raza Negra,* one gets the distinct impression that Carlos Jiménez deliberately planned every phase of the recording's creation: he had wanted to make a tribute to the black race and had needed to introduce something new to the *cuarteto* world in order to keep up with the competition, so he had done both things at the same time. When I interviewed Jiménez shortly after the compact disc was launched, I discovered that none of this was true. To the contrary, almost nothing about *Raza Negra* had been planned at all. Jiménez had not begun recording the disc with the intention of making a tribute to the black race or African slaves, nor had he wanted to "change" the music of Córdoba with his efforts. The recording was the result of several things that had occurred by chance: the addition of three foreign percussionists to the group (and their resulting musical influence), two trips that Jiménez had made abroad, and some foreign musical genres that he had been exposed to.

When I interviewed Jiménez and asked him how *Raza Negra* had come to be created, he began by stating that the three foreign members of his group, Bam Bam, Abraham, and Byron, had been influential in introducing new rhythmic patterns to the band. He then made it very clear, however, that he had not planned to hire these men at all, much less to have made an Afro-Caribbean recording drawing upon their talents. According to Jiménez, Abraham had not been in his plans when he had started recording. Since Byron's contribution had been totally unexpected, his name was not even put into the liner notes. To prove his point, Carlos told me in chronological order the stories of how the three men had come to join his group.

When Carlos and Bam Bam met for the first time, Bam Bam had already been in Argentina for several years. As Carlos explained, it was

Bam Bam who approached him one day—not the other way around: "He came and said to me one day [while I was recording in a studio], 'Mona . . . I would really like to play with you someday.' I answered, 'Well, maybe, call me up around Carnival time. Maybe I can invite you to play on the next album with me. For me it would be a pleasure.' The problem was that I already had another person performing with me. No, excuse me, let me clarify that. The guy who plays guitar was playing congas then" (Jiménez Rufino 1994).

Later, as fate had it, Bam Bam did begin playing with the Jiménez band after Carnival. Keeping in mind the fact that the band members had always wanted to have more percussion, it may be that Bam Bam was hired because he was in the right place at the right time.

When Abraham began playing with the group, it was because he, like Bam Bam, had approached Jiménez. In his case, however, he had asked Carlos for a temporary job. Abraham, who had been brought to Córdoba by Ángel Videla, had been forced to find work with several *cuarteto* groups when Videla's merengue orchestra had been restructured. He approached Jiménez to ask him for work because he was trying to save money in order to go back to his country. Carlos told the story as follows:

So he was here [in Córdoba]. . . . I had a club that was called La Cueva. Well, one day [about a year and a half ago], when I was leaving the club, getting ready to record the album [*Raza Negra*], he showed up. I said hello and he asked if he could come in. I said of course, come in. And there he was. And he said, "This is really great music to play with *tambora.*" And I told him to go and get it— his *tambora.* "I live just around the corner," he said. "Go and get it," I said. So he came with the *tambora* and we rehearsed a tune.

We were going to record it [the tune], but he didn't show up for the recording session. They [the groups that he was working with] didn't let him come or else he stood me up. In other words, we had rehearsed with the *tambora*, but just one tune. And then he didn't come. . . .

When he appeared, I asked him if he was going to come with us. He said, "Fine, but I need some sort of security because I . . . I need to go back to my country. Could you give me work for four months so that I could save money? I don't have money to go back home." I said, "Of course, for four months, of course." . . . "Put together the contract, then," he said. In other words, I did not ask him to come [to play with us]. He came to my house to ask me for work in order to be able to save up money to go back to his country. So I said, "Of course, man, starting immediately. When are you going to start work?" He showed up [at my house] on a Tuesday, and I told him to begin work on Friday. "And what should I do?" he asked. "Do whatever you want," I said. "In the repertoire, play when you think that you should play. When you don't want to play [*tambora*], don't. Stop and play the *güira* then. Do whatever you know how to do, do whatever you want." He got to me. So he didn't come to look for work and I didn't send for him or take him away from another group. I gave him work so that he could save money.

And well, after four months . . . he . . . asked me if I could give him a contract for another four months. "Because I'm saving money," he said. (He's asking me for even more, is what I thought.) "Because I am from a family of fourteen children, and . . ." Fourteen brothers and sisters! But by this time, I had gotten used to his playing and liked it. I had gotten used to his *tu tu tu* coming out of his *tambora*. I had gotten used to it. He said that he would like to stay on with me for eight months. "It's not a problem," I said to him. (Jiménez Rufino 1994)

After having saved up money for eight months, Abraham went to Santo Domingo to rent a house for his family. When he returned to Córdoba, he remained with the band.

When Byron began performing with the group, it was because he, like Abraham, had asked Carlos for a temporary job. In Byron's case, however, one of the band members had suggested that he approach Carlos for work; he had been told that because of a misunderstanding that had occurred while the group was recording *Raza Negra* in Buenos Aires, one of the musicians might be leaving the band and would have to be replaced. Carlos told me the story of Byron's arrival to the group as follows:

He appeared ringing the doorbell [at my house]. Ding. "Hello, I'm from Ecuador," he said. He sat with me back in the lounge and, like you, appeared at two in the afternoon. And I said, "What is it that you do?" "I am a percussionist," he said. One of the band members had told him to come and see me, that I might need a musician.

. . . "Well, what do you know how to play?" I asked. . . . "I dance," he said. "And what do you dance?" I then asked him. "I do African dance," he said. . . . And I thought, What in hell's name? . . . and it was a Wednesday. "Fine," I said, "come to the dance on Friday and watch what the band does. Go to Atenas on Friday and watch." And Byron showed up and watched.

Well, the Ecuadorian, I had him get up on stage and I watched him dance. And I said to him, "Man, what am I going to do with you?" And he said, "I want to go to Ecuador. . . . I left Ecuador with a group of dancers [about a year ago] and I have been traveling around Chile, Ecuador, Peru, Buenos Aires, and lots of places. And well, I am here now and I do not have a job." Oh, the same old trick, I said to myself. And what was I supposed to do? "Well, OK, what do you need?" I asked him. "Work," he said. And I thought to myself, I have to give him work so that he can go back to his country. That's the first thing that I have to do. (Jiménez Rufino 1994)

Carlos then told me that he had never thought about adding dance—African or any other kind—to the group. Due to the circumstances, however, Byron has been allowed to "do his own thing" right from the start.

After Carlos had told me the stories about how the three foreign musicians had joined his group, he spoke more specifically about *Raza Negra* itself. In order to convince me that the whole project had been unplanned, he explained how he had come up with the title of the recording:

I was in Brazil. . . . I heard . . . or . . . I saw [a poster in São Paulo] that said "Raza Negra." And I thought, Well, what . . . a great title for a tune, . . . since I feel as though I were part of a black race that is completely marginalized . . . the black race of *cuarteto* music. Because before, when I walked down the streets of Córdoba, when I walked out on the sidewalk, people yelled "Hey you" at me. This happened to me when I was sixteen or seventeen years old. They knew that I sang *cuarteto* so they would say, "Put your head down. Here comes that black piece of shit who sings *cuarteto*," to me just as loudly as you would talk to someone who was standing across the street. Loudly, so that I would hear them. And I felt very bad. . . . I thought of the title based on what happened to me. (Jiménez Rufino 1994)

In fact, when the band began recording the album that was finally named *Raza Negra,* Carlos had not yet made the trip to Brazil during which he got the idea for the compact disc's title. As he explained to me, before he had made the trip, he had not been planning to record anything that had to do with the black race at all: "No, [the whole thing was unplanned,] because I went to Brazil during the month when we recorded *Raza Negra.* We recorded the compact disc in twenty days. [After I returned from my trip] I said to Tapia, 'Look, I have a crazy idea, we have to do *Raza Negra.*' I told him that we should do something about the black race, but that we would have to speak about things from Argentina; if we used Brazilian names of things [Brazilian crops that are mentioned] in the song, nobody would understand us. We would have to translate 'mandioca' and a lot of other words just like it" (Jiménez Rufino 1994).

Jiménez then explained that some of the Afro-Caribbean musical influences on the recording, the use of merengue and rap, for example, were the result of a trip that he had made to Miami in 1989 or 1990. After the tune "¿Quién Se Tomó Todo el Vino?" had become a tremendous hit, a Mexican impresario had brought him to the United States with the idea of promoting his music in the Latin market. In fact, this man had wanted the whole band to make the trip (which did not happen). When he was in Miami, Jiménez was exposed to merengue and rap for the first time (salsa music had arrived in Argentina long before this time, Carlos said, but not merengue and rap).

Although Carlos said that he had never had any intention of performing merengue music in Córdoba, he had liked a Juan Luis Guerra tune ("Burbujas de Amor") that he had heard in Miami so much that he had done a *cuarteto*-style cover version of it soon after he had returned to Córdoba. But when he was doing *Raza Negra,* he did not consciously try to do merengue on it; instead, since he was still evidently under the influence of his trip to Miami, the use of merengue on it had been done unconsciously. His use of rap mixed with *cuarteto* on *Raza Negra* was consciously planned, however. As Carlos explained it to me, the musical genres that he had heard in Miami were "influences." "Everything you hear can have an influence on you. The only thing that I put on the recording on purpose was a rap tune, just one rap tune. That was on purpose."

Carlos admitted that the foreign members of the group, once they were incorporated, did have an impact on the Afro-Caribbean genres and songs that were recorded on *Raza Negra* as well. For example, Abraham brought him a merengue that he had composed, called "No Soy Dios Para Perdonar" ("I'm Not God So I Can't Forgive You" JIMÉNEZ—ROJO —VÁSQUEZ-MARTÍNEZ). Carlos did accept Abraham's merengue, but he changed it around some, as he normally does when he is brought an original composition. "I'm crazy," says Carlos. "No, it's true, I'm crazy. I change all of the tunes around because if I have to sing a song and I can't feel it, I just can't sing it." In other words, he accepted ideas from band members for the recording, but he added his own personal touch to the Afro-Caribbean genres that were recorded; none of this happened in a calculated fashion so as to "change" *cuarteto* music or to keep up with the competition. Regarding Abraham's merengue, for example, he had the following to say:

> I changed the melody on him a little. Ask him about it someday. He brought it to me like this and I changed it around. "We're going to change it," I said. "The introduction goes here. This part goes in the middle, and the lyrics don't go like this. When I finish singing, you should come in with ta ta ta . . ." Here each person says what he wants to; each person speaks his mind. And after that I say, "No, let's stop." And then I say, . . . "Stop, man, I don't like that arrangement. [I put my stamp on it.] Why? I just don't like it as it is. I don't like it." I don't know anything about music, but I have ideas. (Jiménez Rufino 1994)

The Story of "Penita"

During my stay in Córdoba, I had an unforgettable experience: I recorded one tune, "Penita," on *El Marginal*. I played piccolo in the song, an instrument that had never before been used in either a *cuarteto* recording or on stage. In fact, flutes have not been used in *cuarteto* music, either, and no female instrumentalist had performed with a *cuarteto* group since Leonor Marzano played with the Cuarteto Leo. Augusto Marzano was an amateur flutist, but had mostly played his flute at home with Leonor accompanying him on piano (Mareco 6 June 1993:F1; "Un emblema" 13 January 1993:C1). Before I recorded with the group, which I did on my next to last day in Córdoba, I also rehearsed with the band members and performed live at two dances. Both observing how these performance opportunities arose and becoming one of the musicians gave me an inside look at how all of the individuals in the band are involved in the processes of musical decision-making that have formed the Jiménez style.

I met Carlos Jiménez on 30 September 1994, at the Estadio del Centro, right before he was to perform at a dance. This was just one week after he had launched *Raza Negra*. Since a journalist I had interviewed had already warned Carlos that I would be appearing at a dance at some point, he was not surprised at all to see me. In fact, when he was informed that I was at the dance, he addressed me by name when he came out to greet me. Backstage, the friend who had taken me to the dance told Carlos that I am a flutist; she said that I used to play in the Teatro Colón and the National Symphony Orchestra in Buenos Aires. He sounded surprised, yet was happy to know that he was dealing with a musician.

When I went to my next Jiménez dance, on 11 November, Carlos asked me how long I was planning to stay in Córdoba. When I said that I expected to leave in May, out of the blue he asked me if I would like to record one number with his group on its next compact disc; since the recording would be released in May or June, he said, there would be ample time for me to record with the band before leaving Córdoba. I thought that Carlos was joking until he brought me out on stage, announced in front of the thousands of people at the dance that I would be recording one tune with them on their next compact disc, and that I played the flute. I felt very embarrassed and wondered if he would eventually "forget" about the whole thing. Since his group plays by ear, and I had never attempted to do anything so important without a part, I was quite apprehensive about what could happen. I decided to just put the matter completely out of my mind. That same evening, Carlos and I arranged for a time when I could interview him. We decided to meet at his home on Tuesday, 15 November.

When I got to Carlos's house, he mentioned the fact that I would be recording with the band when he introduced me to his daughter, Lorena. He told her that I was a musician from the United States who was studying in Córdoba, that he had invited me to record one tune with the group on its next compact disc (he kept repeating this over and over), and that I had played in the Teatro Colón. When he asked Lorena how she felt about the idea, she answered, "I think it's wonderful. Look, in the band there are people from all over the world. This would amount to adding another one. Besides, it's a good way to make the band unified." To this Carlos responded, "All the foreigners in the group . . . I love people with new ideas." Since he then said that he already had an idea for the tune, and that it would be nice if I would return to his house to play with Lorena for fun (she plays keyboards), I began to take the matter more seriously. In fact, from that day onward, each time that I saw Jiménez, he spoke of the fact that I was going to record with him. However, it was only when his announcer Tito talked about the matter on a radio program, and told me that when Carlos commits himself, especially in front of a crowd, he never goes back on his word, that I was convinced. The idea began to sink in even more when some of the musicians said that they might be able to write out a part for me.

After Lorena left, Carlos and I continued with the interview. All of a sudden, he changed the subject. Since he is spontaneous, and jumps from idea to idea, I thought that perhaps I had misunderstood something. He said that his band was going to rehearse that Thursday. This rehearsal was necessary because at the dance on Friday, he was going to do a set of tunes that imitated the style of *cuarteto* that was done in the late 1970s, the time when groups played *pasodobles* and *tarantelas*. He said that he was going to "turn people's heads around" by mixing this music with selections from *Raza Negra*, but not because he was trying to make "changes" in *cuarteto* music: "No, I'm going to explain it to you. *Raza Negra* came out two months ago, and I don't play just once a month in Córdoba; I play in Córdoba every Friday, Saturday, and Sunday. So, well, you have to vary things for the people who come. We do this by changing the repertoire around. Instead of always starting the same way, we change the music that we use. Maybe I come up with something new sometimes, and we do it; we play a new tune. This is so that the audience has a good time. It would be very boring by the end of the year if we didn't." He said that since the band has approximately 150 tunes in its repertoire, many of which it does not play very often, it is necessary for the musicians to rehearse when older repertoire is used. Rehearsing helps them remember the keys the songs are in as well as the tunes themselves.

All of a sudden, with what he said next, I fully realized what Jiménez was getting at: in his next compact disc, he planned to go back to the old *cuarteto* style. Carlos explained it to me as follows: "Well, my love, I am going to tell you something. In six months I am coming back with the original *cuarteto* style. Or I should say, I am going to go backwards. I'm crazy. I'm going backwards. And Bam Bam is going to play in only four or five tunes. He won't play on the songs in this '*cuarteto*' set, and it's going to be only Abraham who dances with me—not Byron." He admitted that he was going to do this for the sake of both his audience and the musicians. As I was listening to his explanation, it occurred to me that Jiménez had decided to make this stylistic change deliberately. Not only that, he had made the decision without having consulted anyone else in the process. Although *Raza Negra* had been created without a prior plan, this time there was going to be one.

Another thing suddenly became clear to me as well. When Jiménez had mentioned his love of string instruments in *cuarteto* earlier in the interview, he had mentioned that it had been necessary to replace the violin with a set of keyboards when he had formed his own group. He had also spoken of how wonderful it had been when five string players from the local symphony orchestra had performed live with his band. He had said that this addition of strings to his group was his idea of the perfect way to play *cuarteto* music, and that he had always dreamed of being able to have that many string instruments in his band. "I would be delighted to have that many strings," he said. "Why do you think I talked to you about playing flute with us? Because I love strings [and a flute can be used as though it were a string instrument]. . . . I would love to have a flute in my group. I wish that Tribi knew how to play flute." When I then told him that I also played piccolo, he got very excited. He said that maybe I could record two tunes with the group, one on each instrument. In any case, he made me promise not to tell anyone that I was going to play piccolo with his band.

I was startled because Jiménez had apparently always wanted to have had a flute in his group. I had appeared at the right time, just as had occurred when the band members had been wanting more percussionists and Bam Bam had arrived on the scene. Not only that, Carlos had decided that he was going to return to the traditional *cuarteto* style and was going to use my flute as though it were a string instrument. In other words, he had already made concrete plans for his next recording and I had just happened to fit into them. He was thinking farther ahead as well; he told me that after he had recorded this next compact disc, for the one after that he was going to invite one of five famous Argentine rock stars to record one song with him. His idea of inviting a guest artist to perform with the group had already inspired him to record with another one.

In the ensuing months, I got to know the Jiménez musicians well, much better than those of the other groups, because they knew that I was going to record with them. They occasionally teased me about my up-coming engagement with them and began to ask me about my musical career. For example, they were interested in knowing about sightreading and playing in a symphony orchestra. I also traveled to San Juan, where they performed with Santamarina, and stayed in the hotel with them. One night I remained in the lobby chatting with some of the men until the sun came up. To me, they all seemed sensitive, spontaneous, respect-ful, and a lot of fun. I really felt like I was becoming a part of the band.

As my departure date from Córdoba approached, I kept going to more Jiménez dances; I needed to speak with Carlos there in order to find out when we would be recording. The word finally came down that we would record in Córdoba, not in Buenos Aires (as had originally been planned). It was only two weeks before the date of my departure that I was told when I should first come to rehearse and exactly when I would record with the band. Since the musicians knew that I would be leaving the country immediately after recording with them, they organized ev-erything so that I would spend as little time as possible "working" with them. As Abraham was the composer of the tune that I would be record-ing, I was instructed to keep in contact with him regarding the final details of when they would need me to play with them. Not knowing what was going to happen, I made sure that I had said good-bye to everyone I knew in Córdoba before I began to rehearse with the group. I decided to completely free up my schedule because I knew that the band members often rehearse many hours per day when they are getting new tunes together for a recording session, as has been explained by Ricardo Verón:

> On many occasions, we cannot rehearse because we are perform-ing. . . . But when we devote ourselves to rehearsing, when we have to get the new tunes together, we work an average of ten or twelve hours a day. We do not set down our instruments until a couple of songs have been put together. After that, we do the orchestration and arrangements, finding the best possible way for each person to

play in each song. We do our work seriously: we look for tunes that are catchy and that move people. We address everyday problems in our song lyrics, and we do it with our style so that our music will not be like everybody else's. This is what makes the music of our group identifiable and loved by the public. What is a real problem is that 70 percent of the bands buy tunes from groups in Buenos Aires and adapt them. As a result, they make hybrids that nobody completely accepts. (Verón, quoted in Mero 1988:74)

Verón had told me that they had kept up this type of pace for two months when they had recorded *Raza Negra,* so I wanted to be ready for anything.

Since I had no idea what to expect the day I was first asked to rehearse, I went to Carlos's house with my flute, piccolo, tape recorder, and some staff paper. When I got there, I was led to the *quincho,* the small house on the other side of the swimming pool, in the backyard. I saw that only Verón, Luis Tapia, Tino, Conejo, and Abraham were there rehearsing—not Jiménez. The band members were not yet ready for me, since they were finishing up with a tune that Conejo had composed. Conejo was singing the vocal line of his tune, and the musicians were adding in the instrumental lines one at a time (by ear) as they copied the sequences from a diskette that had been prepared for them. While the rehearsal was going on, maids, children, and other employees and friends of the family walked in and out of the building. Jiménez's bus driver, El Turco (The Turk), also stopped by for a while. Abraham and I sat down at the table inside the *quincho* to wait our turn, and we helped ourselves to *mate* and dry pastries (*criollitas*) that were available for all of the musicians. As we listened, the musicians kept trying out passages, making comments to each other about what they might change or interpret in another way, and redoing details of the arrangements. They had been at the Jiménez house for hours, and had been doing the same thing every day of the week for the past few weeks, in order to prepare the new songs. On weekends, they were performing at dances. Since the disc was to be recorded in Córdoba this time, they were preparing and recording the tunes slowly, only two per week.

Jiménez, who had been sleeping, finally showed up at the rehearsal. The men then played "Penita" (JIMÉNEZ—VÁSQUEZ-MARTÍNEZ—VERÓN) for me, but without all of the instrumental lines and without the vocal part.[1] They had not yet learned all of the sequences on Abraham's demo diskette of the tune (each person had to learn his corresponding part by ear), but they wanted me to at least have an idea of what my participation in the song would entail. Abraham then sang the tune through once for me. I was told that the scale-type passages that were being done temporarily on the keyboards (using a flute sound) were the figures that I was supposed to imitate. Since no part had been written out for me, I tried to grasp the structure of the piece, which had verses and a refrain, in order to figure out where I was supposed to come in. I realized that certain running passages were repeated throughout the song, but that they did not all occur with the same number of measures of rest between them. The passages were not always the same, either.

In order for me to figure out what runs I was supposed to play (Abraham had actually composed them and had put them on his diskette), I was told what key the song was in; I then transcribed the notes onto my staff paper, one by one, as one of the men played them on the keyboards for me. The men were amazed that I could quickly write down what was being played. I decided that I would figure out the proper rhythmic values of the notes at home, but that I would not try to write out a whole part for myself. My plan was to memorize the small fragments that I had transcribed, and to then play my part by memory. I decided that I would make a tape of the group playing "Penita," and that I would practice with the tape enough times at home so that I would be able to "feel" where I should come in. Abraham, who was conducting the rehearsal (since "Penita" was his composition), gave me several indications about what he had in mind.

After we had finished with the runs I was to play, Jiménez told me that he wanted me to come up with a countermelody that would be played in the refrain along with the vocal line. This countermelody was to be sad, slow, and "not like *cuarteto* music"; it was to sound like something that I would normally play "in my country." Since he said that I could figure out this countermelody at home, we went on to the next step: we tried out my instruments with the song.

The first time we went through the tune, I used my flute to play the fragments that I had transcribed. Since the flute was too soft for the other instruments—even when it was played an octave higher—we then tried out my part on the piccolo. My performance with the piccolo was an instant hit with everybody; the men got quite excited about the instrument's tone quality, which they said sounded like a bird, and began talking all at once (they had never seen either a flute or a piccolo up close before). We then tried out both my flute and my piccolo in the refrain section, in the spot where I was to invent the countermelody. Once again, the flute did not sound quite right. We decided that the piccolo sounded better than the flute for the entire song because it matched the timbre and the register of the "flute" sequence that Abraham had put on his diskette.

The band then allowed me to make a tape recording of them playing the unfinished song; Carlos sang the vocal line this time through. While I was making the recording, I danced *cuarteto* with the bus driver and had *mate*. We decided that I would return the following day, Thursday, 11 May 1995, to do a final run through of "Penita" with the band; I was to come with my countermelody already completed. The recording session with the group would take place on the following Wednesday (17 May). I then realized that the band had gone through "Penita" no more than six or seven times in the three hours I had been at the *quincho*, and that the following day would be my only actual rehearsal with them before the recording session. Abraham and I then left the rehearsal because we had finished "our" song. Since I was playing his tune, he made sure that I got home safely and said he would call me later to give me the address and telephone number of the recording studio. He told me that he was very happy with the piccolo part and that he would see me the next day.

At home, I immediately got to work. I listened to "Penita" over and over again. Once I had come up with an idea for my countermelody, I wrote it out on staff paper. (The lower line of figure 6.1 shows how I

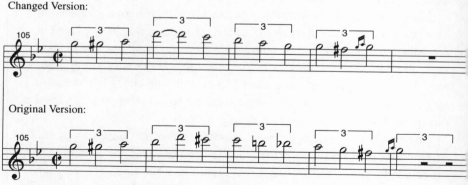

6.1. Piccolo countermelody of "Penita": original and changed versions. By permission of SADAIC, Buenos Aires.

originally wrote these measures of my part, and the top line shows how they were later amended.) I then proceeded to memorize both the runs that Abraham had composed for me and the melody I had invented by playing them in a music-minus-one fashion with the tape recording that I had made. The next day, after I had practiced in a similar way, I went to the rehearsal.

When I arrived at the Jiménez house that day, the band was not yet ready for me; they were still rehearsing another tune. Tribi, Abraham, and I sat out by the pool and talked while we waited for our turn. To pass the time, Abraham asked me to listen to two new pieces that he had composed. We also danced *cuarteto*, had *mate* and *criollitas*, and practiced some dance steps together. Juana, Carlos's wife, and many children were nearby. I was told that Carlos was sleeping. In fact, he did not come to the rehearsal at all—even when I rehearsed my part with its new counter-melody.

The time to rehearse "Penita" finally arrived. Much to my surprise, we went through the tune only three times, from top to bottom, without any pauses. Everyone, including Juana and the children, gathered round to listen. Other people, for example the bus driver, danced and clapped while I played. Since most of the people there had never seen or heard a piccolo before, I saw lots of smiling faces the first time we went through the song. All of the children were especially interested in what I was doing. The musicians all congratulated me and called me *maestra* (teacher) and *profesora* (professor). Their only concern about my performance was that I not allow the final grace note figure of my counter-melody to hang over into the following section of the tune. Since we did not go through the song again, I felt that the rehearsal had ended almost before it had started. I was concerned because Carlos had not heard my countermelody, and worse yet, he would not hear it until I was at the recording studio.

Abraham, Tribi, and I left the rehearsal together in a taxi. After we had dropped Tribi off, Abraham suggested that I go to the dance the next evening and that I try the tune out live, up on stage. He felt this would give me another chance to rehearse the tune before Wednesday and that it would allow Carlos a chance to hear what I had come up with. He asked me to think about his idea and then suggested how I should go dressed to the dance—in a conservative yet stylish dress. After I thought about his idea for a while, it did seem like a good one. Since I did not want to risk having to change my newly invented part during the recording session (if Carlos did not like it), this would be a way to get Carlos's approval before Wednesday.

The next night I went to the dance at Atenas with my piccolo. Since Abraham had not said anything to Carlos or the band members about having me perform with them, he was the only person who knew that I had brought it. In the first set, the band played "Penita" once—without me. In the break afterwards, when I mentioned to Carlos that I had brought the piccolo, he got very excited. Before the band repeated "Penita" in the third set, Carlos introduced me to the crowd; he said it was a shame that I would not be able to perform with them at the record launching. Without warming up, testing the sound system, or trying out Tribi's microphone (they asked me to use his mike), I began to play. The dancers were so startled to see a woman up on stage performing, and on an instrument they did not recognize, that they stopped dancing: I saw the "wheel" temporarily come to a standstill until the dancers' surprise wore off. As I was performing, many people crowded around the stage to listen. I recognized many of their faces and felt that I was among friends. While I was performing, Jiménez smiled and gestured his approval, especially when I played the countermelody that I had invented. Afterward, many people came up to me to tell me how much they had enjoyed the performance.

The next evening, when I went to the dance at the Super Deportivo, I also took my piccolo along. When Carlos saw me at the dance, he just assumed that I had brought my instrument along and that I was going to play with them again. While I was standing around during the dance, many people approached me and asked me if I was going to play "Penita." Since they had heard it the night before and had enjoyed it, they wanted to hear it again, they said. In their opinion, the song was just not the same when the piccolo part was played with keyboards. The band played "Penita" once in both the first and second sets, but without me. People kept coming up to me and asking me why I was not on stage playing with the group. Finally, when Ricardo Verón announced "Penita" in the third set, Carlos asked me to join them. As had happened the night before, I used Tribi's mike without a sound check. This time, though, no one stopped dancing when I played.

On Monday, 15 May, a full-page article about my research was published in *La Voz del Interior* ("La evolución en el cuarteto" 15 May

1995:1C). As a result, I was interviewed by telephone during a major *cuarteto* radio program, was asked for an interview by people from one FM station, and was asked to appear on a cable television program the following day (the same day that I would be recording). All of a sudden, my participation in *cuarteto* music had made me a celebrity and was affecting the music I was studying.

The day I recorded with the band, I arrived at the Pira studio at 4:00 P.M. When I got there, I was told that Carlos would not be coming to the recording session because he was in Buenos Aires. Since the musicians were not exactly sure how fast Carlos wanted to do "Penita," we decided to do two takes of the tune, each at a slightly different speed, to give him a choice. I had to wait for almost thirty minutes before I recorded my part because José Concha was doing the accordion tracks for two tunes when I arrived (he was recording over the keyboard and bass tracks that had already been recorded). Everyone present (Verón, Conejo, Luis, Tribi, Abraham, Carlos's sound technician, and the Pira sound technician) was critiquing his performance. They were asking him to repeat all sorts of small passages over and over because of the tempo not being precise enough or notes being played slightly late.

After José finished, I went back into the soundproof booth where I was to record. As I played my part, I wore earphones in order to be able to listen to the tracks of the song that had already been recorded. Abraham sang the vocal part live for me, with a special microphone that was located in the area where the sound console was, in order that I have the melody line to follow. I began recording by memory, but felt very uncomfortable without the measures I had written out with my part. Since I was having a hard time keeping close to the microphone, the sound was not recorded evenly at first. As a result, I was asked to repeat many passages over and over again. Finally, I decided to put my "cheat sheet" on a stand and to read the measures I had transcribed as I played (see figure 6.2). We then started from the top of the song. I recorded each entrance separately, as many times as were necessary, until I was allowed to move on to the next one. I was asked to repeat passages when some notes sounded weaker than others within a phrase, when the grace note in my countermelody was late, when attacks were not clear, or when notes in the runs were a bit behind. It was quite obvious that these men were after precision and musicality. Since they had never worked with a wind player before, and did not know that a person cannot blow or maintain his embouchure for hours without taking a break, I had to tell them that I needed to rest after about two hours had gone by.

Since I was almost hyperventilating by this time, we had *mate* and crackers while we rested and talked. Meanwhile, so as to not waste time, Tribi and Conejo recorded the *güiro* and tambourine parts of the tunes that were being recorded that week. Once again, all of the band members and the sound technicians critiqued their performances and asked them to repeat certain passages over and over again. If Tribi happened to hit the *güiro* a little too hard on a few stokes, he was asked to do them over. He also had to repeat passages in which he slowed down. When Conejo recorded, the same sort of thing happened. As these two men were recording, the other band members asked me quite a lot of questions about how a symphony orchestra records and performs. Once I had started to feel better, they all took turns dancing with me as well.

By this time, I was ready to finish recording. Everything went well until I got to my countermelody. Although all of the band members had heard me play it before, and had approved of what I had done, the ending now sounded dissonant to them. All of a sudden, they began asking me to change it. Luis Tapia sang me some suggestions, but I got mixed up and flustered because I knew that I would be leaving Córdoba the next day and would not be able to return to the studio if we did not finish "Penita" that same evening. Since all of the men agreed that I would need to change the passage, Luis used the keyboards in order to show me how I could easily "fix" my part. We ended up changing my countermelody slightly (see figure 6.1). I transcribed what Luis had suggested onto staff paper and made no attempt to memorize it. Since I had already programmed the passage so firmly into my brain the way that I had created it, I had a hard time performing the amended part naturally. In any case, we finished recording my two takes.

Out of the blue, Luis Tapia asked me if I could play an octave higher with my piccolo. Since my answer was affirmative, he asked me to demonstrate. Because he liked the upper range of the instrument so much, he asked me to change the endings of both takes by playing them up an octave. At this point, my embouchure was completely shot, and I was almost too tired to stand up. Since changing the passage would mean taking it up to a high B-flat, one of the highest notes on the piccolo, I was not sure that I would be able to comply. Somehow, after having spent five hours in the studio, I managed to redo the endings. I felt that this upper

6.2. Jane Florine recording the piccolo part of "Penita." Photograph by Luis Tapia, Córdoba, Argentina, 1995. By permission of Jane L. Florine.

register of the instrument had sounded too loud, but they said they would be able to tone down what I had recorded when they mixed and equalized the sound.

Relieved to have somehow finished, I relaxed with my friends. We were all quite happy about our shared experience, but we were all very sad as well. To wind down, we talked and danced. When the time came to leave, they said that they would attempt to get me a tape of the song before I left the next day. If that was not possible, they would send me a copy of the recording after it had been released and launched. Bleary-eyed, I left to take a taxi with Tribi, and wondered if I would ever see any of them again.

When I returned to Córdoba for a two-week visit in early August 1995, I discovered that *El Marginal,* as Jiménez had decided to call his new compact disc that had my recording of "Penita" on it, had been launched on July 24. I was amazed to hear "Penita" being played on the radio and when I walked into record stores in downtown Córdoba. When

I was interviewed on Radio Suquía, I was even more surprised to hear that it was one of their most requested tunes. It was truly gratifying to see that my small contribution to *cuarteto* music had evidently been made to a good song.

I went to one Jiménez dance during my stay. Since I had not brought my piccolo with me to Argentina this time (the musicians asked me if I was going to perform with them the minute they saw me), Carlos asked me to get up on stage to sing "Penita" with him. I also danced with him and played Tribi's *güiro*. Verón and the other band members all wanted to know if I had heard the recording yet, and if I liked the way they had mixed the sound. If I had not had to return to the United States in May 1995, I am sure that I would have been included in the mixing process and at the launching ceremony. Verón also wanted to be sure that I had seen the thank-you message they had put on the back of the liner notes to acknowledge my participation with them; he had been responsible for this. All of the band members kept telling me what a good experience it had been for them to have played with me, and Abraham said that my invented countermelody and interpretation added a touch to the finished song that he could not have come up with on his own. At the dance, I was surprised at the number of people who came up to greet me, from policemen to dancers.

When I saw the title of the new disc, *El Marginal*, I wondered if Jiménez had gotten his inspiration for the title (and the title tune) as a result of his recording of *Raza Negra*. I remembered that when I had interviewed him, he had spoken about how the black race has always been marginalized and that he had always felt like a marginal man singing *cuarteto* music. The title also reminded me of a paragraph from a book written about Jiménez: "Jiménez, a true rebel against the established order, is a man faithful to *cuarteto* traditions, which he learned in the school of life, by blows, like millions of men and women who follow and identify with him. They do so because like them, he has suffered, and still suffers, from marginality despite his fame" (Mero 1988:79).

Conclusion

Individual Participation in Musical Decision-Making

From the individual biographies and stories that have been presented in this chapter, some general comments can be made regarding the composition of the Jiménez culture pool, the musical contributions that are made by all of the band members either as a group or individually, how the musicians participate in group operations and policy formation, and the role of Carlos Jiménez and his special personality on the band's musical style. In any case, it is evident that almost all of the members of the Jiménez band are highly involved in musical decision-making; they help to formulate the group's musical style, which is a true fusion of all of the propriospects of the band members. In fact, it would be difficult for a culture pool to be more heavily drawn upon than it is in this group.

Regarding the backgrounds (propriospects) of the Jiménez band members, these men are, generally speaking, older than most of the members of other *cuarteto* groups are: their average age is thirty-four. Most of them have little formal schooling or musical training, but all of them except the three foreigners have grown up with, and like, *cuarteto* music. (The three foreigners say that they like *cuarteto* music, but that they like it because it reminds them of genres from their own countries.) Despite the fact that the men like *cuarteto,* and many would choose it as their preferred genre to perform to make a living, they actively listen to and get musical ideas from many other kinds of music, including salsa, merengue, Latin jazz, African-derived genres, rock, rap, classical (symphonic) music, and romantic vocal music. Most of the men have been working with *cuarteto* bands since their teens (or even longer) and have extensive experience in performing the genre. Only one of the men (Luis) was forced to study music, and only two had parents who were involved with music professionally (Pupi and Conejo). Excluding the three foreigners, all of the other members of the group had been with Jiménez for at least six years in 1994, and some had been working with him for more than twenty years; they describe themselves as being friends and colleagues, not as employees. The men openly say that they are very happy working with Jiménez, that they play a personal role in what the band produces, and that they want to end their careers in his group. They proudly say that they are all highly intuitive (not intellectual), play from the heart, and perform with feeling. In addition, they think that they are highly creative because they play by ear, not with written music.

In the individual biographies, each man spoke of how he and the other band members make musical contributions to the group; only the two announcers said that their involvement in musical decision-making is limited. The musicians mentioned that they have complete freedom to introduce their own ideas, that the band members and Jiménez are always open to what each person has to say, and that there is mutual respect for one another in the group. Abraham, who had felt musically limited in his own country, for example, feels that he has grown professionally by having worked in such an environment. The musicians also spoke of how much they appreciate the fact that they can be creative, that everything down to the last detail, even timbre, is not imposed from above; they enjoy working in a situation in which each person is expected to let his voice be heard and to take the initiative to contribute whatever he can. Pupi, for example, said that he would not be able to work in a group in which he could not come up with ideas on his own or had to read off a part. I saw firsthand how everyone chips in when I rehearsed and recorded "Penita" with the group; for one thing, we all chose to use my piccolo because of its timbre.

All of the band members agreed that almost everyone composes and helps "arrange" for the group, but each man spoke about a special, more personal type of individual contribution that he has made to the band as well. As a result of some of these individual musical contributions, polyrhythm, dance steps, choreography, "positive vibrations," and knowledge of other musical genres (African music, merengue, rock, rap, salsa, etc.) have been incorporated. Individual band members have also been responsible for having consciously and unconsciously added elements from other genres to *cuarteto,* for having made little suggestions (added "grains of sand") to improve arrangements, for having introduced novelties inspired in part from outside listening, and for having come up with ideas inspired by the foreign band members. In addition, Byron mentioned the role he has played in teaching audience members to dance to *cuarteto* music, and Verón pointed out the importance of the bass player in maintaining the band's rhythmic foundation.

A couple of these points regarding the formation of the group's style were mentioned by almost all of the band members. First of all, the men said that most of the changes in the band's present style, and their current ideas, have been inspired by the arrival of the three foreign percussionists, who brought new instruments and novel ways of thinking to the group. They all agreed that they get ideas from a process of mutual inspiration and exchange; by pooling and considering each other's ideas, they come up with even more. The other point highly stressed by all of the musicians was the importance that their listening to genres other than *cuarteto* has had on the band's music. The word "osmosis" was used by Bam Bam to describe this phenomenon. Both Luis and Jiménez spoke of how they have unconsciously used outside ideas in their compositions (in the creation of drum rhythms and *merentetos*, for example), and Pupi spoke of how he intentionally tries to use some of what he listens to (elements from salsa music).

From the biographies and stories contained in this chapter, it can be seen that Jiménez trusts his musicians, gives them much responsibility, and delegates many aspects of musical decision-making to them. For example, each band member supervises the rehearsal and recording of his own tunes. Jiménez is often not present in rehearsals until arrangements have already been put together and does not go to the recording studio until all of his musicians have already recorded their parts; the musicians are left on their own to take care of what must be done. In the studio and in rehearsals, all of the band members critique each other's performances and ideas; Jiménez is not there telling everyone what to do. Everyone has a say in the mixing of the band's recordings as well. Jiménez relies on Verón to arrange the rehearsal and recording schedules, to put liner notes together, to pick the order of the tunes that will be performed each evening, and to test his sound equipment before dances. He has Conejo put the lyrics of each tune to be sung on a stand which he keeps close by his microphone and asks Luis for help when he composes and must make demos. Many more examples than these could be given as well.

At times Carlos asks people to create their own parts. For example, when Abraham joined the band, he was told to play whenever he thought that he should; he was also asked to alternate between *tambora* and *güira* as he saw fit. When Byron joined the group, the same type of thing occurred, and when I recorded with the group, I was asked to come up with a countermelody that sounded like music from my country. Since the band members are encouraged to be creative and to speak up in this fashion, it often happens that they take the liberty of making certain ideas or suggestions without asking Carlos—when they assume that he would agree with what they are proposing. For example, it was Abraham who suggested that I perform live with the group. He assumed that Carlos would not mind, and for some reason I cannot explain, I knew that he was right. And in the studio, it was the musicians, not Jiménez, who took the liberty of asking me to make last-minute changes in my part. Even back in the days of the Cuarteto de Oro, the musicians used to take the initiative to propose their own ideas: it was Verón who had them update their arrangements on their final recording with the group in order to plan for their departure and who insisted that the band needed more percussionists, for example.

It is also evident from the information provided in this chapter that the Jiménez band members are all in agreement with the founding principles the group instated in 1984 and that they all work to maintain them. As a result, they have clear musical goals and ideals from which they do not waver. To begin with, they work as long as is necessary to make good tunes and recordings; they experiment in order to get just the right timbres, for example. They seek precision and musicality, so they will not put up with such things as sloppy rhythm, uneven tone quality, or missed notes. Secondly, they work without a prominent owner-employee relationship; there is little distance among band members and everyone collaborates in a group fashion. As Bam Bam has put it, Jiménez does not suffer from "star syndrome." Band members treat each other with respect, listen to each other's ideas, and try to attend to each other's needs. Everyone is acknowledged on liner notes because each individual is a part of the group and is highly appreciated. Thirdly, they do not distance themselves from their audience. Since they want to reach their followers and play what they want to hear, the band members keep up with the times technologically and use lyrics that address the public's concerns. Lastly, they want their music to "evolve" with the times and to constantly have new, updated features, but they insist that this be done without "changing" it into something that is not *cuarteto;* the *tunga-tunga* in the bass and the piano must remain, and the accordion and "strings" must always play a big role. This also means that they must stick to using original material, not adapt cover tunes.

In truth, much of what happens in the group has to do with the very special personality of Carlos Jiménez, who is warm, open-minded, intuitive, simple, and caring. It is true that the band members make many suggestions and contribute freely because they are both encouraged and asked to, but they also do so because they know that Jiménez will always listen to and consider what they have to say. On top of that, Jiménez just assumes that everyone has something to offer. He might change people's suggestions or compositions around a bit (such as he did with "No Soy Dios Para Perdonar"), but he thrives on new, and especially foreign, ideas. Due to his total open-mindedness, spontaneity, and love of learning new things, he is like a sponge that soaks up any new and interesting musical idea. As soon as he comes across something he likes, he somehow fits it into what he is doing (such as when he asked me to record with the band and how my experience led him to think of recording with a rock star). At some later date, these influences often appear in the band's music, in either a conscious or unconscious fashion, such as how a rap tune was used intentionally in *Raza Negra,* whereas *merentetos* were created without anyone really having planned to do so. Over time, Jiménez's ideas accumulate and feed off each other, such as happened with the creation of *Raza Negra.*

Since Jiménez is always concerned about other human beings, especially people who are in need, some stylistic elements of the band's music have come about because of his generosity. Tribi, Abraham, and Byron were all added to the group because they needed work, but in turn, have contributed to form the band's special Watusi section. Jiménez makes sure that all his band members' needs are met, especially that they have enough money to live on—such as when he did not take the band to the United States—and wonders how they will survive after he retires. It is quite likely that one of the main reasons he asked me to record with the group, which has served to change the band's style somewhat, was in order to help me; he thought I could learn a lot from performing with a *cuarteto* group firsthand and wanted me to be able to finish my project. Since he was not able to finish his own schooling, yet values formal education, he appreciated the fact that I was working on a university degree and wanted to help me achieve my goal.

Musical Innovation (Change) That Is Stimulated from Within a Culture

Based upon what has been related in the individual biographies and stories presented above, it is possible to make some general observations about how musical innovation arises from within a culture. Firstly, as was observed in the previous chapter by applying the ideas of Goodenough, power relationships and access to decision-making are critical factors which determine to what degree a group's culture pool (i.e., who will be allowed to make individual contributions and exactly how and to what degree this will be permitted) is drawn upon over time. In this particular case, as has been discussed above, the open-minded, egalitarian personality of Carlos Jiménez makes the individual backgrounds of each person in his group highly important in his band's overall musical style. Since members are encouraged to introduce new ideas and arrange repertoire in a group fashion, and are given ample opportunity to do so, individual ideas are quickly absorbed by all of the band members and are used to stimulate further innovation; as a result, personal styles of performing, musical preferences, and musical knowledge can easily be introduced into the band's music, especially because the group plays by ear. Every single person in the band, except the two announcers, plays a role in musical change. In the last few years, however, the role played by the three foreign percussionists in the band has been critical in the evolution of the group's style.

The Jiménez band fits in very well with much of what Barnett has said about the occurrence of innovation. According to Barnett (1953:20–22), the amount of innovation that arises in a culture depends upon opportunity differentials, concepts held toward change, and attitudes toward experimentation that might exist. For example (Barnett 1953: 40–46, 56–57), innovation occurs most often when it is expected, when members of a group collaborate in order to create, when people of differing backgrounds come together, when group members have breadth and depth of personal knowledge, and when a wide cultural base is present (i.e., when many "ingredients," which are often obtained by communicating with others, are available in a person's or a group's pool of knowledge). Innovation increases when constraints are not placed on creativity, when people have freedom to explore on their own, and when authority restrictions are not present as well, says Barnett (1953:65–67).

Since all of these conditions are present in Jiménez's band, it is not surprising that his group's music is so original and is a true composite of the band's culture pool. Many of the comments made by the band members also confirm what Barnett (1953:97–127) has said about the role of self-wants in innovation: they come up with new ideas because they have creative needs and want to avoid routine and boredom (1953:152, 156–57); Jiménez and Luis, in particular, spoke about how playing the same material night after night is hard on both band members and audiences. Their comments about the role of combining new material picked up through "osmosis" with old material serves to confirm Barnett's (1953:9, 181–291) idea that all innovation is based on recombinations of old and new ideas (Bam Bam, Pupi, and Luis all spoke of this process). It is also evident that these men have the proper character and personality to be innovative (Barnett 1953:20): they are very observant of what is around them, remember what they have heard and/or liked, and have a talent for analyzing everyday occurrences and updating them. Their sensitive, intuitive nature and curiosity about new things certainly play a role in this process.

Barnett (1953:72) has also written that innovation occurs more often in an environment in which there is competition than in one where there is not. Since the *cuarteto* world is such big business, and new ideas must constantly be created in order to keep one's market share, it is not surprising that all of the band members are so openminded and are continually trying to add new elements to their music. Since bands are expected to record two compact discs a year, and to do something different on each one, they are forced to be innovative to keep up with the competition.

Secondly, what happened during the period of time comprised in this study can be used to make certain conclusions regarding "externally stimulated" and "internally stimulated" change. According to what was seen in this case study, it would appear that as Kubik (1986:54) has said, both of these types of change usually occur to some degree simultaneously, and externally stimulated change can play a big role in internally stimulated change. For example, all of the musicians mentioned in this chapter say that they listen to many genres of music, most of which are foreign; they consciously use what they have heard at times and on other occasions unconsciously use what they have absorbed by osmosis as the springboard for new creations. The most obvious occurrence of this concerns the foreign percussionists, who have introduced musical knowledge from their own countries and have inspired the other band members to innovate in new ways; everyone in the group agrees that the biggest stylistic evolution in their music has occurred since these three men have joined the group.

I can also say that my appearance in Córdoba, which happened completely by chance, has perhaps stimulated other changes in the group's music; I brought new ideas about playing and thinking about music to them and introduced a new instrument. My answers to the men's questions about playing a wind instrument, working in a symphony orchestra, and sightreading have given them new insight on ways to perform music, for example. The fact that I was able to transcribe a portion of my part and perform both with or without it also gave them food for thought;

they had always assumed that a person who plays with music cannot play with feeling. My presence also inspired Jiménez, who had not before recorded with a guest wind player, to think about inviting a rock performer to record with him on his next compact disc.

Some of the other foreign influences that band members have absorbed have been the result of technological advances, such as newly invented electronic instruments, which they have become aware of through recordings that have reached them (those of the Beatles, for example). Kubik (1986:54) has pointed out that technology introduced from external sources can have a great effect on internally stimulated musical change, just as it has had in this case. The band's style could not have evolved to what it was in 1984, or even today, without these innovations. Since one of the group's founding platforms in 1984 was to keep its music instrumentally and harmonically up-to-date, the band members are still in tune with all types of new technological influences. Now that cable television and imports (compact discs, audiocassettes, videos, instruments, and music magazines) are common to Argentines, band members can keep abreast of all of the latest trends in international popular music and technology more easily. This trend also confirms Kubik's (1986:55) idea that internally stimulated cultural change can arise from commercial pressures that arise and are imposed by external sources.

Contact that the Jiménez band members have had with foreign genres of music has occurred in other ways as well. Travels of band members abroad and visits made by famous musicians to Argentina have had an impact on the group's music, for example. Jiménez's trips to both Brazil and the United States played an important role in the music that was recorded on *Raza Negra,* as did the visit of Juan Luis Guerra and his introduction of merengue to Argentina. In this modern world, internal musical change, or innovation, is thus inspired by a combination of personally learned musical knowledge, knowledge of music obtained through enculturation, and musical knowledge picked up from contact with the music of other cultures, as Goodenough (1981:112) would put it. Even Barnett (1953:40) has stated that many elements essential to innovation may come from distant sources.

Thirdly, from the stories that have been told in this chapter, it can be seen that not all musical decision-making that leads to evolution of musical style is carefully and/or consciously planned. It is possible for change to be planned, however, and for it to occur due to a combination of consciously and unconsciously made decisions which occur in a chain-like fashion as a result of each other. As a consequence, it is sometimes not possible to identify one moment in time during which a conscious decision has been made to implement musical change, as Blacking (1986:6) would have one believe. To the contrary, Barnett (1953:16) has stated that innovation is not always a "deliberate and closely reasoned process." According to Barnett (1953:16), "thousands of innovations are unpremeditated, and innumerable others are both unplanned and unwanted. Many appear on impulse and multitudes go unnoticed by either their creator or anyone else."

For example, the production of *Raza Negra* was almost totally a product of chance from start to finish, not an attempt to consciously "change" the music of Córdoba or to introduce Afro-Caribbean music to the city; very little conscious decision-making was involved in its creation. The appearance of the three foreign musicians, Jiménez's contact with foreign genres, and his trips abroad were the stimuli for the recording. The title was added after the musicians were already in the recording studio working, Abraham and Byron were not part of the original plans, and only one tune, a rap one, was intentionally placed on the compact disc as being something different from *cuarteto;* the merengue influences that appeared in the *merentetos* were unconscious, according to Jiménez. In fact, *Raza Negra* was in part a result of the longtime desire of the band members to add more percussion to their group and to do a more *tropical* style of composition.

On the other hand, Jiménez's decision to return to the old style of *cuarteto* playing in *El Marginal* was a consciously planned one. Even so, at least part of what was recorded on the compact disc came about by chance, just as had occurred with *Raza Negra*. It is true that Jiménez had intentionally decided to return to the old *cuarteto* style in *El Marginal,* but he had no clue that a foreign, female piccolo player was going to appear on the scene. Although women do not play in *cuarteto* groups and neither flute nor piccolo had ever before been used in the genre, Jiménez did not have me record with his group in order to be the "first" person to add these elements to *cuarteto* music or to make a statement. Instead, the fact that I play piccolo happened to fit into his personal agenda; he had always wanted to have a flute in his band and had long considered it to be a string instrument. By treating the flute/piccolo as though it were a violin, it was quite appropriate to use it in traditional *cuarteto* music. If I had appeared when Jiménez had been recording *Raza Negra*, I most likely would not have been asked to record with him at all. The fact that he invited me to perform with the group also fits in with his personal history of accepting foreign musicians and helping those who are in need: he thought that it would be helpful for me to record with the band.

Regarding the issue of consciously imposed "changes" made in *cuarteto*, all of the musicians in the Jiménez band have a similar opinion: they say they are consciously trying to "improve" *cuarteto* music, or that they want to help it to "evolve," but that they do not want to "change" it. They insist that despite any "improvements" that are made to *cuarteto*, its basic essence (the presence of the accordion) and the *tunga-tunga* (played only in the bass and piano parts) must always remain. In other words, their deliberate innovations must fit within the comfort zones of their audience and the parameters of the *cuarteto* style.

The musicians explain that additions and improvements to *cuarteto* are intentionally made so as to avoid boredom and routine for both the musicians and the listeners as well as to keep up with the times; music dies if it does not "evolve," they say. As has been stated above, part of these "improvements" that are consciously made are done in order to ensure commercial success; since all the bands are competing with each other for their share of the *cuarteto* market, they must constantly come up with something new. However, now that Argentines have easy access to other styles via recordings and television, it is also audiences that demand that *cuarteto* keep up with this international level of professionalism. In other words, the foreign influences that have motivated musicians to innovate have also influenced audience members to demand a certain level of musical expertise, creativity, and adaptation to international standards from *cuarteto* groups. External pressures that originate from outside a culture can thus produce musical change via both those who consume the music and those who create it.

Lastly, the influence of individual personalities should not be underestimated in the study of musical change (Barnett 1953:63, 321–23). In the case of Jiménez, the importance of his management style, generosity, openmindedness, spontaneity, and love of learning on the band's style have already been described. It should not be forgotten that Jiménez is an idol who has great influence on the masses that follow him, however; he has a large number of fans largely because of his rags-to-riches life story and the fact that he has not turned his back on the poor—not because he is a great singer or because of the music that his band plays. Since his admirers look upon him as a symbol of what they would like to become, they are willing to accept almost anything that he comes up with just because he is Carlos Jiménez. I once told Jiménez that his fans would buy his recordings even if he sang opera arias on them; they love him for who he is—not for what he sings—is what I actually meant. A rock performer, Julio Anastasía of Los Navarros, has made a similar comment about Jiménez: "I don't think he has anything to worry about [if he introduces musical changes]; any changes that he might try to make will be well-received by the public because everything he produces comes from the heart" (Gregoratti 27 September 1994:3C). In other words, some individuals can introduce musical change more easily than others just because of who they are.

The *Cuarteto* World Revisited: Córdoba in 1998

After an absence of three years, I returned to Córdoba in the summer of 1998. The main reason for going to Argentina during the months of June and July was to get the copyright releases I would need to publish this book, but I was also anxious to see what had become of my friends in the *cuarteto* world. Although part of my plan was to visit the six bands with whom I had worked in 1994–95 to see what might have developed over time, I was especially curious to see what had happened with the group of Carlos Jiménez. Before going to Córdoba, where I stayed four weeks, I spent two weeks starting the copyright-release procedure at SADAIC (Sociedad Argentina de Autores y Compositores), the national songwriters' and composers' association, in Buenos Aires. After my stay in Córdoba, I returned to Buenos Aires for three weeks in order to finish up paperwork at SADAIC.

Initial Impressions

When I arrived in Córdoba, the city appeared to be much the same as it had been in 1994–95; I found most of the same locales in business and the same employees working in them. The bus routes had not changed, my close friends all lived in the same places, and life was still economically difficult. I walked the same paths as I used to, admired and sat in the same churches, and generally felt quite at ease. It was as though time had stopped. On the other hand, I did note some subtle signs of change and excitement in the city. I could now go to fast-food restaurants and make phone calls from a bevy of public communications centers; I even found a travel agency with electronic mail service. Since the soccer World Cup championship was in full force and Argentina was still a contender, there was much talk of upcoming games. The founding of Córdoba and Independence Day were soon to be celebrated.

When I began to inquire about developments in the *cuarteto* world, I had quite the opposite impression; many changes had taken place. The genre was still flourishing and several new groups had appeared, but some important bands from my prior stay in the city had pretty much ceased to exist. Because of all the changes I observed, I was motivated to speak with Emeterio Farías shortly after my arrival. Once I had gotten a general overview of what had happened during my absence, I then proceeded to speak with the owners of the groups I had studied in 1994–95, attended several dances, went to some rehearsals of Jiménez's group, chatted with the *cuarteto* crowd at cafes, and watched television to find out about the rest.

Generally speaking, I discovered that Emeterio Farías was still the power in charge of the *cuarteto* industry in Córdoba. Farías's advertising agency, Mejor Propaganda, was still the main vehicle for groups in producing their television and radio commercials, and he continued to sponsor weekend dance events at Atenas and the Super Deportivo. Radio Suquía, his *cuarteto* radio station, had moved to just around the corner from his office, and he was now also running a *cuarteto* television program, Ritmo Punta, once a week. Another television program that included *cuarteto* music, Telemanía, was being shown on Saturday and Sunday; there had not been this much open television coverage of *cuarteto* in the past. As far as radio coverage was concerned, the same stations and programs I had encountered in 1994 were still in existence.

My friends told me that economically speaking, 1995 had been the worst year in the history of *cuarteto;* the normal commercial situation had returned in 1996, with good profits being made in the *cuarteto* world since that time. Most of the same dance halls continued to be used and the same weekend dance circuit was being followed as before, but two new halls, Maipú Juniors (a small locale) and Bogos, an athletic club similar to Atenas and the Deportivo, had been added to the list. Maipú Juniors was being used by smaller groups, for example, Marejada, Rodrigo, and Cachumba—three new bands I had not heard of. The same number of people were attending dance events as during my initial visit, but a method of adjusting ticket prices had been found to keep this figure steady: *cuarteto* fans could now enter dances for only five pesos if they arrived before a fixed hour (i.e., early).

In the summer of 1998, Jiménez was by far "number one" in the city, a privileged position he had held for the past couple of years, I was told; people were being turned away from his dances in droves, and no hall was big enough to hold all his admirers. Tru-la-lá, after having taken a real nosedive in 1995, had gained in status to become number two. Number three was a new band called Cachumba, a group of young neighborhood boys that imitated the *cuarteto-cuarteto* style and Jiménez's manner of singing. Even the song lyrics used by this youthful band were of the Jiménez type, addressed to the lower stratum of society and its everyday concerns.

A group called Jean Carlos was number four at the time. Its solo singer, Jean Carlos Sánchez from the Dominican Republic, was formerly a member of Tru-la-lá. When Jean Carlos had left Tru-la-lá to form his own band in 1995, he had stressed merengue and dancing in his group. The year 1995 was a tremendously successful one for him, as it was for La Barra, but his departure had almost caused Tru-la-lá to disband. Miraculously, Tru-la-lá had managed to recover from this loss with the hiring of a new singer, Cristián Amato, and La Barra was now approximately fifth in the rankings. One new group I was told about was Marejada, which was formed in the wake of *moderno* singer Jorge Quevedo's departure from Chébere. Two other new bands also mentioned frequently were that of Rodrigo, a singer from Córdoba who had worked in the *bailantas* and had decided to return home (he was now performing in the Jiménez vein), and that of Los Zarza. I was told that Videla was in the process of forming a new band, that Santamarina had new management, and that Gary was performing in the interior and Buenos Aires. There were fewer active *cuarteto* groups than before, only between twenty and twenty-five.

Musically speaking, I quickly noticed some changes in format and style. For one, few of the groups had two singers or alternated *tropical* and *moderno* as strictly as I had remembered. The *tropical* style seemed to be overshadowing the *moderno* one in dances by far, and bands were also playing several *cumbias* per evening; at times I wondered if I would hear any *moderno* selections at all. From what I was told, much of this move toward the *tropical* style was due to the initial success of Jean Carlos in

1995, which had now worn off to a degree. Latin percussion was used much more profusely than before, and it was now quite commonplace to see a *tambora* player on stage. Although *melódico* was still being sung, often times with a *tropical* flavor, at the same time there seemed to be a return to the original *cuarteto* ideal of emphasizing the *tunga-tunga*. Some groups had as many as four singers—not the two I was expecting.

I noticed that some *cuarteto* groups were beginning to return to Buenos Aires and the *bailanta* scene. A trend to use playback in Buenos Aires had turned off fans there, so *bailanta* administrators had begun to recruit *cuarteto* groups again—even allowing them to work with both chains simultaneously. It was mostly groups who could not make it in Córdoba that were performing in the *bailantas* to survive, but there were exceptions. Jiménez, for example, had performed in one in June 1998, but on a sole Friday evening, to pave the way for other bands from Córdoba.

Another thing I quickly found out is that several bands had now adopted different office locations: some had not moved far, others had moved from the outskirts of the city to downtown, and yet others were now running their businesses from quite far away. As a result, rehearsal operations had changed for most of these same groups. The majority of the bands, however, were performing in the same locales as before.

During my three-year absence, big changes had occurred with how *cuarteto* groups made recordings. Some owners had changed labels, for example, and most were now recording in studios in Córdoba—not in Buenos Aires, as before. Many bands had signed with a new label called JM, which was part of the MJ Musical record store: Santamarina, Aldo Kustin, the Cuarteto Leo, Orly, and Cachumba to name a few. MJ Musical, which was still the main *cuarteto* record store in the city and had the same management, was also handling record distribution for its artists. The biggest change of all involved studio recording procedures: for the most part, bands had returned to recording each member's part live—not using sequences put on diskettes as before and/or having only the singers and a handful of instrumentalists go to Buenos Aires to record live over sequences already put on a diskette.

Instead of doing business in the El Padrino bar on Tuesday afternoons, the *cuarteto* crowd had returned to the Bon Que Bon. Owners and those hiring bands for their locales—for both Córdoba and the interior—would meet after lunch to discuss what had happened at dances during the past week and to do business. Some *cuarteto* musicians, such as the composer and band owner Aldo Kustin, were still using the Bon Que Bon as their personal office, making and receiving necessary telephone calls. It really amazed me to see that all these men now used cellular telephones, the perfect solution for their hectic and transient lifestyle.

I was surprised to see so many of the same fans I had met in 1994–95 at the dances; quite a few of these people remembered me and came up to greet me. These "friends" all asked how my dissertation had turned out and wanted to know if I had found a job. The musicians, arrangers, and owners were curious about my present situation as well. I received a warm welcome from all of the groups and their owners and was surprised to be given several compact discs of current material. For the most part, owners agreed to meet with me the same day I called them to set up appointments, another surprise considering their busy schedules. When I went to the Bon Que Bon to visit with the groups, I was invited to more dances than I could possibly attend. I was also given permission to record dances, tape part of a radio program, use parts of commercial recordings if I could manage to put together a compact disc with my book, and much more. This treatment made me realize that I had been truly accepted into the *cuarteto* world.

Update: The Six Bands Revisited

Besides my general observations about what had happened in the *cuarteto* scene, I also noted the specific changes that had taken place in each of the six bands I had studied. Some of the groups had gone through major upheavals over the three-year period involved, yet others had made it through the same period of time almost untouched. What I discovered about each band is presented below.

Chébere

Group History

During my absence, Chébere had gone through quite a lot of turmoil: not only had it had fallen from its privileged status, it had almost died. After going through a whole series of changes, the same three owners as before eventually remained in control of the band. Lugones and Guillén still perform with the group, but Pizzichini has retired from performing;

all three carry out the same functions as before (public relations, musical leadership, and administration). As always, it was Pato Lugones who met with me, gave me recordings of the group, and acted as the band's official spokesperson. The only other person remaining from Chébere as it had existed in 1994 was a percussionist, who now plays both *timbales* and drum set.

Chébere's downfall began when Jorge Quevedo, its *moderno* singer, left the band to become the solo singer of his own group toward the end of 1995. After making one unsuccessful compact disc, he had disappeared from view. Daniel Guardia, a singer from Córdoba who had been working in the *bailantas,* was hired to replace Quevedo. Since Chébere fans did not like Guardia's style, the owners had to come up with yet another replacement. Meanwhile, Rubinho Da Silva ("Rubinho" is the diminutive of "Rubens"), the band's *tropical* singer, along with the four brass players and the drum set player, left to start their own group, called Marejada. They formed their band following the Chébere tradition, having Rubinho alternate sets with a *moderno* singer, and have continued to imitate Chébere in all that they do.

Because of these developments, Chébere could no longer function as a band. To remedy the situation, the owners decided to hold a musical reunion inviting two former Chébere singers, Videla and Pelusa, to join what was left of their ensemble. As a result, they drew up a working agreement and put together a program called "El Reencuentro" ("The Reunion"). At first crowds came to the performances of this new business venture in record numbers: La Vieja Usina was full for the first dance, with 4,000 to 5,000 people forced to remain outside the building owing to lack of space, and the evening was recorded live by BMG. A second "Reencuentro" with new material was later done, but the two singers involved still kept working with their own bands; the owners of Chébere were waiting to see what would happen. Finally, in June 1997, all three groups (Chébere, Videla, and Pelusa) decided to unite on a semi-permanent basis to keep doing "Reencuentro" dances. This new group went to many places in the province of Córdoba to perform, but began having problems quickly; only old fans of Videla and Pelusa were interested in listening to the band. At the end of 1997, the enterprise was dissolved.

The three original Chébere owners decided to start over from scratch, reforming their group. Gabriel Ferrer, who had experience singing in pubs, was chosen as the *moderno* singer, and Ramoncito Meléndez, a Dominican, was selected as Chébere's new *tropical* voice. It was thought that Meléndez, with his Caribbean roots, would be able to add authenticity and a special foreign touch to Chébere's *tropical* selections. Due to the growing interest in merengue, the owners wanted to begin doing their *tropical* tunes in that style. Almost the same instrumentation as before was decided upon, but the two trombones were exchanged for one trombone and a saxophone. The owners also hired two keyboard players (one on piano and one on synthesizer), two percussionists (one on drum set and the other on congas), an electric guitar player, a bass guitarist, and two trumpet players.

The administrative makeup of the group, such as the number of assistants, sound technicians, and bus drivers and buses, was not changed. The full-time status of the musicians was also maintained. Chébere abandoned its office downtown, however, and began to use the building where it had always rehearsed (in the Ayacucho neighborhood) as its center of operations. Since the building had been sold just a few days before my 1998 visit, the owners were not quite sure what their next step would be. The band was performing only sporadically—in the same halls as before and with a university-type of crowd as its audience—while its management was getting things organized.

Musical Decision-Making

The three owners of Chébere still select the band's repertoire with the same criteria as before: they use the best material possible (a combination of original and cover tunes) and choose quality lyrics. A compact disc on which all but one of the selections were cover versions of songs they liked had just been released before my 1998 visit. The owners still allow the musicians to suggest possible tunes to record and to contribute their own material.

Osvaldo Ferri left the group in 1995 because of health problems, so it was necessary for the Chébere owners to find a new arranger. A keyboardist named Gustavo Pollioto, who is not a member of the group, did part of the arrangements for the compact disc that the band had just released, and another outsider, Daniel Grifo, also helped. The rest was done by Chébere's new keyboardist, Pachi Moyano, along with Pepe Garnero, who did the wind parts. Moyano and Garnero now share the arranging duties. Moyano uses computer equipment to put together complete scores of his arrangements and to put diskettes together, but the parts are hand-copied for the musicians. As is customary, the singers do not know how to read music, and chord symbols are used in the parts for the guitarists and keyboardists.

Rehearsals are run as before, putting together the instrumental parts and then calling in the singers, who do not read music. The two new arrangers now direct the rehearsals. The percussionists operate as before, adding what they want, and performing without a part. The guitarist often has no part, either. There is no special choreography, but the Dominican singer moves around while he sings. Everyone can make comments and give ideas on changing and/or improving the band's arrangements.

The "new" Chébere has released one recording, on the SUM label, which will produce and distribute their compact discs. SUM, a single-owner enterprise, has signed Chébere to make five compact discs over a four-year period. The group records and mixes its products in Córdoba; the masters are made abroad and then pressed in Buenos Aires. Each person records his part live, without the use of any machines or sequences, and the singers record over the tracks that have been recorded for them by the instrumentalists in the group; no plans have been made to record with any guest artists. No photos appeared in the compact disc that had been released; only the arrangers' names—not the band members'—were listed on it, and both *tropical* and *moderno* selections were featured in equal number. Before the "new" Chébere was formed in 1998, the "Reencuentros" were recorded with BMG, and the band had thought that it was going to launch its recordings in the U.S. Latin market. This latter project did not work out because the record label wanted to have Chébere on staff recording in the United States and then planned to market the group's compact discs in Argentina.

Besides the owners, who are middle-aged, the average age of the musicians in the band is between 25 and 30 years old; the two youngest ones are 18 and 20. The members of the group come from the same personal and educational backgrounds as before and have many types of musical experience: few were ever real *cuarteteros,* some are presently or were formerly university students, some are members of the local symphony orchestra, and some have conservatory degrees. I discovered that one Chébere musician is a classical guitarist who occasionally plays formal recitals.

Videla

Group History

In 1995, Videla and Emeterio Farías had jointly owned Sazón. When Videla joined Chébere to do the "Reencuentros," he was obliged to dismiss all of his musicians. After this project was dissolved, he began to form his own group once again. His former announcer joined him as orchestra manager, and a couple of musicians from Gary's group were hired to play in his new band, but little other information was available in July 1998 regarding his plans. Videla no longer had an office at Mejor Propaganda, so it was necessary to call him at home for information.

Videla's new group had been performing at locations in the interior, but with little success. His band had also been going to Buenos Aires to play in the *bailantas* and had signed a contract with the *bailantas*' record label to do a compact disc. Since the group had not yet made a recording and details about Videla's plans were being kept secret, it was not possible to find out any more about his band. It was speculated by many, however, that Videla would soon be retiring from active performance to produce recordings, compose, and arrange. He was, in fact, already acting as a producer for some groups.

Tru-la-lá

Group History

Although Tru-la-lá was doing well in 1998, it had gone through a real crisis in my absence. Shortly after my prior departure, the *tropical* singer Jean Carlos had decided to leave the band to form his own group. At first he had enjoyed great success by concentrating on merengue (with an occasional *moderno* number and some *cumbia* thrown in) and singing everything himself, but after one really good year, his popularity had begun to fade. He put only his own photograph on his recordings.

Once Jean Carlos had left Tru-la-lá, La Barra had become tremendously successful—it became first in the standings—and Tru-la-lá had declined in popularity to sixth or seventh. Cánovas had hired a singer to replace Jean Carlos, but he did not dance or have Jean Carlos's presence. When it was decided that this new singer should be asked to leave the group, Sandro, the *moderno* singer, abandoned Tru-la-lá to form his own band. At the time of my 1998 trip, Sandro had not yet achieved any real success, and the singer asked to leave the band had formed a group called Los Venados. When Cánovas then added a trumpet and a saxophone to Tru-la-lá, things only got worse. He eventually chose to have a trumpet and a trombone in the group.

When Jean Carlos had left Tru-la-lá, the band's accordion player and one of the keyboardists had decided to join him; the keyboardist later left Jean Carlos and formed a group called La Clave along with some musicians who were leaving other bands. One of Tru-la-lá's keyboardists had joined his brother in La Barra at the same time, and other personnel changes had occurred as well. Two brothers of one of the orchestra managers were hired to play percussion when the *timbales* player became one of the band's singers. One of them, who used to be a *plomo* for Jean Carlos, was now playing *tambora* in Tru-la-lá. The former conga player, who had been playing electronic *tambora,* was asked to play *güiro* when Cánovas decided only to announce and sing (Cánovas had formerly played *güiro* as well). The original drum set player had stayed with the band, and an electric guitar player from Videla's group had been taken on (he had been with Chébere meanwhile). One of Videlas's former keyboardists who had lost his job was also hired.

In July 1998 Tru-la-lá consisted of 16 members, four of whom were singers who did not play any instruments while they performed (one of these was Cánovas, who was still the group's announcer). One of the singers was doing only a few numbers per night, either slow or *moderno*-style ones, and Cánovas was singing a couple of tunes per evening at most. The other two singers, Cristián Amato and Alejandro Severio, were taking turns and singing tunes that sounded *tropical* (some were *cumbias*). There was a *tambora* player who also played congas, a *timbales* player, two keyboards, two trumpets, one trombone, *güiro,* another percussion player, drum set, bass guitar, and electric guitar; the accordion had been eliminated from the band.

Tru-la-lá's office had been moved from downtown to Cánovas's house, a much more peaceful location. The band was still playing in the same dance halls as before and had pretty much stopped going to the *bailantas* to perform.

Musical Decision-Making

Manolo still has the final say in what gets recorded by Tru-la-lá. Selections include a combination of cover tunes (international hit songs, recommended ones, or tunes brought from abroad) and original material, including compositions done by Tru-la-lá members and other composers living in Córdoba, who are still allowed to collect royalties. Before making a recording, Cánovas takes a few days to get together some songs that have good potential; he has the singers listen to them to see if they like them and asks for their opinions. Lalo, the new arranger who has replaced Victor Scavuzzo, is also consulted.

One of the Tru-la-lá keyboardists I met in 1994, Dard "Lalo" Kaczorowski, eventually became the group's arranger; he has continued to perform on keyboards as well. Lalo was given the band's arranging duties only gradually, as a result of Manolo's giving Scavuzzo less and less to do; Cánovas had wanted to try a different approach. For reasons of economy, Scavuzzo had used many of his own tunes on recordings, but little by little this practice came to a halt, and he and Cánovas went their separate ways. This change in arranger, as well as the departure of the band's accordion player, who used to copy out the parts for the musicians, caused slight changes in how the group rehearses and learns tunes. Although Scavuzzo worked with computerized equipment, Lalo does not. Since Lalo does not have time to copy parts for everyone, some of the material the band plays is done by ear. For the pieces that Lalo arranges, he invents and hand-copies parts for the brass players (and sometimes for the keyboardists); the keyboard parts contain chord symbols whenever possible. The electric guitarist and percussionists play by ear.

In rehearsals, the material given to Tru-la-lá on diskettes (prepared with sequences) is changed around a bit to make it suitable for performance and recording. Rehearsals are often held on Tuesdays or Wednesdays in the Estadio del Centro, but are sometimes held on weekends in the same location where the band will be playing its dance. Rehearsals are run by Lalo, who plays the accordion part on one of the keyboards and especially supervises the pieces that must be learned by ear.

Although Tru-la-lá continues to record with BMG, only Manolo's face now appears on the front of its compact discs—not a photograph of the whole group as before—and almost all of the material performed by the band sounds *tropical*. The names of the musicians and singers do not appear on the liner notes. Everyone now records live, without the use of any sequences, and the band's 1998 compact disc was very successful.

Gary

Group History

Not much had changed with Gary's group during the time I was away. Two musicians who had left his band for Videla's had been replaced, and one of the female singers was new, but there had been no other changes of personnel. Gary even had the same secretary and agent. Instead of Gary's office being located in its former luxurious quarters, however, it had been moved to a small apartment on Chacabuco Avenue in downtown Córdoba. Gary's operating procedures had remained the same, as had the places where the group performed (in the interior and the *bailantas*), but he was coming to Córdoba much more seldom than before. While I was visiting in 1998, he did have one special event planned for the city of Córdoba and was placing all sorts of ads in the newspaper to promote it. He was still recording a combination of *tropical, moderno,* and *melódico* selections on his compact discs and felt that his group was doing quite well.

Gary was now setting his sights more on Chile, Peru, Central America, and perhaps the United States instead of Argentina; he was hoping to be able to record a compact disc in the States. His former plan of recording slow, ballad-type tunes in the States had not worked out, but he had won the "Tropicana Golden Award," given out by the International Association of Entertainment Journalists in Las Vegas, Nevada, in 1998. He had traveled to Nevada to receive the prize and had sung two tunes during the award ceremony.

Santamarina

Group History

During my 1998 visit, I found that few of the 1994 members of Santamarina were still with the band: only Fernando Bottalló, the group's drum set player, and the band's announcer had remained. I also discovered that Santamarina's orchestra and box office manager, Roberto Ramis, had become a joint owner of the group along with Fernando. Roberto had decided to continue on as both orchestra and box office manager in addition to carrying out his new duties. The other two Bottalló brothers who had been owners, Rubén and Carlos, were no longer associated with the group. Rubén had left to devote himself to rental properties and Carlos was selling cars; they were no longer involved in musical endeavors. Julio "El Turco" ("The Turk") Manzur was no longer singing, nor was he an owner, either; he was running a drug store instead. Along with the change in ownership, the band's office had been moved right downtown, only a few steps away from Radio Suquía's new location and Mejor Propaganda.

The very day I called the band's new office, I was given an appointment. Since news of my visit had spread quickly, Fernando and Roberto already knew that I was in town. I discovered that the new owners do their advertising with Farías and broadcast their commercials on several radio stations: LV3, LV2, Radio Popular, and Radio Suquía. Although the band's formation had remained the same, with the same number of musicians and the same instrumentation, the personnel had changed. Both of the new singers, Charly and Cristián, were around twenty years old and sang *tropical melódico;* the band was doing much less of the *moderno* style than before. Charly, in particular, had added dancing and a show aspect to the band's performances. Just as before, the band was playing mostly in the province of Córdoba, neighboring provinces (including the province of Buenos Aires), and the *bailantas* of Buenos Aires. Some of their longer trips had included performances in Comodoro Rivadavia and San Carlos de Bariloche. They were still using the same style of uniform as before.

Musical Decision-Making

Now that Fernando Bottalló has taken over most of the musical leadership of Santamarina, more of an emphasis is being placed on *tropical* selections than before; only one set of *moderno* tunes is sung at dances, and some of the *tropical* songs are sung in the *melódico* style. Other new developments are that the *tunga-tunga* is being emphasized more than before and that some song lyrics have social content. One big Santamarina hit written by one of the new singers, for example, discusses abortion. Another addresses child abuse. The "new" group has recorded both original material and cover tunes (consisting of successful "oldies," Central American hits, and a merengue) and is now performing *cumbias* regularly, as many as five or six per evening. Band members are now encouraged to offer their own compositions or to suggest cover tunes to perform; all suggestions are considered and/or tried out. Contrary to the time when Carlos Bottalló composed almost all of the band's material, the policy is now more open.

Fernando Bottalló now does all of Santamarina's arrangements, which are simpler, more popular, and easier to dance to than before. Some tunes are arranged in the unsophisticated, early style of Santamarina in order to better reach the band's audience.

Since Santamarina no longer has its former office and rehearsal space, rehearsals are now held in Toledo, where the band has a warehouse and the bus driver lives. Fernando runs rehearsals, in which everyone is allowed to make suggestions for changes. Since most of the musicians know how to read music—the way it has always been in this group—written-out parts are prepared for the rehearsals.

Contrary to what happened in the past, all names and faces of the members of Santamarina now appear on the covers of the band's compact discs and in the liner notes. Another change made in the group is that everyone now records live in Córdoba with the JM label; each singer does approximately half of the disc. On Santamarina's compact disc recorded in June 1996, *Olé Olá,* sixteen songs had been recorded instead of the usual ten or eleven. All performing at dances is done live as well.

Jiménez

Group History

In July 1998, the group of Carlos Jiménez was enjoying tremendous success; it was the top band in the city by far, having to turn away many fans from its dances for lack of space. The group had also returned to playing in the Sargento Cabral Club, a somewhat dangerous locale where it had always drawn many admirers and which had been closed due to too much noise. I discovered some changes in the band's operations as well. For one, Jiménez had built an annex to his house in which he now had an office and a rehearsal room. Tito Avedaño, who had retired from announcing for the band, was now the group's office manager. The office itself was a true haven of memorabilia portraying the accomplishments and career of Jiménez: all of his gold and platinum records were displayed on its walls and many trophies and important photographs were in plain view. A door from the office led to the rehearsal space now used by the band; they no longer used the family's *quincho* by the pool to rehearse, nor did they need to enter the Jiménez house. The band had also begun playing in the *bailantas* of Buenos

Aires again and was planning a trip to Chile to break ground for other *cuarteto* groups.

The Jiménez family was still heavily involved in Carlos's career: his wife was still managing his finances along with the couple's lawyer, and their son, Carlitos, had decided that he wanted to be a *cuarteto* singer. Much to my surprise, Tribi had recently left the band (Byron and Pupi had left long before, in 1995) and three young singers by the names of Juan Carlos Olmos, Marcos Bainotti, and Hugo Dante Merlo had been hired to help Carlos out. From talking with these three young men at rehearsals and dances, I saw that their presence had helped to change the style of the group a bit by giving it a more youthful image. Since Jiménez is now middle-aged, these fellows were helping him to rest by taking care of some of the singing duties; they began each set (of which there were usually three per evening) by taking turns singing, after which Carlos would come on. The new singers did approximately three or four tunes per evening apiece, including the likes of *cumbia* and rap music, and I noticed that each young man had his own special group of fans. Jiménez had updated his own image a bit as well. Although La Mona was still doing the same stage antics as before, he was now changing his quite sophisticated clothes before each set and was coming onto the stage wearing a long coat each time. After a few numbers, he would remove the coat to reveal the matching outfit underneath it. As soon as he would throw the coat to the floor, it would be picked up by his personal valet and taken backstage, where a cooler of nonalcoholic drinks was also located. Carlos had not changed as far as generosity goes: he went out of his way to help me, and on one occasion, I saw him invite a female singer who had lost her job to sing at one of his dances to get exposure.

Because of the copyright permissions I needed from this group for my book, I spent much of my time in Córdoba with this band and those who worked with it during June and July 1998. It was necessary for me to meet with Jiménez's lawyer several times for me to find out which tunes were still registered with his own publishing company, called Jimdel, and which ones belonged to Warner and BMG (Jiménez has changed labels, which own the rights to some of his songs, many times). Another thing I had to do was find the musicians and composers who had written the tunes and/or granted me the interviews I wanted to use, which involved locating people without telephones, waiting in living rooms for hours at a time, going to rehearsals and dances, and creating forms for the

7.1a. Juan Carlos Olmos, Omar "Conejo" Rivarola, and Ricardo Verón (named from left to right) take time out to eat steak sandwiches at a rehearsal at the new Jiménez studio. Photograph by Jane L. Florine, Córdoba, Argentina, 1998.

songwriters to sign. This quest for signatures involved me in all sorts of activities because the men wanted both to help and include me in what they were doing. I was invited to eat *lomitos* (steak sandwiches) one evening at a rehearsal, for example (see figures 7.1a and 7.1b). I was also allowed to go to songwriters' and interviewees' homes to collect the signatures I needed.

Musical Decision-Making

The repertoire used by Jiménez is more or less the same as before, but with the addition of more *tropical* elements and *cumbias*. The three new singers, in particular, sing this more *tropical* type of tune. One of these young men was singing a rap-type song at dances as well. The tunes are still selected by a joint effort of the entire group, and the singers are all allowed to perform what they like; if necessary, they may change around the material they are given to sing as well. All of the members of the band continue to compose, some with computerized equipment (sequences) and some without. It is common to find members of the group getting together outside of rehearsals to put songs together in home studios.

7.1b. Luis Tapia, Abraham Vásquez-Martínez, Hugo Dante Merlo, and Marcos Bainotti (named from left to right) take a dinner break at a rehearsal in their new studio. Photograph by Jane L. Florine, Córdoba, Argentina, 1998.

Everyone in the Jiménez band still contributes his ideas in rehearsals, which are still held only when a recording needs to be produced. There is much open discussion of all suggestions. On these occasions, the group begins to rehearse in the early evening and may continue to do so almost all night. Musicians commonly get together during the mornings of rehearsal days to put their tunes together on diskettes, but rehearsals are suspended on the days the band performs at dances or must travel.

At the end of 1997, Jiménez had changed from BMG to the Warner label. He had signed a contract for several recordings with Warner, the first of which was released in early 1998 when his contract with BMG had expired. During my July 1998 visit, the band was in the process of composing and rehearsing the tunes to be recorded on its next compact disc. As in the past, everyone who participates in the production of a recording has his name listed in the liner notes, but only Jiménez's image appears on the cover. Now that the three new singers have been added to the group, each has been allowed to record a solo number on Jiménez's compact discs. The last two or three compact discs released by the band have been extremely successful and have gained them many fans.

Since I already knew most of the men in the band well, I enjoyed getting caught up on what had happened to them in the last three years. The major changes in the group regarding personnel were Tribi's departure (he had not been replaced) and the hiring of the three new singers. It was interesting for me to meet and talk with these three young men, who allowed me to interview them. What I found out about them follows.

Juan Carlos Olmos

Juan Carlos Olmos, whose nickname is "Muñeco" (Doll), does not play any instruments in the group—not even when he is resting his voice (see figure 7.1a). Twenty-four years old in 1998, he was born in the city of Córdoba. Although he is not really from a family of musicians, he told me, his Italian grandfather played the organ and sang in church. Juan Carlos feels that his interest in music did not come from his grandfather; it was something that came from within, he thought, since he had liked to sing even when he was small. He described himself as a solitary person with few friends and said that music had made him strong. Juan Carlos has always listened to a variety of music, including *cuarteto*, but he began to study music seriously only at the age of eighteen; in his last year of high school, he started taking lessons in lyric singing (classical music), including opera and tango. He has now begun to take lessons in singing popular music with a private voice teacher who is a phonologist, and he has learned how to read music. Someday he would like to learn how to play piano, or an instrument with which he could prepare sequences, in order to help himself in composing songs. He plays no instruments at present.

Juan Carlos had planned to attend college after finishing high school, but when the opportunity arose to work with the Jiménez group, he changed his mind. The manner in which he was hired was like a dream come true: "On a radio program that Carlos Jiménez has on Saturdays, *El Club de los Bailarines,* which is broadcast on Saturday afternoon at two P.M., they were announcing [a contest] for singers who had their own style; a photograph and a demo cassette with tunes [had to be submitted to enter the competition]. I signed up. I brought my photograph and my cassette tape [of songs] to [the radio station]. As it turned out, I ended up in the group along with my colleague, Marcos." According to Juan Carlos, the two young men had joined the band at the same time. Prior to this, he had done some odd jobs to help out his family, with whom he lives, such as working as a mailman.

Being hired by Jiménez turned out to be a traumatic experience for Juan Carlos. Since he had never sung with another group or in public before joining the band, his lack of experience made him suffer from immense stage fright. Fortunately, he at least had knowledge of what went on at dance halls before taking the job, which had helped him some: he had gone to *cuarteto* events to dance from the time he was fifteen and had always liked *cuarteto* music, but he had not been interested in the musicians' scene at the time. Since he liked being exposed to new things, he had also gone to discos, other sorts of dance places, and concerts of classical music when he was younger.

Juan Carlos is allowed to choose the songs he sings in the Jiménez group and helps in rehearsals when the tunes meant for him are being put together. He has also written some song lyrics of his own, to which he has mentally created melodies, and has received help in arranging them by singing them a cappella to his colleagues; he does not work with computer equipment. Given a choice, there are many styles of music that Juan Carlos likes to sing: classical music, *boleros,* Mexican music, *tropical,* and especially *melódico (tropical melódico),* which has real feeling to it, he says. Regarding *cuarteto,* he thinks that he will have to develop his own special way of singing it if he ever becomes a solo singer.

In his two years and six months with the Jiménez band, Juan Carlos has contributed his "good vibrations" to the audience. He has attempted to learn how to dance to better mesh with the group as well, he mentioned. As to the future, Juan Carlos said that he always wants to continue singing—whether it be on a big stage or just for a few people in a pub. Seeing how the Jiménez organization with its thirty or so employees works has been fascinating, he said; he has learned that what a singer transmits is very strong. His initiation into the band was doubly difficult, he recalled, both because of his inexperience and Jiménez's popularity: "Taking the place of Carlos Jiménez was very difficult. What happened is that Jiménez is even more than a god for the public. Since many people think he is a god, being up on stage replacing him wasn't easy at all. The first time I got up on stage there was a deafening lot of whistling and catcalling. Bottles were flying, [and] just about anything was being thrown. But as time went by, and the dances went by, people began accepting the [situation]. They realized that Carlos Jiménez was not going to retire from singing [or be replaced]; instead, we were just there to help him out."

Juan Carlos expressed gratitude for the opportunity he has been given and compared it to the one Jiménez had at the age of fifteen upon winning a singing contest. He was glad to be part of the Jiménez clan, although like any family, its members can have their differences, he said (Olmos 1998).

Marcos Bainotti

Marcos Bainotti, whose nickname is "Glaciar" ("Glacier") or "Pecho Frío" ("Cold Chest") plays *güiro* and tambourine in the Jiménez band when he is not singing. He began his musical career long before starting in the Jiménez group; at the time of my 1998 visit, he was twenty-three (see figure 7.1b). Marcos was born in the province of Córdoba, in Porteña. Although he is not from a family of professional musicians, he grew up with a lot of music in his home: his father, who played folk music on his guitar, had formed a family group along with an uncle of Marcos's who played string bass. Marcos did go to dances when he was younger, but he was never a very good dancer, he said. He went mostly to listen to the groups and to look for a "model" to follow.

Marcos, who has liked to sing from the time he has been small, later learned how to play trumpet and read music in the Youth Municipal Band in the town where he lived. He also attended a local conservatory for two years and took private voice lessons with an opera teacher in a town called San Francisco. Although he has always liked classical and many other types of music, he would choose to sing *boleros* were he given a choice.

Marcos finished high school but did not go on to college because he started performing professionally. At first he played trumpet in a *cuarteto* group (for one and one half years), but he has not done so for quite a long time now. Then, after he had sung for three years with a group from his home town, the possibility of singing with Videla's band came about. This had happened because Marcos's group had performed jointly with Videla's band one time that the latter had played in a nearby town called Freyre. Once Videla had heard him sing there, Marcos made a trip to Córdoba. The two of them talked, after which Videla auditioned and hired him. Marcos was only nineteen at the time.

When Marcos was small, he liked lyric, slow music (*melódico*). He preferred Argentine singers over foreign ones because he could understand the lyrics sung in Spanish, but he did like the music of people like

Julio Iglesias. Nowadays he prefers to listen to classical music because it helps him to relax, but he still likes *melódico*. He likes *cuarteto,* too, but does not feel comfortable singing the *tropical* style. Marcos has never sung folk music.

Although Marcos likes to sing, he would like to learn how to play an instrument in order to be able to work as an arranger someday or to be able to arrange his own tunes. He learned to play a bit of piano at the conservatory, but that was all. He is glad that he can read music because this knowledge gives him "a little more freedom and ability to hear things that others who don't know music theory can't." His ability to read music has helped him to learn how to sing new tunes faster than other singers, for example (Bainotti 1994).

It was quite by accident that Marcos became a member of the Jiménez group, as he explained to me during my visit:

> Videla became affiliated with another venture and with another singer, Pelusa, a singer here in Córdoba, and I went back to the town I'm from, Porteña, which is located about 260 kilometers from the capital. [At that same time], Jiménez had announced a contest to find some singers because he was going to begin singing in a theater in Carlos Paz and wouldn't have time to get to the first set of his dances. Since he would finish at the theater [in Carlos Paz] quite late, he held a contest. I hadn't found out about this contest because I was in Porteña; the information hadn't arrived there. And then a friend who worked for a radio station here let me know about it, and I came to speak with Carlos. Juan Carlos had already won the contest. In other words, I came to talk to him on my own behalf. He had me audition, and well, we rehearsed. [That's how] both of us ended up being hired.

Long after this had happened, Carlos began paying attention to Hugo, the third of the young singers to be hired, stated Marcos, and saw that he had a different style from what the others in the group were doing; he decided to hire him. Marcos wasn't sure why Carlos had chosen three singers, but said "there are three different things to listen to." He, like the other two fellows, does two or three songs in each set, and then Carlos comes on to sing. Marcos chooses the tunes he performs with the group and also does some composing. When he joined the Jiménez band, he was surprised to find out that all the band members are allowed to compose songs for Carlos as well.

Marcos explained what it was like to begin singing with the group once he was hired: "In the beginning it was quite hard because Carlos is a singer who is a strong idol here in Córdoba and across the entire country. Well, it sort of rubbed people the wrong way that there would be someone else singing in his group. But over time, after about a year and a half, I think, everything changed. But not in the beginning." According to Marcos, the older members of the group treat him "just like one of the guys." He does not feel out of place, since they are all working toward having the dances go well. Marcos has no immediate plans; he is young, is comfortable in the group, and has a lot left to learn from his colleagues, he feels (Bainotti 1998).

Hugo Dante Merlo

Hugo Dante Merlo, whose nickname is "Chuqui," has studied all kinds of dance, even classical; he was twenty-three in 1998 (see figure 7.1b). Besides singing, he plays hand percussion, *güiro*, and tambourine in the group. Born in the city of Córdoba, he moved to Mexico when he was eight years old. He later lived in many other places for short periods of time, such as California and Puerto Rico, but returned to Córdoba every year after he left the country in order to visit his family. When he returned for his yearly visit to Argentina a year and a half before the date I spoke with him, he had ended up staying. He had come to visit his parents, as usual, but Jiménez had heard of him and had asked to meet with him. Since the two men got on well, he had joined the band. At the point Hugo was hired, Juan Carlos and Marcos had already been with the group for quite some time; for this reason, he felt well-received. He had never gone to a *cuarteto* dance before he began performing with Jiménez.

Hugo's father and mother, who were from Santa Fe and the littoral region, respectively, are professional singers who do Paraguayan music with harp. As a result, Hugo became quite interested in Argentine folklore and later began to teach it. In fact, he considers himself to be a dancer—not a singer. He was a member of the national ballet of Mexico for seven years (in the School of Fine Arts in Mexico City), and later, when he worked with a salsa group in Puerto Rico, he sang and played congas. Besides being a percussionist, he has had some training in singing, has had two years of conservatory training in Paris, where he lived for many years (he studied classical guitar and piano), has studied four years at a university in Paris, and is a language teacher.

The music Hugo likes best is salsa, whether it be for listening, singing, or performing. *Cuarteto* doesn't bother him because "it is part of the same type of music, kind of like merengue, a mixture." He feels that his varied background has allowed him to make a contribution to the Jiménez group: "Here I contribute a little bit of knowledge, a little bit of experience, since I have been in Puerto Rican and Cuban groups. I was in the percussion school in Cuba for eight months, in the national school of percussion in Havana."

Hugo plans to go back to dancing professionally someday, but feels that he cannot do so in Córdoba. "Here there is no future in dance; at the professional level you don't earn much of anything at all," he remarked. Hugo is also a composer. He creates the melody in his head, plays it on keyboards for his colleagues, and then develops it with them. His knowledge of music theory, solfège, and transposition allows him to make scores and parts for his own compositions (Merlo 1998).

The Figure and Image of Carlos Jiménez

The fact that Carlos Jiménez is still number one in Córdoba after so many years is a phenomenon that merits analysis; in the changing history of the genre, his presence has been a given. Observing his continued success in 1998 only emphasized his importance.

It has been said that Carlos Jiménez possesses more attraction and magnetism than any one person has ever had (Mero 1988:65). His antics onstage, such as his body gyrations and interaction with the public, make it impossible not to feel his enthusiasm and energy. People often talk about his special wardrobe—especially since he rarely wears a particular outfit more than once—and the disreputable people found at his dances. Jiménez is the only *cuarteto* figure about whom an entire book has been written and the only one to have his own radio program; he used to have his own television programs as well (Mero 1988:146, 162). In Córdoba, one routinely hears his name mentioned in all types of social circles. Much of what is said about him has reached preposterous proportions, such as remarks to the effect that he has a piece of platinum in his head and is fighting cancer (Hepp 1988:21–22).

Jiménez's generosity, especially with the poor, is well-known. At dances, he occasionally raffles off motorcycles and houses; he has even given away taxis to create employment possibilities for the winners (Mero 1988:68). One Mother's Day, he had toys delivered to the children of female convicts at the local prison (Mero 1988:163). On Mondays and Tuesdays, the only days of the week that he is at home, he supposedly receives people who come to ask him for money and/or personal advice (Mero 1988:163).

Another unique aspect of Jiménez's persona is that he consistently draws large crowds. The leader of the General Confederation of Labor in Buenos Aires had the following to say about the singer: "It just can't be. I've never seen such a thing. In this country, nobody can get more than two thousand people together, yet he does what he wants. We, at the CGT (General Confederation of Labor), have free convocations, but people go to see Jiménez and pay. It's not easy to find this capacity to mobilize people, and this charisma. Even less so when people are demobilized and demoralized" (Mero 1988:182).

When at these mass events either the police or his fans have gotten out of hand, it has been only Jiménez himself who has been able to restore order (as occurred at Cosquín). On another occasion he stopped the police—not his fans—by saying "These are my people and you're not going to hit them" (Barei 1993:53). During the years that *cuarteto* was banned by the military government, *cuarteteros* continued to attend his dances, which were held secretly, as much as ever—despite risking arrest or being taken to jail. Jiménez himself insisted upon remaining at the dance hall for an entire four hours during this same era of *cuarteto*—even when the police had taken all of his followers away (Mero 1988:54; Jiménez Rufino 1994).

Analysis of Jiménez's Power and Influence

How is it possible that one mortal has such influence over so many people? The first answer to this question lies in the total personality of Jiménez as a singer, his presence, in a concept Simon Frith calls "the voice." The voice is the sign of an individual personality: "In discussing the narrative devices of contemporary pop in particular, we are not just talking about music but also about the whole process of packaging. The image of pop performers is constructed by press, and television advertisements, by the routines of photo-calls and journalists' interviews, and through gesture and performance. These things all feed into the way we hear a voice; pop singers are rarely heard 'plain' (without mediation). Their vocals already contain physical connotations, associated images, echoes of other sound. All this needs to be analyzed if we are going to treat songs as narrative structures" (Frith 1987a:145–46).

The tone of a voice is even more important than the lyrics of a song; words are only a sign of the voice. Since the voice is also a transparent reflection of feeling so intimately connected with the person that sound and image cannot be separated (Frith 1987b:98), all of the aspects of Jiménez's background and performance style described above constitute his voice. Despite his ready admission that he cannot sing well (it is often pointed out that he sings "out of tune"), Jiménez fans love La Mona's "voice" (as opposed to his singing voice), that is, what he represents (SADAIC 1992:20).

Secondly, those who adore Carlos Jiménez do so because they can identify with him. Richard Middleton describes the "domain of identification" as follows:

> Certain aspects of the psychopathology of our society . . . produce both individuals with the desire to act as representatives, focuses of identification, scapegoats, and so on, and mass audiences who need such individuals to offer them subject-positional opportunities for identity-confirmation, catharsis, wish-fulfillment, cannibalistic consumption or whatever. The star singer, so close and yet so impossibly far away, invitation to a life of unmatched intensity yet at the same time an institutionalized function in the ideological structure, is the most obvious transmission belt for the interpellative dialectic. . . . the star is the focus of what we can call the domain of identification. (Middleton 1990:249)

As Frith says, "we come to feel that we 'possess' the performer, making him part of our identity and our lives" (1987a:143). In this case, the ability to identify with Jiménez involves three elements: authenticity (or truth), ordinariness, and revenge.

Authenticity

Regarding authenticity, "Good music is the authentic expression of something—a person, an idea, a feeling, a shared experience, a Zeitgeist. Bad music is unauthentic—it expresses nothing" (Frith 1987a:136). For a performer to be authentic, he must be true to the experiences or feelings he is describing (Frith 1987a:136). Jiménez says that he sings for popular culture and his fans; he is one of them. La Mona's fans say they like him because he has not changed despite his success (Mero 1988:42,

50, 65–67, 79, 97). Contrary to what has happened with some other singers who have become rich and famous, Jiménez does not behave any differently than before: he still socializes with those from whose ranks he came (*negros* and those who are marginal), still performs every weekend in Córdoba, and sincerely performs *cuarteto* because he likes and feels it. In fact, *cuarteto* is Jiménez's favorite kind of music (Jiménez Rufino 1994). He is authentic because "he's a total *cuartetero,* body and soul, of whom there are few," "the only person who you end up believing" (Mero 1988:71). The fact that he loses three kilos per dance via physical effort (Barei 1993:53) is perhaps also a sign of truth, sincerity, and authenticity (Frith 1987a:147). Many *cuarteto* groups try to imitate Jiménez's success. Since he is authentic, however, and they are often merely trying to make money from *cuarteto* without really liking the genre, fans find out; these "imitators" are usually unsuccessful and are abandoned by *cuarteteros.*

Jiménez is an idealist who has never compromised himself for the purpose of making money; he sticks to his own personal standards of professionalism and constantly seeks to follow his fans' wishes. This can be seen in the reasons why he left Ramaló's group and how he has updated *cuarteto* while maintaining its essence, keeping the accordion and trying to use violin in his band.

Regarding song lyrics, Jiménez is also the exception to the norm. As has been shown above, he adopts special topic matter in serving the needs of his crowd, the marginalized class. So as to not abandon his fans, Jiménez has always been careful to perform in Córdoba every weekend. Although he did perform in Buenos Aires for a time, he eventually stopped going there because he missed his supporters in Córdoba and did not like the working conditions or commercialized "show" aspect of performing in *bailantas.*

Jiménez is also devoted to his band members; most of them have been with him for many years and are considered friends—not "employees." One of his greatest worries is to see that their needs are met, as occurred when he declined an offer to go to Miami for a month with the band because they would have lost a month's worth of income from dances, and when he has taken on new band members only because these men have needed work. La Mona's democratic workstyle ensures that no one person is more important than anyone else and that everyone contributes ideas.

In order to remain true to himself and his followers, Jiménez has continually refused to have an agent (he likes to be his own boss) and has created his own publishing company; lead sheets are given away to those who request them. When at one point he was being crowded out of the major locales in the city because he did not want to concede to club owners' demands, he created his own dance establishment, La Cueva, where he could be in control of his efforts (Jiménez Rufino 1994).

La Mona has even challenged the recording industry in order to maintain his ideals. The story of how *Raza Negra* came to be shows many ways in which Carlos Jiménez is his own boss, remaining true to himself instead of bending to commercial pressures. With *Raza Negra,* Jiménez was merely following his own agenda and desires—not following the crowd. When he felt that PolyGram, the label he had long recorded with, was not properly distributing his recordings, he switched to BMG— his choice of the four labels that courted him (Ábalos 23 September 1994:21).

Ordinariness

Besides being attracted by his authenticity, Jiménez fans can identify with their idol because of his ordinariness: he is just like the next guy. Although he has become rich and famous, he still associates with them just as before. This fact is emphasized in some of his song lyrics, such as "La Mona es un Muchacho de Barrio" ("La Mona Is a Neighborhood Boy"; C. JIMÉNEZ—A. KUSTIN) and "La Mona, es como Ud." ("La Mona, He Is Like You"; JIMÉNEZ—ARÉVALO—VERÓN), in which he emphasizes that he is just one of the boys (a member of a circle of neighborhood friends), says he got his schooling in the street, and promises that he will never change. In one commercial video, La Mona can be heard singing "my friend, I am like you" as he appears as a factory worker, a taxi driver, a bus driver, and a fruit vendor (Barei 1993:63). In another, *El Bailarín* (1993), he mixes with children and the elderly at a local hospital.

Although Carlos Jiménez is now very wealthy, *cuarteto* fans prefer to judge the man based upon how he treats them instead of thinking about his money or where he lives. They look at his human qualities and actions toward them, wishing that they could also become successful; he is a model, a symbol of what they could become. Most of all, they appreciate the fact that he still considers himself to be a *negro* and has not forgotten about the prejudice and discrimination either he or they have had to endure: he has not renounced his origins or begun to look down upon them. Paradoxically, Jiménez is still seen as a member of the working class.

As Pablo Vila has stated (1992:131), popular music has always offered ways in which people could enjoy and appreciate identities they yearned for or believed themselves to possess. Simon Frith (1987a:140–42) explains this creation of identity as follows:

> Music can stand for, symbolize and offer the immediate experience of collective identity. Other cultural forms—painting, literature, design—can articulate and show off shared values and pride, but only music can make you feel them. . . . We use pop songs to create for ourselves a particular sort of self-definition, a particular place in society. The pleasure that pop music produces is a pleasure of identification—with the music we like, with the performers of the music, with the other people who like it. And it is important to note that the production of identity is also a production of non-identity—it is a process of inclusion and exclusion. . . . Only music seems capable of creating this sort of spontaneous collective identity, this kind of personally felt patriotism. . . . Music also makes one's feelings seem richer.

In the case of *cuarteto*, dancers experience a feeling of solidarity and belonging to a social space in which a strong type of identification is produced between participants. This identification is an imaginary value that is linked with ideas of fidelity (people normally follow only one group), class, and of authenticity in enjoyment; the subject and the denied object come together (Barei 1993:63). Because *cuarteto* has always helped its fans to create a group identity among people who are all of a low, marginal class, it is very important for *cuarteteros* that Jiménez be "one of them."

Revenge

Because Carlos Jiménez acts like he is one of their same social class and is a seen as a fellow *negro* who has not rejected his past, *cuarteto* fans are proud that he has "made it." Since they most likely will not succeed, he is their revenge (Mero 1988:163–64): "La Mona represents the sector he sings for because he sings about what his sector represents. . . . the conditions of Jiménez, like those of his sector, are very strict as to revenge. The most direct way of getting even with reality is with crazy dress, with which he makes fun of those who made him marginal. In other words, he is telling them that he can have those luxurious clothes and jewels on although the society that made him marginal never planned on giving them to him" (Mero 1988:79).

As part of a group, the *cuarteto* fan is then ready to show the world that despite his marginality, he is important. This was the sentiment that was expressed when so many fans went to hear Jiménez at Cosquín. There the "hidden" marginal men and women of Córdoba made it clear (on national television) that they exist and cannot be ignored; although they are low-class sewer cleaners, garbage collectors, errand boys, and domestic servants whose duties may be looked down upon, they are necessary. These people also demonstrated that they have their pride, just as they have their own music and their own leader (Hepp 1988:128). They showed that they have come to "possess" *cuarteto*, which is now a part of their identity and is built into their sense of self (Frith 1987a:143–44). Jiménez himself has expressed this feeling of marginality that his fans experience in *El Marginal*, which he made in remembrance of how marginal he felt in the early days of *cuarteto* (Jiménez Rufino 1994).

Carlos Jiménez has gone much farther than putting his feelings of marginality into words through song in *El Marginal:* he has publicly ridiculed elitists who have made fun of *cuarteto* and those he represents. For example, on talk shows filmed in Buenos Aires and broadcast nationally, he has openly embarrassed famous hosts who have invited him on their programs in order to make fun of him. Through his own rebellious actions, he has empowered his followers to feel better about themselves (Mero 1988:164–65).

In the 1980s, many middle-class university students who knew virtually nothing about *cuarteto* music or dancing began to use the music of Carlos Jiménez to express their social concerns; they drew upon his popularity with the marginal class and came to identify with him for a period of several years. Many of these young people wanted to help the poor, had opposed excesses committed by the military government, and had backed the return to democracy in 1983 (Mero 1988:129–36). It seemed only natural to work in conjunction with La Mona when justice was being demanded for the same social sector in which he sang and was revered. In addition, the students could relate to the concept of marginality: as far as they were concerned, an unemployed doctor or psychologist was just as marginal as an unemployed person from the working class (Mero 1988:89).

After Alfonsín had been in power for a time, and it was evident that he was not going to live up to his promises (regarding the economy and the prosecution of those involved in the *Proceso* for excesses that they had committed during the "Dirty War"), these disenchanted students needed a new type of music for their protest songs. Since they were protesting about a democracy—not a military government—they felt they could not use the same genres of protest music that they had used in the past. Because Jiménez was seen as being a defender of the poor, and they themselves felt marginalized, they used his tunes as a vehicle for expressing their disillusionment during this time period. Before using these songs, however, they changed their lyrics to refer to the causes they were championing (Mero 1988:88–89, 129–30). In 1987–88 these students also staged two massive *cuarteto* dances at the Universidad Nacional de Córdoba, at which Jiménez performed (Mero 1988:129–331, 153–54); this was a setting in which *cuarteto* had never before been heard.

Conclusions Regarding the Power of Jiménez

As has been shown here, the success of superstar Carlos Jiménez is due to a combination of factors. His figure alone, and his total personality, are important to his followers; by identifying with his "voice," which includes his outlandish costumes, his onstage antics, his personal history, his generosity, his sociocultural background, and everything else about him—not just the quality of his singing voice—Jiménez admirers are able to transcend their daily problems and dream of a better life. An idealist, La Mona is admired for his authenticity and his total commitment to his audience. This sincere devotion to his fans is seen in the lines he sings at the end of "La Mona Is a Neighborhood Boy": "I am a neighborhood boy who is grateful / To life for all it has given him / And I have millions of friends / And I carry them all in my heart" (Hepp 1988:14).

Because Jiménez has remained true to his kind despite his fame, his ordinariness has made him a symbol of what many *cuarteteros* would like to become. Merely by being himself he has won the support and love of his fans. The fact that he still feels just as marginal (both racially and socially) as his followers do—despite his current wealth and fame—allows them to identify with him as well; they vicariously live out his successes and experience revenge through his triumphs. It is for the same reason that others, such as university students, have come to admire Jiménez for what he represents. Important to his followers are Jiménez's humble beginnings, mixed racial background, and true love of *cuarteto;* he has come to symbolize the genre as well as those who perform and dance to it.

Through his success as a *cuarteto* singer, Jiménez has taught his admirers that it is possible for a *negro,* a *cabecita*—as some might call him—to beat the odds and triumph over prejudice. He has also shown them that they should value and feel proud of themselves—not bow down to and internalize what elitists say. By his own personal example, Jiménez has helped pave the way toward self-empowerment and self-respect for those of his same sociocultural background. During his lifetime, he has fought back against the military, ignored racial slurs and comments made in order to ridicule him, refused to sell out to commercial concerns, maintained his concern for his band members, followers, and friends, and been his own man. He has also performed the music he loves in his own way—even experimenting with new fusions such as in *Raza Negra* and expressing his sensitivity toward past prejudice and discrimination in *El Marginal.* Most significantly, he managed to overcome the bad publicity resulting from his performance at Cosquín, eventually bringing his own name and knowledge of *cuarteto* music into many Argentine households across the country. Since 1988, the *cuarteto* world has gained in press and visibility because of him.

From the time of its creation in 1943, Argentine *cuarteto* music and those associated with it have gone through a struggle for acceptance and respectability owing to their low-class and racially marginal status; *cuarteto,* like other forms of mass popular music that have preceded it, has been the object of prejudice and intolerance. The first steps the genre made toward recognition were small and gradual: its move from immigrant communities to the fringes of Córdoba, its eventual arrival to the center of the city with internal migration and industrialization, and its transmission to other areas throughout Argentina, including Buenos Aires, took more than forty years. Much of what *cuarteto* has become is the product of one man's efforts: without a doubt, it has been Carlos

Jiménez who has helped this music to achieve its present somewhat more elevated status, put it on the road toward eventual acceptance, and given *cuarteteros* more personal dignity.

Afterthoughts

With these reflections on the importance of Jiménez over the years, thus ended my trip to Córdoba; I had experienced the latest developments in an ever-changing and innovative musical world. Some change was to have been expected, as happens in all types of popular music, so part of what I found did not surprise me. While taking in both the subtle changes and major upheavals that had occurred in three years, I rediscovered many of the same bands I remembered and friends I had made from my fieldwork days. It was refreshing to see that *cuarteto* was still going strong, with younger groups coming into force, and that large crowds were still attending dances.

Although Jiménez was still king, it became obvious that *cuarteto* was not in danger of dying with his passing; in fact, La Mona was already planning for his eventual exit from the scene by having hired three young singers for his group. I saw that outside influences, such as Jean Carlos with the Dominican merengue, had continued to enrich and add further innovative elements to *cuarteto*. Groups continued to look outside their ranks for new ideas, yet the essence of *cuarteto*, the *tunga-tunga*, remained.

As to the bands I had studied in 1994–95, Jiménez's seasoned one had become rejuvenated with new blood. Santamarina, with its change of management, had become less autocratic and was enjoying a new success that reminded one of its earliest years. Chébere, sadly, was almost nonexistent, and Tru-la-lá had risen from the ashes of defeat. Gary was maintaining his position, yet Videla had encountered new problems to solve. I could not have predicted in 1995 the results of this most recent trip.

I enjoyed seeing that the tight-knit culture I had observed in Córdoba was still there, albeit with a new twist; the core elements had remained, but with enough added innovation to keep the music alive. I became convinced that I would be able to make yet another journey to visit my *cuarteto* friends at some other point far in the future; the *cuarteto* tradition would remain strong and would embody the heart of

Córdoba for many years to come. As Jiménez has put it in "Nuestro Estilo Cordobés," the people of Córdoba will be dancing *cuarteto* as long as they live: "They are never going to bury the *tunga, tunga, tunga,* / the *cuarteto* rhythm will never, never, die. / No, no, no, it will never die, / no, no, no, it will always be immortal. / Yes, yes, yes, it will always live. / Yes, yes, yes, I can assure you of that."

APPENDIX A

Places Where *Cuarteto* Recordings
May Be Purchased in Córdoba

MJ Musical
San Martín 114
5000 Córdoba, Argentina
Telephone/Fax: (54-351) 421-2365, 421-4794, 426-0960,
426-0961

Eden
Opispo Trejo 15
5000 Córdoba, Argentina
Telephone: (54-351) 421-3143

Disca, S.R.L.
San Martín 86
5000 Córdoba, Argentina

Círculo Músical
25 de Mayo 186 or San Martín 418
5000 Córdoba, Argentina

La Suiza, S.A.
San Martín 360/74
5000 Córdoba, Argentina
Telephone: (54-351) 422-4483, 422-9631, 422-8858

APPENDIX B

The Major Record Companies in Buenos Aires That Produce *Cuarteto* Recordings

BMG Ariola Argentina, S.A.
Talcahuano 750—piso 6
1013 Buenos Aires, Argentina
Telephone: (54-11) 4373-6631/4051
Fax: (54-11) 4814-2415

PolyGram Discos, S.A.
Av. Córdoba 1345—piso 14
1055 Buenos Aires, Argentina
Telephone: (54-11) 4813-0916/7361/1169/6169;
    4815-4890/4891/4892/4893
Fax: (54-11) 4812-0034

Sony Music Entertainment (Argentina), S.A.
Bartolomé Mitre 1986
1089 Buenos Aires, Argentina
Telephone: (54-11) 4953-7938/7144/9607/0105
Fax: (54-11) 4953-2030

Warner Music Argentina
Castro Barros 848
1217 Buenos Aires, Argentina
Telephone: (54-11) 4931-5666/7881/0326

NOTES

1. Introduction

1. Most of the other provinces or areas of Argentina also have their own special musics associated with them. Many of these provinces (Buenos Aires, La Rioja, Salta, Corrientes, Santiago del Estero, San Luis, San Juan, Mendoza, Jujuy, Patagonia, Santa Fe, Entre Ríos, and Misiones), and their corresponding regional musics, are mentioned in the epigraph to this book.

2. In my article called *"Cuarteto:* Dance-Hall Entertainment or People's Music?" which appeared in the *Latin American Music Review* (see the bibliography for details), I discuss in depth my personal dilemma of how to classify and write about *cuarteto.*

3. A copy of *El Marginal,* cataloged as Mus CD 7613, can be found at the Florida State University's Warren D. Allen Music Library.

2. The History and Musical Evolution of *Cuarteto*

1. See figure 3.2, p. 399, of my Ph.D. dissertation, which is listed in the bibliography of this book, for examples of these connecting passages. Examples can also be found in the paper by Leonardo Waisman, "Tradición e innovación en el cuarteto cordobés," listed in the bibliography.

2. See figure 3.3, p. 399, of my dissertation for examples of rhythmic cells found in early *cuarteto* music. My examples are based upon those provided in "Tradición e innovación en el cuarteto cordobés," by Leonardo Waisman.

3. See figure 3.4, p. 399, of my dissertation for examples of typical *bailaló* endings.

4. See figure 3.7, p. 402, of my dissertation for examples of how the bass line of the contemporary *tunga-tunga* can be varied.

5. For a transcription of *cumbia,* see Peter Manuel's book *Popular Musics of the Non-Western World* (New York and Oxford: Oxford University Press, 1988), 51.

6. For a transcription of a typical merengue passage, see Manuel, *Popular Musics of the Non-Western World,* 45.

7. For a transcription of the entire song of "Penita," including the piccolo part, see figure 3.16, pp. 427–40, of my dissertation. A copy of *El Marginal*, on which "Penita" is recorded, can be found at the Florida State University's Warren D. Allen Music Library. Its catalog number is Mus CD 7613.

8. For transcriptions of the fragments of the four songs discussed from *Raza Negra*, see figures 3.18, 3.19, 3.20, and 3.21, pp. 442–52, of my dissertation.

4. Dancing *Cuarteto*-Style

1. Many of the ideas discussed in this section about the ritual function of *cuarteto* were first presented (in a slightly different format) in a paper read at the annual meeting of the Society for Ethnomusicology held in Toronto, Canada, in 1996; this same paper was later read at conferences in Ybor City, Florida, and Bowling Green, Ohio (see bibliography). A similar paper was later presented in Spanish at the II Congreso Latinoamericano IASPM in Santiago, Chile, in 1997. The IASPM paper was published as part of the conference proceedings in 1999 (see bibliography).

6. Carlos Jiménez and the Process of Musical "Change" (Innovation)

1. See figure 3.6, pp. 427–40, of my dissertation for a complete musical transcription of "Penita." A copy of *El Marginal*, on which "Penita" is recorded, can be found at the Florida State University's Warren D. Allen Music Library. It is cataloged as Mus CD 7613.

BIBLIOGRAPHY

Ábalos, Gabriel. "Ángel Videla, el 'Beatle' cuartetero." *A diario* (Córdoba, Argentina), 9 September 1994, p. 21.
———. "Chébere, un premio bien cuartetero." *A diario* (Córdoba, Argentina), 18 November 1994, pp. 1–3.
———. "Cuando el tunga-tunga incorporó un Bam-Bam." *A diario* (Córdoba, Argentina), 9 December 1994, pp. 1–3.
———. "Cuando 'La Barra' viene marchando." *A diario* (Córdoba, Argentina), 11 November 1994, pp. 1, 8.
———. "Diez años de baile en el país de la alegría." *A diario* (Córdoba, Argentina), 25 November 1994, pp. 1–3.
———. "Eduardo Gelfo tiene alma de tunga-tunga." *A diario* (Córdoba, Argentina), 7 October 1994, p. 21.
———. "El bastión cuartetero." *A diario* (Córdoba, Argentina), 2 September 1994, p. 21.
———. "Emeterio Farías, el rey del baile." *A diario* (Córdoba, Argentina), 30 September 1994, p. 21.
———. "Noelia: 'Siempre quise ser la Mona Jiménez en mujer.'" *A diario* (Córdoba, Argentina), 4 November 1994, pp. 1–3.
———. "Nuevo grupo bailable cordobés." *A diario* (Córdoba, Argentina), 16 September 1994, p. 20.
———. "'Raza negra,' el nuevo de la Mona." *A diario* (Córdoba, Argentina), 23 September 1994, p. 21.
———. "Todo el país bailó con Heraldo Bosio." *A diario* (Córdoba, Argentina), 2 December 1994, pp. 1–3.
———. "Una cuestión de piel." *Página 12* (Buenos Aires, Argentina), 8 September 1993, pp. 30–31.
———. "Una superbanda sabe mantenerse." *A diario* (Córdoba, Argentina), 16 December 1994, pp. 1–3.
Adam, Barbara. "Perceptions of Time." In *Companion Encyclopedia of Anthropology*, ed. Tim Ingold, 503–26. London and New York: Routledge, 1994.
Agulla, Juan Carlos. *Eclipse of an Aristocracy: An Investigation of the Ruling Elites of the City of Córdoba*. University, Ala.: University of Alabama Press, 1968.

Alderete, Néstor, and Silvana Zanelli. "Las noches de Córdoba, al son vivo de las orquestas." *La Voz del Interior* (Córdoba, Argentina), 27 June 1994, sec. C, p. 1.

Alegría (Buenos Aires). July 1991–February 1995.

"Alegría cuartetera." *Alegría* 2 (December 1990): n.p.

Andrews, George Reid. *The Afro-Argentines of Buenos Aires, 1800–1900.* Madison, Wis.: University of Wisconsin Press, 1980.

"Aquí nadie aterriza." *Crónica con ritmo* (Buenos Aires, Argentina), 21 December 1990, n.p.

Arcondo, Aníbal. "Mortalidad general, mortalidad epidémica y comportamiento de la población de Córdoba durante el siglo XVIII." *Desarrollo Económico* 33, no. 129 (April–June 1993): 67–85.

Arrascaeta, Germán, et al. "El rock en el interior es una lucha." *La Voz del Interior* (Córdoba, Argentina), 22 February 1995, sec. C, p. 1.

Avedaño, Pedro. Interviews by author. Tape recordings. Córdoba, Argentina, 30 December 1994 and 25 February 1995.

Bainotti, Marcos. Interviews by author. Tape recordings. Córdoba, Argentina, 30 December 1994 and 23 June 1998.

Ball, Deirdre, ed. *Insight Guides: Argentina.* 2nd ed. Singapore: APA Publications, 1990.

Barei, Silvia N. *El sentido de la fiesta en la cultura popular: los cuartetos de Córdoba.* Córdoba, Argentina: Alción Editora, 1993.

Barnett, H. G. *Innovation: The Basis of Cultural Change.* New York: McGraw Hill, 1953.

Bascom, William. "Main Problems of Stability and Change in Tradition." *African Music* 2, no. 1 (1958): 6–10.

"'Basta de discriminación.'" *La Voz del Interior* (Córdoba, Argentina), 3 July 1995, sec. C, p. 1.

Béhague, Gérard. "Musical Change: A Case Study from South America." *The World of Music* 28, no. 1 (1986): 16–28.

Bellas, José. "¡Ésta es la bomba musical!" *Clarín* (Buenos Aires, Argentina), 28 April 1995, sec. *Sí*, pp. 4–5.

Bertino, Rosa. "La crecida cordobesa." *La Voz del Interior* (Córdoba, Argentina), 10 December 1991, sec. C, p. 1.

Bischoff, Efraín U. *Historia de Córdoba: cuatro siglos.* Buenos Aires, Argentina: Editorial Plus Ultra, 1979.

———. *Historia de los barrios de Córdoba: sus leyendas, instituciones y gentes.* Córdoba, Argentina: Lerner B. Editores, 1992.

Blacking, John. "Identifying Processes of Musical Change." *The World of Music* 28, no. 1 (1986): 3–15.

———. "Some Problems of Theory and Method in the Study of Musical Change." *Yearbook of the International Folk Music Council* 9 (1977): 1–26.

Boria, Adriana. "La representación de lo cotidiano en el discurso amoroso de Carlitos Mona Jiménez." In *Arte y vida cotidiana: la cultura del entretenimiento en Córdoba*, 145–80. Córdoba, Argentina: Alción Editora, 1993.

Brennan, James P. *The Labor Wars in Córdoba, 1955–1976: Ideology, Work, and Labor Politics in an Argentine Industrial City*. Cambridge, Mass.: Harvard University Press, 1994.

Bunkley, Allison Williams. Introduction to *A Sarmiento Anthology*, by Domingo F. Sarmiento. Edited by Allison Williams Bunkley. Translated by Stuart Edgar Grummon. Princeton, N.J.: Princeton University Press, 1948.

Byron R.M.A. Interviews by author. Tape recordings. Córdoba, Argentina, 16 December 1994 and 24 February 1995.

Camps, Sibila. "Un fenómeno cordobés invadió el Luna Park." *Clarín* (Buenos Aires, Argentina), 12 December 1988, p. 30.

Carámbula, Rubén. *El Candombe*. Biblioteca de Cultura Popular, no. 21. Buenos Aires, Argentina: Ediciones del Sol, 1995.

"Carlitos Jiménez presenta una selva de ritmos." *La Voz del Interior* (Córdoba, Argentina), 18 September 1994, sec. C, p. 4.

"Carlitos Jiménez: 'un muchacho de barrio.'" Photocopy.

Chá, Ercilia Moreno. "Alternativas del proceso de cambio de un repertorio tradicional argentino." *Latin American Music Review* 8, no. 1 (spring–summer 1987): 94–111.

"Chébere: veinte años con la música de Córdoba: 1974–1994." 1994. Photocopy.

"Chicas de fuego, (ex) voces del silencio." *La Voz del Interior* (Córdoba, Argentina), 8 March 1995, sec. C, p. 2.

"Chita, la mona que ya cumplió sesenta años." *La Maga* (Buenos Aires, Argentina), 26 July 1995, p. 43.

"Choque esos cinco . . . mil." *La Voz del Interior* (Córdoba, Argentina), 19 February 1995, sec. C, p. 3.

Cinti, Roberto. "Córdoba, la rebelde." *Nueva* (1992): 20–23.

"Clausuran hoy la 'marcha por la vida y contra la droga.'" *La Voz del Interior* (Córdoba, Argentina), 19 November 1994, sec. A, p. 9.

Clifford, James, and George E. Marcus, ed. *Writing Culture: The Poetics and Politics of Ethnography—A School of American Research Advanced Seminar*. Berkeley, Calif.: University of California Press, 1986.

Cohen, Anthony P. *Self Consciousness: An Alternate Anthropology of Identity*. London and New York: Routledge, 1994.

Comisión Municipal de Folklore. "Festival nacional de folklore." N.d. Photocopy.

"Como ellos, no hay dos." *Crónica con ritmo* (Buenos Aires, Argentina), 4 January 1991, n.p.

Concha, José. Interviews by author. Tape recordings. Córdoba, Argentina, 30 December 1994 and 24 February 1995.

"Córdoba no para de cantar." *La Voz del Interior* (Córdoba, Argentina), 12 February 1995, sec. C, p. 1.

"Córdoba sigue siendo productora de música." *Así es crónica* (Buenos Aires, Argentina), 20 July 1989, p. 2.

"Cordobeses inauguran el 'febrero musical.'" *La Voz del Interior* (Córdoba, Argentina), 5 February 1995, sec. C, p. 2.

Cragnolini, Alejandra. "Reflexiones acerca del circuito de promoción de la música de la 'bailanta' y de su influencia en la creación y recreación de estilos." Photocopy.

Crawford, Richard. "Response to Tim Rice." *Ethnomusicology* 31, no. 3 (fall 1987): 511–13.

"Crónica de un oscuro capítulo." *La Voz del Interior* (Córdoba, Argentina), 29 January 1988, sec. 3, p. 9.

"Cuando lo latino llama a la puerta." *La Voz del Interior* (Córdoba, Argentina), 31 October 1994, sec. C, p. 1.

"Cuarteto Leo, cincuenta años y un gran fervor." *La Voz del Interior* (Córdoba, Argentina), 4 June 1993, sec. C, p. 1.

De Fleur, Lois B. *Delinquency in Argentina: A Study of Córdoba's Youth.* University, Wash.: Washington State University Press, 1970.

de Pedro, Roque. "¿Existe una música popular argentina?" *Clarín, Cultura y Nación* (Buenos Aires, Argentina), 3 January 1985, pp. 1–3.

"Diez años y sigue creciendo." *El Diario* (Villa María, Argentina), 2 April 1994, p. 26.

"Discos novedades: Súper Santamarina: extraordinario." *Diario Popular* (Buenos Aires, Argentina), 4 October 1990, p. 8.

"'Doña Jovita,' el éxito del verano." *La Voz del Interior* (Córdoba, Argentina), 6 March 1995, sec. C, p. 1.

Elbaum, Jorge. "Los bailanteros. La fiesta urbana de la cultura popular." In *La cultura de la noche: la vida nocturna de los jóvenes en Buenos Aires,* ed. Mario Margulis and others, 181–210. Buenos Aires, Argentina: Compañía Editora Espasa Calpe Argentina, 1994.

"El humor de los cordobeses, una chispa que hace llama." *La Voz del Interior* (Córdoba, Argentina), 17 February 1995, sec. C, p. 1.

"El redescubrimiento de América." *La Voz del Interior* (Córdoba, Argentina), 23 March 1992, sec. C, p. 1.

Endrek, Emiliano. *El Mestizaje en Córdoba: Siglo XVIII y Principios del XIX.* Córdoba, Argentina: Universidad Nacional de Córdoba, 1966.

"Escándalo en la plaza." *La Voz del Interior* (Córdoba, Argentina), 28 January 1988, sec. 3, p. 7.

Estrellas (Córdoba, Argentina). September 1992–September 1993.

Falcoff, Mark, and Ronald H. Dolkart. *Prologue to Perón: Argentina in Depression and War, 1930–1943.* Berkeley, Calif.: University of California Press, 1975.

Ferrero, Roberto A. *La mala vida en Córdoba.* Córdoba, Argentina: Alción Editora, 1987.

"Flash en la música." *Flash* (Buenos Aires, Argentina), 4 January 1991, p. 28.

Flores, Marta. *La música popular en el Gran Buenos Aires.* Buenos Aires, Argentina: Centro Editor de América Latina, 1993.

Florine, Jane L. "Carlos Jiménez: Reflecting the Power of the People in Argentine *Cuarteto* Music." *Popular Music and Society* 22, no. 3 (fall 1998): 61–115.

———. "*Cuarteto:* Dance-Hall Entertainment or People's Music?" *Latin American Music Review* 19, no. 1 (spring–summer 1998): 31–46.

———. "Cuarteto Dancing: Demystification of a Mass Phenomenon." Paper presented at the annual meeting of the Society for Ethnomusicology, Toronto, Canada, October 31–November 3, 1996, the joint meeting of the Society for Ethnomusicology, Southeastern Chapter, and the Florida Folklore Society, Ybor City, Fla., February 8–9, 1997, and at the Midwest Chapter Meeting of the Society for Ethnomusicology, Bowling Green, Ohio, April 17–19, 1998.

———. "El cuarteto cordobés: análisis de un fenómeno social, masivo, y bailable." In *Actas del II Congreso Latinoamericano IASPM International Association for the Study of Popular Music,* [held] by IASPM and FONDART (Fondo de Desarrollo de las Artes y la Cultura, Ministerio de Educación de Chile), March 24–27, 1997. Santiago, Chile: Rama Latinoamericana IASPM, 1999, 177–90.

———. "Musical Change from Within: A Case Study of *Cuarteto* Music from Córdoba, Argentina." Ph.D. diss., Florida State University, 1996.

Fogal, Robert E. "Traditional Music and the Middle Class in Argentina: Context and Currents." In *Discourse in Ethnomusicology: Essays in Honor of George List,* ed. Caroline Card et al., 267–88. Bloomington, Ind.: Ethnomusicology Publications Group, Indiana University, 1978.

"Folklore en el agua." *La Voz del Interior* (Córdoba, Argentina), 13 January 1995, sec. C, p. 6.

Frith, Simon. "Towards an Aesthetic of Popular Music." In *Music and Society: The Politics of Composition, Performance and Reception,* ed. Richard Leppert and Susan McClary, 133–49. Cambridge: Cambridge University Press, 1987.

———. "Why Do Songs Have Words?" In *Lost in Music: Culture, Style and the Musical Event,* ed. Avron Levine White, 77–106. London: Routledge and Kegan Paul, 1987.

"Gary es el boom que estalló en las sierras." *Alegría* 1, no. 9 (July 1991): 56–57.

"Gary: de Córdoba a Latinoamérica." *Alegría* 3, no. 50 (December 1994): 20–23.

Gerard, Charley, and Marty Sheller. *Salsa!:The Rhythm of Latin Music.* Tempe, Ariz.: White Cliffs Media, 1989.

Gómez, Marcelo. "¿Qué pito tocamos?" *Aquí vivimos* 2, no. 14 (May 1993): 58–64.

González, Juan Pablo. "'Inti-Illimani' and the ArtisticTreatment of Folklore." *Latin American Music Review* 10, no. 2 (fall–winter 1989): 267–86.

Goodenough, Ward H. *Culture, Language, and Society.* Menlo Park, Calif.: Benjamin/Cummings, 1981.

———. "Multiculturalism as the Normal Human Experience." In *Applied Anthropology,* ed. Elizabeth M. Eddy and William L. Partridge, 79–86. New York: Columbia University Press, 1978.

Gregoratti, Luis. "Carlitos Jiménez, el cordobés de plata." *La Voz del Interior* (Córdoba, Argentina), 24 May 1993, sec. C, p. 1.

———. "Carlitos Jiménez, 'un artista de la calle.'" *La Voz del Interior* (Córdoba, Argentina), 27 September 1994, sec. C, p. 3.

———. "Cosquín '95, un festival a la defensiva." *La Voz del Interior* (Córdoba, Argentina), 1 February 1995, sec. 3, p. 2.

———. "Dos alegrías y un malestar." *La Voz del Interior* (Córdoba, Argentina), 11 March 1995, sec. C, p. 2.

———. "El merengue mueve montañas." *La Voz del Interior* (Córdoba, Argentina), 1 June 1992, sec. C, p. 1.

———. "El satélite sacude el baile." *La Voz del Interior* (Córdoba, Argentina), 11 March 1995, sec. C, p. 2.

———. "Júbilo esquina alegría." *La Voz del Interior* (Córdoba, Argentina), 22 September 1994, sec. A, p. 15.

———. "La evolución en el cuarteto es ineludible, pero . . . " *La Voz del Interior* (Córdoba, Argentina), 15 May 1995, sec. C, p. 1.

———. "Los discos giran a menos revoluciones por minuto." *La Voz del Interior* (Córdoba, Argentina), 21 March 1995, sec. C, p. 1.

———. "No sentí jamás, esta sensación." *La Voz del Interior* (Córdoba, Argentina), 13 September 1992, sec. F, p. 1.

Gregoratti, Luis, and Germán Arrascaeta. "Más que un fenómeno, una realidad excluyente: qué tendrá el cuarteto para ser el rey de esta región." *La Voz del Interior* (Córdoba, Argentina), 25 July 1994, sec. C, p. 1.

Grimes, Ronald L. *Beginnings in Ritual Studies.* Lanham, Md.: University Press of America, 1982.

"Guerra actuará en Mendoza." *La Voz del Interior* (Córdoba, Argentina), 28 May 1992, sec. C, p. 4.

"Guerra, el conquistador." *La Voz del Interior* (Córdoba, Argentina), 8 September 1991, sec. C, p. 3.

Gutnisky, Gabriel. "Buen día, Bienarte." *La Voz del Interior* (Córdoba, Argentina), 21 October 1993, sec. C, p. 1.

Guzmán, José Aldo. "El cuarteto: un proyecto de resistencia y crecimiento." 1993. Photocopy.

Hanna, Judith Lynne. *To Dance Is Human: A Theory of Nonverbal Communication.* Austin, Tex.: University of Texas Press, 1979.

Harris, Marvin. *Cultural Materialism: The Struggle for a Science of Culture.* New York: Random House, 1979.

Harwood, Dane L. "Interpretive Activity: A Response to Tim Rice's 'Toward the Remodelling of Ethnomusicology.'" *Ethnomusicology* 31, no. 3 (fall 1987): 503–10.

Hepp, Osvaldo. *La soledad de los cuartetos.* Córdoba, Argentina: Editorial Letra, 1988.

Iglesias, Analía. "Películas, deportes y música son el alma de la TV por cable." *La Voz del Interior* (Córdoba, Argentina), 19 March 1995, sec. C, p. 1.

———. "Todo cambia, incluso la música de cuartetos." *La Voz del Interior* (Córdoba, Argentina), 6 July 1993, sec. C, p. 1.

Jiménez Rufino, Juan Carlos. Interview by author. Tape recording. Cerro de las Rosas, Córdoba, Argentina, 15 November 1994.

"Jóvenes marchan contra la droga." *La Voz del Interior* (Córdoba, Argentina), 18 November 1994, sec. A, pp. 1, 15.

"Juan Luis Guerra sacude con otro ritmo caribeño." *La Voz del Interior* (Córdoba, Argentina), 16 August 1994, sec. C, p. 1.

Kaemmer, John E. *Music in Human Life: Anthropological Perspectives on Music.* Austin, Tex.: University of Texas Press, 1993.

Kartomi, Margaret J. "The Processes and Results of Musical Culture Contact: A Discussion of Terminology and Concepts." *Ethnomusicology* 25, no. 2 (May 1981): 227–49.

Keil, Angela, and Charles Keil. "In Pursuit of Polka Happiness." In *Popular Culture in America,* ed. Paul Buhle, 75–83. Minneapolis: University of Minnesota Press, 1987.

Keil, Charles. "People's Music Comparatively: Style and Stereotype, Class and Hegemony." *Dialectical Anthropology* 10 (July 1985–April 1986): 119–30.

Koskoff, Ellen. "Response to Rice." *Ethnomusicology* 31, no. 3 (fall 1987): 497–502.

Kubik, Gerhard. "Stability and Change in African Musical Traditions." *The World of Music* 28, no. 1 (1986): 44–69.

"La banda Santamarina en la noche de carnaval." *La Séptima* (San Juan, Argentina), 5 March 1994, p. 3.

"La Barra, del desafío a la revelación." *La Voz del Interior* (Córdoba, Argentina), 16 January 1995, sec. C, p. 1.

"La Barra de oro." *La Voz del Interior* (Córdoba, Argentina), 10 December 1994, sec. C, p. 3.

"La comisión y su versión de los desmanes del miércoles." *La Voz del Interior* (Córdoba, Argentina), 31 January 1988, sec. 3, p. 5.

"La cultura popular." *El Diario* (Villa María, Argentina), 14 April 1985, n.p.

"La Leo es todo un símbolo de Córdoba." *Alegría.* Photocopy.

"Lamentable saldo de los incidentes en Cosquín." *La Voz del Interior* (Córdoba, Argentina), 29 January 1988, sec. 1, p. 1.

"¿La Mona eternamente?" *La Voz del Interior* (Córdoba, Argentina), 24 July 1995, sec. C, p. 1.

"La Mona y la dueña del circo." *La Voz del Interior* (Córdoba, Argentina), 9 August 1994, n.p.

"La solidaridad afina con clásico y cuarteto." *La Voz del Interior* (Córdoba, Argentina), 14 December 1994, sec. C, p. 1.

"La 'usina' del cuarteto." *Alegría* 3, no. 48 (October 1994): 4–9.

La vieja usina reciclada como centro cultural y recreativo." *La Voz del Interior* (Córdoba, Argentina), 20 May 1992, sec. C, p. 2.

Leuco, Alfredo. "En defensa de 'La Mona' Giménez." *Clarín* (Buenos Aires, Argentina), 17 February 1988, p. 13.

Lewin, Hugo D. "Siga el baile: el fenómeno social de la bailanta, nacimiento y apogeo." In *La cultura de la noche: la vida nocturna de los jóvenes en Buenos Aires,* ed. Mario Margulis and others, 211–34. Buenos Aires, Argentina: Compañía Editora Espasa Calpe Argentina, 1994.

"Llegó la gran bailanta del año." *Diario Popular* (Buenos Aires, Argentina), 20 December 1990, p. 3.

"Los Fabulosos Cadillacs se robaron los ACE." *La Voz del Interior* (Córdoba, Argentina), 16 November 1994, sec. C, p. 2.

"Los festivales, una tormenta de verano." *La Voz del Interior* (Córdoba, Argentina), 25 February 1995, sec. C, p. 1.

"Los grandes aciertos de Luis Gómez." *Diario Popular* (Buenos Aires, Argentina), 10 January 1991, p. 3.

Loza, Steven. *Barrio Rhythm: Mexican American Music in Los Angeles.* Urbana and Chicago, Ill.: University of Illinois Press, 1993.

Lugones, Eduardo. "Chébere—historia musical." 1995. Photocopy.

Luna, Rodolfo. "50 años de cuartetos." *Umbrales* 1, no. 1 (December 1993): 30–33.

Luna, Rodolfo Daniel, and Daniel Alejandro Boidi. "El tunga-tunga cordobés." *Licenciatura* thesis, Escuela Superior de Periodismo Obispo Trejo y Sanabria, Córdoba, Argentina, 1991.

Machado, Néstor Cires. "Para Córdoba, con amor." *Papeles de Córdoba* (December 1990): 24.

Manuel, Peter. *Popular Musics of the Non-Western World.* New York and Oxford: Oxford University Press, 1988.

Marcus, George E., and Michael M. J. Fischer. *Anthropology as Cultural Critique: An Experiential Moment in the Human Sciences.* Chicago: University of Chicago Press, 1986.

Mareco, Alejandro. "El cordobés de los bailes." *La Voz del Interior* (Córdoba, Argentina), 6 September 1992, sec. F, p. 7.

———. "La leyenda del 'tunga-tunga.'" *La Voz del Interior* (Córdoba, Argentina), 6 June 1993, sec. F, p. 1.

"Martí negó haberle entregado una chapa a Carlitos Jiménez." *La Voz del Interior* (Córdoba, Argentina), 5 March 1992, n.p.

Martín, Manuel, and Marcelo Gómez. "¿Qué pito tocamos?" *Aquí vivimos* 2, no. 14 (1993): 58–63.

Martínez, Jorge Oscar. "Después de Cosquín." *Universidad* 10 (March 1988): n.p.

"Marzo suena sinfónico y urbano." *La Voz del Interior* (Córdoba, Argentina), 10 March 1995, sec. C, p. 2.

Marzullo, Osvaldo, and Pancho Muñoz. "Historia del rock nacional." *Todo es historia* 19, no. 239 (April 1987): 6–29.

"Más cordobeses: Santamarina." *Crónica con ritmo* (Buenos Aires, Argentina), date illegible.

"Más que satisfechos." *Tropi show* (Buenos Aires, Argentina), 30 May 1991, n.p.

Mauleón, Rebeca. *Salsa Guidebook for Piano and Ensemble.* Petaluma, Calif.: Sher Music, 1993.

Merlo, Hugo D. Interview by author. Tape recording. Córdoba, Argentina, 27 June 1998.

Mero, Roberto. *La Mona va! Carlos Jiménez y el fenómeno social del cuarteto.* Buenos Aires, Argentina: Editorial Contrapunto, 1988.

Merriam, Alan P. *The Anthropology of Music.* Evanston, Ill.: Northwestern University Press, 1964.

Middleton, Richard. *Studying Popular Music.* Milton Keynes and Philadelphia, Pa.: Open University Press, 1990.

Ministerio Evangelístico "Cita con la Vida." *América latina nuestra herencia.* Córdoba, Argentina: Fundación Cita con la Vida, 1995.

Miranda Matienzo, Miguel A. Interviews by author. Tape recordings. Córdoba, Argentina, 16 December 1994 and 24 February 1995.

Moreno, Albrecht. "Violeta Parra and La Nueva Canción Chilena." *Studies in Latin American Popular Culture* 5 (1986): 108–26.

316 / Bibliography

Mörner, Magnus. "Immigration into Latin America, Especially Argentina and Chile." In *European Expansion and Migration: Essays on the Intercontinental Migration from Africa, Asia, and Europe,* ed. P. C. Emmer and M. Mörner, 211–43. New York and Oxford: Berg, 1992.

"Multitudinario acto de clausura de la marcha contra la droga." *La Voz del Interior* (Córdoba, Argentina), 20 November 1994, sec. A, p. 13.

Murdock, George Peter. "How Culture Changes." In *Man, Culture, and Society,* ed. Harry L. Shapiro, 247–60. New York: Oxford University Press, 1956.

Nettl, Bruno. "Historical Aspects of Ethnomusicology." *American Anthropologist* 60 (1958): 518–32.

———. "History and Change in Blackfoot Indian Musical Culture and Thought. " *The World of Music* 28, no. 1 (1986a): 70–85.

———. "Recent Directions in Ethnomusicology." In *Ethnomusicology: An Introduction,* ed. Helen Myers, 375–99. New York: Norton, 1992.

———. "Some Aspects of the History of World Music in the Twentieth Century: Questions, Problems, and Concepts." *Ethnomusicology* 22, no. 1 (January 1978): 123–36.

———. *The Study of Ethnomusicology: Twenty-nine Issues and Concepts.* Urbana, Ill.: University of Illinois Press, 1983.

———. "World Music in the Twentieth Century: A Survey of Research on Western Influence." *Acta musicologica* 58 (1986b): 360–73.

"¿Nos devoran los de afuera?" *La Voz del Interior* (Córdoba, Argentina), 10 November 1994, sec. C, p. 1.

Olmos, Juan Carlos. Interview by author. Tape recording. Córdoba, Argentina, 23 June 1998.

Ortiz, Dirty. "Larga vida a los cuartetos." *El Ojo con Dientes* (Córdoba, Argentina), fall 1993: 23–25.

Ortiz, Raúl. "Populares sí, cuarteteros no." *Página 12* (Buenos Aires, Argentina), 20 October 1993, p. 31.

Ortiz, Raúl, and Sergio Zuliani. "La Mona, aunque se vista de seda." *Córdoba* (Córdoba, Argentina), 13 July 1988 (?), n.p.

Ortiz, Raúl Dirty. "La música pop es parte de la religión." *La Voz del Interior* (Córdoba, Argentina), 27 January 1995, sec. C, p. 1.

———. "Pidamos, total pagan los Reyes." *La Voz del Interior* (Córdoba, Argentina), 5 January 1995, sec. C, p. 1.

Ortiz, Raúl Dirty, Luis Gregoratti, and Germán Arrascaeta. "La libre competencia con ritmo cordobés." *La Voz del Interior* (Córdoba, Argentina), 11 March 1995, sec. C, p. 1.

Pacini Hernández, Deborah. *Bachata: A Social History of a Dominican Popular Music.* Philadelphia, Pa.: Temple University Press, 1995.

Peña, Manuel H. *The Texas-Mexican Conjunto: History of a Working-Class Music.* Austin, Tex.: University of Texas Press, 1985.

Pintos, Víctor. "El merengue llega al sur." *La Voz del Interior* (Córdoba, Argentina), 1 September 1991, sec. C, p. 2.

Platía, Marta. "Bailando con la más fea." *Aquí vivimos* 2, no. 14 (May 1993): 38–45.

"Premios ACE." *La Voz del Interior* (Córdoba, Argentina), 14 November 1994, sec. C, p. 2.

Pujol, Sergio A. "Música e intolerancia." *Todo es historia* 23, no. 262 (April 1989): 66–75.

Quinteros, Mario. Interviews by author. Tape recordings. Córdoba, Argentina, 16 December 1994 and 24 February 1995.

Rapoport, Amos. "Spatial Organization and the Built Environment." In *Companion Encyclopedia of Anthropology*, ed. Tim Ingold, 460–502. London and New York: Routledge, 1994.

Ratier, Hugo. *El Cabecita Negra.* Buenos Aires, Argentina: Centro Editor de América Latina, 1971.

"Recitales, murgas y comparsas para recibir la primavera." *La Voz del Interior* (Córdoba, Argentina), 21 September 1994, sec. A, p. 14.

Reyna, Roberto. "La Mona no se viste de seda." *Página 12* (Buenos Aires, Argentina), 7 February 1988, p. 19.

Rice, Timothy. "Tim Rice Responds." *Ethnomusicology* 31, no. 3 (fall 1987b): 515–16.

———. "Toward the Remodelling of Ethnomusicology." *Ethnomusicology* 31, no. 3 (fall 1987a): 469–88.

"Ritmo cordobés en la plaza del folklore." *La Voz del Interior* (Córdoba, Argentina), 8 February 1995, sec. C, p. 2.

Rivarola, Héctor O. Interviews by author. Tape recordings. Córdoba, Argentina, 17 December 1994 and 24 February 1995.

Rivas, Mario. "¡Bailaló!" *La Voz del Interior* (Córdoba, Argentina), 9 April 1989, sec. 3, p. 1.

Rojo, Eduardo. Interviews by author. Tape recordings. Córdoba, Argentina, 16 December 1994 and 24 February 1995.

Romero, José Luis. *A History of Argentine Political Thought.* Translated by Thomas F. McGann. Stanford, Calif.: Stanford University Press, 1968.

Rosaldo, Renato. *Culture and Truth: The Remaking of Social Analysis.* Boston: Beacon Press, 1993.

Rossi et al. (ECI group). "El tunga tunga es algo más que un ritmo." Escuela de Ciencias de la Información, Universidad Nacional de Córdoba, Córdoba, Argentina, 1992. Photocopy.

Royce, Anya Peterson. *The Anthropology of Dance.* Bloomington, Ind.: Indiana University Press, 1977.

SADAIC (Sociedad Argentina de Autores y Compositores). *Música y Letra* 5, no. 10 (1992): 3–50.

Salinas, Mario. Interviews by author. Tape recordings. Córdoba, Argentina, 6 January 1995a and 24 February 1995b.

Salton, Ricardo. "El tango Milonguita: un caso de intolerancia desacreditado por la realidad musicológica. Cierto paralelo con otro caso reciente." 1988. Photocopy.

———. "Un furor que va cediendo." *Noticias.* Photocopy.

Salzano, Daniel. *El alma que canta.* Córdoba, Argentina: Ediciones Fundación Silvestre Rafael Remonda y María Reina Loustau de Remonda, 1993.

"Santamarina: conmoción." *Crónica con ritmo* (Buenos Aires, Argentina), 24 May 1991, p. 9.

"Santamarina ¡mata!" *Diario Popular* (Buenos Aires, Argentina), 12 September 1991, p. 5.

"Santamarina y Julio: con la onda del cuartetazo." *El sur de Córdoba* (Villa María, Córdoba), 7 January 1988, p. 5.

Schechner, Richard. "Ritual and Performance." In *Companion Encyclopedia of Anthropology,* ed. Tim Ingold, 613–47. London and New York: Routledge, 1994.

Schmucler, Héctor. "Los cuartetos, entre la tragedia y la farsa." *Plural 13,* no. 4 (May 1989): 15–18.

Scobie, James R. *Argentina: A City and a Nation.* 2nd ed. New York: Oxford University Press, 1971.

———. *Secondary Cities of Argentina: The Social History of Corrientes, Salta, and Mendoza, 1850–1910.* Stanford, Calif.: Stanford University Press, 1988.

Seeger, Anthony. "Do We Need to Remodel Ethnomusicology?" *Ethnomusicology* 31, no. 3 (fall 1987): 491–95.

———. "Ethnography of Music." In *Ethnomusicology: An Introduction,* ed. Helen Myers, 88–111. New York: Norton, 1992.

———. "Music and Dance." In *Companion Encyclopedia of Anthropology,* ed. Tim Ingold, 686–705. London and New York: Routledge, 1994.

"Separados, en Montevideo." *La Voz del Interior* (Córdoba, Argentina), 26 March 1992, sec. C, p. 2.

"... Se viene Santamarina." *Tropi show* (Buenos Aires, Argentina), 15 November 1990, n.p.

Shay, Anthony V. "The Functions of Dance in Human Societies." M.A. thesis, California State College, Los Angeles, 1971.

Shelemay, Kay Kaufman. "Response to Rice." *Ethnomusicology* 31, no. 3 (fall 1987): 489–90.

Shiloah, Amnon. "The Traditional Artist in the Limelight of the Modern City." *The World of Music* 28, no. 1 (1986): 87–99.

Shiloah, Amnon, and Erik Cohen. "The Dynamics of Change in Jewish Oriental Ethnic Music in Israel." *Ethnomusicology* 27, no. 2 (May 1983): 227–52.

"Siempre el número uno." *Alegría*. Photocopy.

"Siempre hay lugar para uno más." *La Voz del Interior* (Córdoba, Argentina), 9 January 1995, sec. C, p. 1.

Sierra, Luis Adolfo. *Historia de la orquesta típica: evolución instrumental del tango.* Buenos Aires, Argentina: A. Peña Lillo, Editor, 1976.

"Sobre las palabras, el mismo cielo." *Córdoba* (Córdoba, Argentina), 7 July 1990, pp. 2–3.

"Sobre los cuartetos y la contemplación de la cultura." *La Voz del Interior* (Córdoba, Argentina), 17 March 1994, sec. D, p. 2.

"Sólo quiero que la gente se divierta." *Puntal* (Río Cuarto, Argentina), 13 November 1992, p. 24.

Soria, Adrián. "La Mona Jiménez: La 'usina' del cuarteto." *Alegría* 3, no. 48 (October 1994): 4–9.

"SUM Records y Barca: catálogos nacionales de música caribeña." *La Maga* (Buenos Aires, Argentina), 17 August 1994, p. 31.

"Super Santamarina." *Hechos, periódico regional* 43 (May 1993): n.p.

Szuchman, Mark D. *Mobility and Integration in Urban Argentina: Córdoba in the Liberal Era.* Austin, Tex.: University of Texas Press, 1980.

"Tangos, cuartetos y música clásica en concierto solidario." *La Voz del Interior* (Córdoba, Argentina), 15 December 1994, sec. A, p. 1.

Tapia, Manuel Luis. Interviews by author. Tape recordings. Córdoba, Argentina, 30 December 1994 and 24 February 1995.

"Terminó como 'La Mona.'" *Página 12* (Buenos Aires, Argentina). Photocopy.

"Todo cuarteto es divisible por dos." *La Voz del Interior* (Córdoba, Argentina), 26 September 1994, sec. C, p. 1.

Tribilín (L.M.A.). Interviews by author. Tape recordings. Córdoba, Argentina, 30 December 1994 and 24 February 1995.

Tumas-Serna, Jane. "The Nueva Canción Movement and Its Mass-Mediated Performance Context." *Latin American Music Review* 13, no. 2 (1992): 139–57.

Turkovic, Robert J. "Race Relations in the Province of Córdoba, Argentina, 1800–1853." Ph.D. diss., University of Florida, 1981.

"Una euforia demencial quebró la quinta luna." *La Voz del Interior* (Córdoba, Argentina), 29 January 1988, sec. 3, p. 9.

"Un despropósito." *La Voz del Interior* (Córdoba, Argentina), 29 January 1988, sec. 3, p. 9.

"Un emblema de la música más popular." *La Voz del Interior* (Córdoba, Argentina), 13 January 1993, sec. C, p. 1.

"Un mensaje sin agresión mejorará al cuarteto." *La Voz del Interior* (Córdoba, Argentina), 10 September 1994, sec. C, p. 1.

"Un sacudón llamado cuartetazo." *La Voz del Interior* (Córdoba, Argentina), 15 March 1994, Revista 90° aniversario de la Voz, pp. 76–77.

Van Maanen, John. *Tales of the Field: On Writing Ethnography.* Chicago and London: University of Chicago Press, 1988.

Vásquez-Martínez, Abraham. Interviews by author. Tape recordings. Córdoba, Argentina, 16 December 1994 and 24 February 1995.

"Verano con Jiménez." *La Voz del Interior* (Córdoba, Argentina), 12 January 1995, sec. C, p. 3.

Verón, Ricardo. Interviews by author. Tape recordings. Córdoba, Argentina, 17 December 1994a and 30 December 1994b.

Vila, Pablo. "Rock Nacional and Dictatorship in Argentina." In *Rockin' the Boat: Mass Music and Mass Movements,* ed. Reebee Garofalo, 209–29. Boston: South End Press, 1992.

"Vuelve Santamarina." *Tropi show* (Buenos Aires, Argentina), 20 December 1990, n.p.

Wallace, Anthony F. C. *Culture and Personality.* 2nd. ed. New York: Random House, 1970.

Waisman, Leonardo. "Jiménez Rufino, Juan Carlos." Photocopy.

———. "Tradición e innovación en el cuarteto cordobés." 1993. Photocopy.

Waterman, Christopher Alan. *Jùjú: A Social History and Ethnography of an African People.* Chicago and London: University of Chicago Press, 1990.

Weinberg, Félix. *El salón literario de 1837.* Buenos Aires, Argentina: Librería Hachette, 1977.

Wheaton, Kathleen, ed. *Insight Cityguides: Buenos Aires.* Singapore: APA Publications, 1990.

Wynia, Gary W. *Argentina: Illusions & Realities.* New York: Holmes and Meier, 1992.

DISCOGRAPHY

Así Me Gusta a Mí. La Barra. Sony (Columbia) compact disc 2–478679, 1995.

Chébere: Premio A.C.E. '94. Chébere. Clave Records compact disc CD 51413, 1994.

Chébere en LaVieja Usina. Chébere. Clave Records compact disc CD/E 51313, 1994.

Con Todo Respeto. Gary. BMG compact disc 74321–19813–2, 1994.

Cuarteto Leo: 20 Grandes Éxitos. Cuarteto Leo. CBS audiocassette 580–708, 1973–1986.

Dalila. Gary. BMG compact disc 74321–25385–2, 1994.

El Marginal. Carlos Jiménez. BMG compact disc 74321–30538–2, 1995.

El Nuevo Santamarina. Santamarina. Sony (Columbia) compact disc 2–478675, 1995.

Exageradísimo '95. Various groups. BMG compact disc 74321–27011–2, 1995.

La Barra. La Barra. Sony (Columbia) compact disc 2–470463, 1994.

Nueva Magia. Ángel Videla and Grupo Sazón. BMG compact disc 74321–29687–2, 1995.

Para Toda América. Carlos Jiménez. PolyGram audiocassette 63263, 1984.

Raza Negra. Carlos Jiménez. BMG compact disc 74321–23116–2, 1994.

Santamarina de Oro. Santamarina. Sony (Columbia) compact disc 2–470455, 1994.

Se Siente Tru-la-lá. Tru-la-lá. BMG audiocassette 74321–21169–4, 1994.

Sound archives of Chébere, La Ranchada radio station, Radio Suquía, and Santamarina.

Tru-la-lá: 10 Años. Tru-la-lá. BMG compact disc 74321–24649–2, 1994.

Trulalazo. Tru-la-lá. BMG compact disc 74321–29135–2, 1995.

Viva La Música. La Banda del "Negro" Videla. BMG compact disc 74321–22647–2, 1994.

VIDEOCASSETTES

Bohmetter, Mario. *Cuartetos.* 3 volumes. Unpublished, no number or date.

Chébere en La Vieja Usina. Chébere. Clave Records videocassette VH 60013, 1994.

Cuando Se Acaba El Amor. Gary. Training Productora videocassette, no number, 1995.

La Mona Jiménez: El Bailarín. Carlos Jiménez. Visión Video videocassette, Lomas de Zamora, Argentina, 1993.

Loza, Santiago. *La Mona.* Unpublished, no number or date.

Raza Negra Record Launching. Carlos Jiménez. Mejor Propaganda. Unpublished (no number), 1994.

Tru-la-lá. From Tru-la-lá archive. Unpublished (no number), 1994.

INDEX

Locators in boldface type refer to pages with illustrations.

328 / Index

298; newspaper commentary about, 205, 210–12; "Penita," story of, 242–56. *See also* "Penita"

El Padrino, 106, **167**, 271

"El Paraguas": instrumentation, form, and texture, 36; lyrics, 41–42; melodic/harmonic features, 36–39; rhythmic elements, 39–41; title, use of, 18; transcription of, **37–40**; *tunga-tunga,* 40

El Proceso, 31, 32, 297

El Reencuentro (Los Reencuentros), 273, 275, 276. *See also* Chébere; La Banda del "Negro" Videla; Videla, Ángel "Negro"

"El Turco" (bus driver), 248

"Esta Noche Me Voy de Caravana" ("Tonight I'm Going Out from Place to Place"), 80–81

Evolution, *cuarteto,* 3, 11, 18, 19, 30–31, 35–83, 119–20, 298; during 1995–98, 269–90, 299–300; Goodenough, application of theories of, 163–64; of Jiménez band, 238–43, 243–56, 256–61, 261–67; Jiménez musicians, comments about, 212–30; newspaper reports about, 205–12

Facundo (singer), 188

Falklands/Malvinas War, 31, 32

Farías, Emeterio (impresario): in 1998, 269, 276, 280; importance of, 17, 105–7; with Tru-la-lá, 175; with Videla, 172–75, **173**

Fernando (singer), 92, 165

Ferrari, Ariel (*cuarteto* group), 226

Ferrer, Gabriel (singer), 273–74

Ferri, Osvaldo (arranger), 167–70, **169**, 274

Festival Nacional de Folklore: *cuarteto,* heard at, 97, 119, 195, 229; Cuarteto Leo, performance at, 24; founding of, 119; humor, use of, 5

Florine, Jane L.: approach of, 11; countermelody in "Penita," 78, 249–

54, **250**, 256, 259; goals of, 11–21; participation, musical, 20, 108, 211, 258, 259, 261 (in "Penita," 243–56; in *Raza Negra/El Marginal,* 238–43); research role of, 17, 108, 263–66

Fraga, Leo (singer), 165

Fuentes, Edgar (Gary), **132,** 181–87, **182**; Buenos Aires, travel to, 157–59; Tropicana Golden Award, 279; in Tru-la-lá, 176–77, 182–83. *See also* Gary

Fuentes, Karina, 157, 158, 183, 184

Garnero, Pepe (arranger), 274

Gary (band): activities, 92; arrangements, 185–86; *bailantas,* performance at, **112,** 155–56, 157–59; decision-making, musical, 184–87; Goodenough, application of theories to, 163, 202–4; group history, 181–83, 276, 279; hats, used by fans, 131, **132;** members, **182, 185,** 187, 279; in 1995, 183–84; in 1998, 270, 299; reason for working with, 17; recording, 186–87, 279; rehearsals, 186; repertoire and composition, 184–85; Unquillo, **182,** 186; women in, 108, **182**

Gelfo, Eduardo (son of Miguel Gelfo), 24

Gelfo, Miguel (musician), 24

Gómez, Luis (musician), 231

Gómez, Sandro (singer), 177, 276–77

Goodenough, Ward: application of model of, 163, 197–204, 261–67; cultural change model of, 14–15, 19, 161–64

Grande, Héctor (radio announcer), 106

Gregoratti, Luis (journalist), 206–7, 209–10

Grifo, Daniel (arranger), 274

Groups, *cuarteto. See Cuarteto* groups, membership of; *and names of individual bands*

Guardia, Daniel (singer), 273

Jane L. Florine is assistant professor of ethnomusicology/musicology at Chicago State University. She has published articles on *cuarteto* in the *Latin American Music Review, Popular Music and Society,* the *Garland Encyclopedia of World Music,* and the *Actas del II Congreso Latinoamericano IASPM International Association for the Study of Popular Music.*